What People Are Saying About *The Nonprofit Consu*

Increasingly, we rely on consultants to meet the nonprofit sec... *particular, fundraising needs. Linda Lysakowski and Susan Schaefer provide aspiring and veteran consultants with a range and depth of advice about how consultants can best strengthen this sector. That experience is yours to command through* The Nonprofit Consulting Playbook.

Andrew Watt, FInstF
President and CEO, Association of Fundraising Professionals

The Nonprofit Consulting Playbook *offers practical lessons and suggestions for realistically beginning or continuing a career as a consultant in the sector. The proven techniques, time-tested strategies, and foundational guidance shared by the authors touch on the key areas of building and sustaining a consulting practice. Whether you're new to the field or have several years of experience, I have no doubt that you'll find this a useful primer for the future.*

Geoffrey E. Brown, CAE
Executive Director, The Giving Institute
(formerly the American Association of Fundraising Counsel)

If you're thinking about becoming a consultant, the information in these essays will help you determine the right path and guide you along the way. If you're a new consultant, the honesty in these articles will reassure you that even some of this field's best wondered early on whether they would succeed. And if you're a veteran consultant, this is one of the few books in our sector that will give you fuel for your next reinvention.

Amy Scanlon
Owner, Amy Scanlon Consulting

I laughed out loud when I read this book because all of the questions I wrestled with in my consulting career were right there! From the early questions like "What should I name my business?" to the more complicated questions like "How in heaven's name should I deal with this x#!!xx##!! client?" This book brings the clarity, wisdom, and good humor I hungered for during much of my consulting career. Thank you, Linda and Susan, for pulling together such a stellar group of consultants to share their stories and advice. You've created a first-rate resource for our field.

Andrea Kihlstedt
Author of *Asking Styles: Harness Your Personal Fundraising Power*

This is the book I wished for when I began my consulting career. It's a fun, practical look at the business side of nonprofit consulting. For those of us who "grew up" in the nonprofit sector, it should be required reading if you are considering moving from staff to consultant.

Barbara L. Ciconte, CFRE
Donor Strategies Inc.

As a professional newer to the field of consulting, I found The Nonprofit Consulting Playbook *to be an informative resource that provides lived examples (and solutions!) to issues I have already tackled in setting up my new business; strategic, values-based, and operational points I should consider in running my consulting practice; and ideas and topics to ponder and reflect on to further my business and plan for the future. What struck me most while I was reading* The Playbook *was the significance of* relationships. *The value of seasoned consultants sharing their personal and professional experiences is priceless and so appreciated! I am thankful to have "forever access" to these individuals through their stories, and it will remind me of the incredible supportive and giving nature of this work.*

DeDe Esque
Owner, DDSQ Consulting

I found the book to be very helpful as someone who is considering becoming a consultant but hasn't made a final decision. The book's credibility lies in hearing from so many individuals who have years of consulting experience. It touches on issues I had not even considered and led me to create several checklists that will help me evaluate my decision. I would suggest this book to anyone starting out for the first time as well as experienced consultants considering expanding their business.

Anissa Holmes
Aspiring Consultant

Wow!!! Home run, touchdown! The editors and authors of The Nonprofit Consulting Playbook: Leading Strategies from 25 Leaders in the Field *have put together a compilation of excellent guidance about building a new consulting practice for us novices. Chapter Four, "What's in a Name," really hit home, as I am starting my own consulting company. I wish I had this information some two years ago when I began this journey. The book is chock full of excellent advice. This is great information from some of the most respected leaders in our field. I highly recommend it if you are thinking about starting a consulting practicing.*

Glen W. Cosper, MA ACFRE
President, Relationship Fundraising

Linda Lysakowski and Susan Schaefer have pulled together a fantastic resource for anyone engaged in the nonprofit consulting business. From the mouths of experienced consultants who've seen it all and done it all come words of encouragement, frank tales of caution, and practical tips for success. It's like having a corps of mentors right there on your bookshelf! I've had my own business for thirteen years now, and I took away a number of useful suggestions about how I can improve my practice and focus on my own personal goals for being a consultant. This is definitely not just a book for startups and those thinking about making the leap into consulting. The diverse authors in The Nonprofit Consulting Playbook *remind us that it's business we're building and that there are many pathways to success. Chapters range in topics, style, and voice—from starting and marketing your firm to considering how to wind things down and move on to the next big thing in your life. It's almost conversational in shape, with the authors taking you along on their personal journeys through the ups and downs of consulting. It's an approachable and easy-to-use resource, one to which readers can turn again and again. Better watch out! If you take time to follow up on all the good ideas and helpful tips in this book, you might not have time to take care of your clients!*

Marshall H. Ginn, CFRE
Managing Director, Capital Development Strategies LLC

As the president of a writing service company that provides grant research and writing, I face many of the challenges my more seasoned counterparts describe in this insightful book. How helpful to have a road map for success! From Simone Joyaux and Jean Block, I got the nudge to write the articles I've been contemplating. Betsy Baker showed me what to add to my LinkedIn strategy, and Marti Fischer gave me the missing piece for making proposals that will inspire clients to close. Ellen Bristol made me realize I'd been wasting too much time on unqualified and low-value prospects, and Susan Schaefer got me hooked in to all the right associations where I could meet prospective clients and referrers. Thank you, all!

Katherine Metres
President, Your Edge for Success Inc.

As a development professional in the field for thirty years getting my feet wet in consulting, this book is a terrific resource. It answered all of my questions and raised other critical issues that I would never have thought of—such as an honest assessment of who you are, how you appear to others, who you want to be, and how to carve your niche—all of which are all fundamental to embracing consultancy. Every critical area is thoroughly and creatively presented with multiple viewpoints to ponder. It's soup to nuts, but it's also a rich and satisfying meal!

Marjorie Spitz Nagrotsky, MSSS
Development Consultant

This book will help new consultants avoid pitfalls and provide experienced consultants with ideas to help both their businesses and their personal lives thrive. The diversity of contributing authors shows that "listening to your own drummer" can lead to success—even if your path looks different from everyone else's.

Chris Stacey
President, Sapphire Consulting

The Nonprofit Consulting Playbook

Winning Strategies from 25 Leaders in the Field

Edited by:

Susan Schaefer, CFRE

Linda Lysakowski, ACFRE

The Nonprofit Consulting Playbook: Winning Strategies from 25 Leaders in the Field

One of the **In the Trenches**™ series
Published by
CharityChannel Press, an imprint of CharityChannel LLC
30021 Tomas, Suite 300
Rancho Santa Margarita, CA 92688-2128 USA
http://charitychannel.com

Copyright © 2013 by CharityChannel LLC.

All rights reserved. No part of this book shall be reproduced, stored in a retrieval system, or transmitted by any means, electronic, mechanical, photocopying, recording, or otherwise, without written permission from the publisher. No patent liability is assumed with respect to the use of the information contained herein. This publication contains the opinions and ideas of its editors and contributors. It is intended to provide helpful and informative material on the subject matter covered. It is sold with the understanding that the editors, contributors and publisher are not engaged in rendering professional services or advice (including legal services or advice) in the book. If the reader requires assistance or advice, a competent professional should be consulted. The editors, contributors, and publisher specifically disclaim any responsibility for any liability, loss, or risk, personal or otherwise, which is incurred as a consequence, directly or indirectly, of the use and application of any of the contents of this book. Although every precaution has been taken in the preparation of this book, the publisher and author assume no responsibility for errors or omissions. No liability is assumed for damages resulting from the use of information contained herein. The characters portrayed in this book, and the events associated with them, are fictitious. Any similarity to real persons, living or dead, is coincidental and not intended.

In the Trenches, In the Trenches logo, CharityChannel Press logo, "C" logo, and book design are trademarks of CharityChannel Press, an imprint of CharityChannel LLC. *New Yorker* Cartoon of Trojan Horse, 7/4/2011, Media ID 134800, Copyright © Christopher Weyant/*The New Yorker* Collection/www.cartoonbank.com.

ISBN Print Book: 978-1-938077-17-3 | ISBN eBook: 978-1-938077-28-9

Library of Congress Control Number: 2013938000

13 12 11 10 9 8 7 6 5 4 3 2 1

Printed in the United States of America

This and most CharityChannel Press books are available at special quantity discounts for bulk purchases for sales promotions, premiums, fundraising, or educational use. For information, contact CharityChannel Press, 30021 Tomas, Suite 300, Rancho Santa Margarita, CA 92688-2128 USA. +1 949-589-5938

About the Editors

Linda Lysakowski, ACFRE

Linda is one of fewer than one hundred professionals worldwide to hold the Advanced Certified Fund Raising Executive designation. In her twenty years as a philanthropic consultant, she has managed capital campaigns, helped dozens of nonprofit organizations achieve their development goals, and trained more than 25,000 professionals in Mexico, Canada, Egypt, Bermuda, and most of the fifty United States, in all aspects of development.

Linda is an AFP Certified Master Trainer and serves on the board of the AFP Foundation for Philanthropy. She has received two AFP research grants. She is also a prolific writer and is always working on another book (or two, or three). Linda has received the Outstanding Fundraising Executive award from both the Eastern Pennsylvania and the Las Vegas chapters of AFP (Association of Fundraising Professionals) and in 2006 was recognized internationally in Atlanta, Georgia with the Barbara Marion Award for Outstanding Service to AFP. Linda is also a graduate of the Lay Ecclesial Ministry Program, Diocese of Las Vegas and is active in her church in Boulder City, Nevada.

Susan Schaefer, CFRE

Susan is a consultant, writer, and speaker who is passionate about the nonprofit sector. Her practical approach to fundraising and board development has made her a frequent speaker at conferences and in classrooms. She founded Resource Partners LLC in 2001 with a mission to help nonprofits excel. Her work with executives, development staff, and boards has empowered dozens of organizations to reach and exceed their financial goals. Susan brings integrity and proven results to all her work, resulting in clients who return to her again and again.

Prior to founding Resource Partners, Susan helped lead the design and implementation of the billion-dollar Gates Millennium Scholars Program, funded by one of the largest private grants in history. Throughout her career, she has held seats on nonprofit boards, regularly holding leadership positions. Her next adventure includes serving as adjunct faculty at Johns Hopkins University, where she is slated to teach fundraising. Susan holds a master's degree in Not-for-Profit Management and a bachelor's degree in English, both from the University of Maryland.

About the Contributors

Helen B. Arnold, CFRE

Helen is president and CEO of Arnold Olson Associates, a nonprofit consultant firm, and is a principal of Clearly Compliant, which provides state registration services for nonprofit organizations. Clearly Compliant also aids consultants in negotiating their state registration processes. She is a member of CharityChannel and a contributing author to *You and Your Nonprofit*. Helen is an AFP Certified Master Trainer, a Certified Webinar Facilitator, and holds the Certificate of Nonprofit Management from Iowa State University. She has served on fifty-eight nonprofit boards in her forty-five year involvement in the nonprofit industry. Helen serves as a trainer, faculty, and speaker to audiences nationally on a wide array of fund development topics.

Leo Arnoult, CFRE, MA

Leo established Arnoult & Associates Inc. in 1987 to help nonprofit organizations strengthen their development programs. He was the founding president of the Memphis chapter of the Association of Fundraising Professionals (AFP), and has served on its national board of directors. Since 1995, his firm has been a member of the Giving Institute, formerly the American Association of Fund Raising Counsel (AAFRC), and he is past chair and current board member of the Giving USA Foundation, which publishes *Giving USA*, the annual report on charitable giving and philanthropic trends.

Betsy Baker, MPA

Betsy is President of YourGrantAuthority.com and CoachWithBetsy.com. She has a master's degree in public administration from Auburn University and is an author, trainer/coach, public speaker, and grant writing consultant, having raised $10 million in grant funding. Betsy is a regular presenter for the Association of Fundraising Professionals, The Foundation Center, the Grant Professionals Association, the Georgia Center for Nonprofits, and United Way agencies and is a regular contributor to Opportunity Knocks!, CharityHowTo, and CharityChannel. She also hosts webinars, workshops, and other educational opportunities concentrating on grant writing and how to successfully market a nonprofit consulting business.

Jean Block

Jean turned her direct experience as a nonprofit staff and volunteer leader into two profitable nonprofit consulting firms. She is a nationally recognized consultant and trainer on nonprofit management, board development, fundraising, and social enterprise. She has written books on nonprofit subjects, speaks at national and regional conferences, and presents webinars on these topics. Visit her websites to learn more, take advantage of free downloads, and sign up for her e-newsletter: www.jblockinc.com and www.socialenterpriseventures.com.

Jan F. Brazzell, PhD, ACFRE

Jan leads Advancement Consulting, a firm she founded in 2001 to provide customized, professional solutions and practical advice in governance, fundraising, strategic planning, and management. Based in Tacoma, Washington, Advancement Consulting has served more than sixty organizations spanning the fields of health, education, social services, recreation, wildlife, arts, economic development, and culture. Prior to becoming a consultant, Jan led the MultiCare Health Foundation as executive director; served as vice president for development and university relations for Pacific Lutheran University; and directed corporate and foundation relations for the Franciscan Foundation for Health Care. She holds a certificate in education management from Harvard University, an MA and PhD in sociology from Indiana University, and a BA in sociology from the University of Alabama.

Ellen Bristol

For the past twenty years, Ellen has helped hundreds of nonprofit agencies achieve fundraising success. She is an expert on managing fundraising for optimum performance using a scientific approach built on the continuous improvement model.

Ellen designed the Leaky Bucket Assessment for Effective Fundraising, an online survey that measures the level of maturity of nine fundamental business practices that either contribute to or detract from the effectiveness of the fundraising effort. She is also the developer of the methodology for effective fundraising, Fundraising the SMART Way™, and its software-based toolkit, the SMART Way™ Scorecard 2.0. Her most recent publications include the e-book *De-Mystifying Fundraising*, and *What's Wrong With Your Fundraising—And How You Can Fix It*, co-authored with Linda Lysakowski, ACFRE. Ellen has also published articles for two CharityChannel Press compilations.

Pamela A. Cook, ACFRE

Pamela is the founder of Pamela Cook Development Search, www.pamelacook.com, a firm that assists Northern California nonprofits in recruiting senior development staff. Prior to establishing her firm, Pam was a fundraiser for Stanford University, California Academy of Sciences, University of Virginia, and United Way. She also managed the Clorox Foundation. Pam is a graduate of Duke University and University of Virginia and was a Fulbright Scholar at Australian National University. She holds the Advanced Certified Fundraising Executive (ACFRE) credential. She was selected as Hank Rosso Outstanding Fundraising Executive by the Association of Fundraising Professionals (AFP) and served as president of the Golden Gate Chapter of AFP.

Michelle Cramer, CFRE

Michelle is president & CEO of CRAMER & ASSOCIATES, a full-service fundraising consulting firm. Michelle is passionate about fundraising, entrepreneurism, and the power of philanthropy, often referring to her profession as "her life's calling." In 1987, she co-founded Hodge Cramer & Associates and over the course of twenty-two years, grew the practice into a nationally recognized consultancy. In 2009, she and her colleagues launched CRAMER & ASSOCIATES. True to the firm's brand, *Forward Thinking Forward Fundraising*, Michelle and her team bring an entrepreneurial mindset when developing fundraising strategies and spearheading campaigns. Michelle serves as dean of the AFP GI International Consultants School and is on the board of directors of the Giving Institute. She is a graduate of The Ohio State University. www.cramerfundraising.com.

Bob Crandall

Bob has been active in the nonprofit community for over twenty-eight years, working in a wide variety of positions with responsibilities encompassing the creation of new fundraising and planned giving programs, developing capital campaigns, growing annual support, spearheading major special events, and more. Bob has been a Certified Fund Raising Executive for twenty years and owns his own consulting firm: Crandall, Croft Associates. In addition to serving on the board of AFP Northeast Indiana Chapter, Bob has been a member of the Christian Leadership Alliance and other professional fundraising organizations. Most recently, he served for six years on the AFP Foundation for Philanthropy board and as the foundation's vice chair for fundraising. Bob also enjoys international fundraising—speaking in Brazil, India, Jordan, Israel, Mexico, and Puerto Rico. Bob was awarded the Barbara Marion Award for leadership and service to AFP.

Marti Fischer

Marti founded Marti Fischer Grant Services with the personal commitment to help nonprofits become vital partners that enhance the social and cultural fabric of their communities. Marti works with organizations to define their core work and purpose, develop strategic and fundraising strategies, and guide them in implementing practical applications. Marti has worked with groups of all sizes, but gravitates toward the enthusiastic optimism of start-up and small organizations. Have a question or need some advice? Please feel free to contact Marti through her website at www.mfgrants.com. Marti is grateful for the opportunity to collaborate on this book and wishes its readers success in their endeavors.

Gayle L. Gifford, ACFRE

Described as "strategic, bright, insightful, fearless, and principled," Gayle is president of Cause and Effect, Inc. and a nationally known consultant whose lifework is to help nonprofits improve the quality of life for all people. Gayle challenges conventions to find practical solutions to the problems nonprofits face. Her expertise includes governance, strategic and business planning, organization and fund development, and public engagement design. Gayle is one of a select number of fundraisers who have earned the advanced credential ACFRE. Gayle is the author of *How to Make Your Board Dramatically More Effective, Starting Today*. Follow her on Twitter @gaylegifford or at www.ceffect.com and her blog The Butterfly Effect.

Mary Hiland, PhD

Mary has over thirty-five years of experience in the nonprofit sector—both as a board member and executive director. Mary's consulting, speaking, workshops, and training focus on strengthening nonprofit leaders, and executive and board teams, as powerful forces for community impact. Mary assists with effective governance, board and leadership development, and strategic alliances. She has extensive experience with nonprofit mergers. She is an executive coach for new and experienced executives and board leaders. Mary is a researcher and published author. She has a PhD in human and organizational systems with a focus on nonprofit leadership and governance. You can learn more about her at www. hiland-assoc.com.

Margaret M. Holman

Margaret is president of Holman Consulting, a full-service fundraising consulting firm she founded in New York City in 1991. She served as senior vice president for development & communications at America's first and largest humane society, the ASPCA. She has also held senior fundraising management positions at a variety of arts, health, and educational institutions throughout the country. She has published numerous articles on fundraising and nonprofit management, lectured widely, and served as faculty for institutes and conferences, including the Partnership for Philanthropic Planning, the European Association for Planned Giving, the Association of Fundraising Professionals, and the International Conference for Fundraising Managers in the United Kingdom.

Simone P. Joyaux, ACFRE

Simone is described as "one of the most thoughtful, inspirational, and provocative leaders in the philanthropic sector." A consultant specializing in fund development, strategic planning, and board development, she works with all types and sizes of nonprofits, speaks at conferences worldwide, and teaches in a graduate program for philanthropy. Her books, *Keep Your Donors* and *Strategic Fund Development*, are standards in the field. Her feature articles, *Nonprofit Quarterly* (NPQ) web column, and blogs receive rave reviews. She founded the Women's Fund of Rhode Island, chaired CFRE International, and regularly serves on boards. Simone gives at least 10 percent of her income annually and has bequeathed her entire estate to charity. www.simonejoyaux.com.

Alexander "Sandy" Macnab, FAHP, CFRE

Sandy is president of Alexander Macnab & Co. (AlexanderMacnab.com), which he founded in 1994. The creator of nationally-respected annual and planned giving programs, he provides on-going annual and campaign counsel, development audits, board self-assessments, feasibility studies, and planned and major gift support. His workshops, seminars, webinars, and audio conferences have helped hundreds of professional fundraisers and nonprofit board members increase financial and volunteer support. A Master Trainer, he was invited to join the inaugural AFP Faculty Training Academy class, represents the Association of Philanthropic Counsel to the CFRE International Advisory Council, and is an adjunct professor in the graduate school of Business and Nonprofit Management teaching Planned Giving for Nonprofit Organizations at Chicago's North Park University.

Stephen C. Nill, JD

Stephen is the founder and CEO of CharityChannel, established in 1992 as a community of nonprofit sector professionals who work together to advance philanthropy. He founded CharityChannel Press (www.CharityChannel.com), the publishing arm of CharityChannel and the publisher of the *In the Trenches*™ series of books, of which this book is a part. He also founded For the GENIUS® Press (www.ForTheGENIUS.com), publisher of books on just about any subject people want to learn. He is a practicing attorney in his fourth decade advising nonprofit organizations and educational institutions. He has also served as chief development officer of a large west coast university, as CEO of a large healthcare foundation, as senior vice president of a west coast nonprofit hospital chain, and as the co-founder and development director of a thriving parochial school. He also composes symphonic music that has been performed internationally.

Meri K. Pohutsky, MA

Meri is currently the national program manager for resource development at Goodwill Industries International. She is the lead grant writer, resulting in $80 million in awards to date. She also provides consultation and training in all resource development strategies for the 158 affiliated US Goodwill agencies. Meri operated her own consulting firm, Meri and Associates, for sixteen years. She honed her skills as a leader in several nonprofit organizations, including service as a CEO. In each position, she was able to expand services and increase revenues significantly. She has also served as a grant reviewer and chairperson for federal, state, and United Way grant reviews. Meri has a long history of volunteer service on boards and in local service groups.

Sandy Rees, CFRE

Sandy is founder of GetFullyFunded (www.getfullyfunded.com), where she helps nonprofit leaders raise the money of their dreams and build successful boards. She started her career in nonprofit work in 1998 at Knox Area Rescue Ministries and spent five years at Second Harvest

Food Bank. During her time at Second Harvest, the organization nearly tripled its budget, based largely on her efforts in fundraising. Sandy is the author of *Get Fully Funded: How to Raise the Money of Your Dreams, Fundraising Buffet,* and *Simple Success Fundraising Plan.* She co-authors the column "Little Shop" for *Fundraising Success* magazine and authors the blog *Get Fully Funded.* Sandy is an accomplished presenter and an AFP Master Trainer. She has led fundraising seminars for the Association of Fundraising Professionals, the Chattanooga Center for Nonprofits, and many local and regional conferences.

Eugene A. Scanlan, PhD

Gene recently retired after forty-two years in the nonprofit sector. He served as a consultant for over twenty-five years, including as senior staff of a major national firm and as president of eScanlan Company. Additionally, he served as foundation officer for a major think tank, development director for an environmental organization, and senior staff of a grant-making foundation as well as in other positions. He has taught graduate-level online and in-person courses, authored two books, book chapters, and several articles, and served in various volunteer positions with his professional association at the chapter and international level. He has been a frequent speaker at conferences, workshops, and programs and lives in British Columbia.

Martha H. Schumacher, ACFRE

Martha is president of Hazen Inc. Hazen specializes in campaign and major gift strategy, solicitation and training; development planning; and board, staff, and organizational development (hazeninc@earthlink.net). Martha's current and recent clients include the American Red Cross, National Aquariums in Washington DC and Baltimore, Best Buddies International, and Safe Kids Worldwide. Before launching Hazen, she led the Defenders of Wildlife fundraising team as vice president for development. Martha serves on the Association of Fundraising Professionals (AFP) International Board of Directors and was recently named the AFP DC Chapter Outstanding Professional Fundraiser of the Year.

M. Kent Stroman, CFRE

Regarded as America's ASKING Coach, Kent is a talented speaker, insightful advisor, effective communicator, and published author. Kent's purpose in life is to equip, inspire, and encourage. He accomplishes this through speaking, writing, teaching, consulting, and executive coaching. After a twenty-five year career in higher education, Kent launched Stroman & Associates, consulting in fundraising, board governance, strategic planning, and leadership development. He holds numerous credentials, including Certified Fund Raising Executive. Kent is a popular speaker and presenter to regional, national, and international audiences. Learn more at www.StromanConsulting.com.

Justin Tolan, CFRE

Justin, a fundraising veteran since 1995, serves as chief fundraising adviser at ME&V Fundraising Advisers (www.MEandV.com) in Cedar Falls, Iowa. His guiding fundraising philosophy is to treat donors as you would like to be treated. Justin has counseled successful campaigns for hospitals, community centers, endowment building, and state associations. Justin raised major gifts for a youth organization prior to joining ME&V in 2001. He is a long-time mentor with Big Brothers/Big Sisters and serves as treasurer of the Bremer County Community Foundation. He is a past president of the Eastern Iowa Chapter of the Association of Fundraising Professionals and graduated from the University of Iowa.

Sandra Migani Wall, PhD

Sandra is the founder of TELESIS, a resource development consulting firm in Maumee, Ohio, providing an array of services and creative solutions tailored to meet each individual client's needs. Sandra has developed people, boards, programs, and resources over thirteen years in health education, fourteen years as a member of local and national boards, and eighteen years of part-time consulting. She has helped raise over $20 million from grants, sponsorships, and individuals for nonprofits of all sizes, in all life cycles, with local, regional or national geographical boundaries, and in varied sectors—education, human services, justice, arts, health, wildlife, zoological, botanical.

Deborah Ward, MA, CFRE

Deborah is a nationally recognized proposal writing consultant whose services include project development, prospect research, RFP analysis, writing and editing of proposals, and evaluation of grants programs. Deb is also the grant writer for Gundersen Lutheran Medical Foundation in La Crosse, Wisconsin. She is a monthly columnist for *eSchool News* and the author of Writing *Grant Proposals that Win, 4th Edition* and *Effective Grants Management*, published by Jones and Bartlett Learning. In addition to grantsmanship, Deb has experience with individual donor and corporate solicitations, direct mail appeals, special events, and annual funds. She has her graduate degree in philanthropy and development from Saint Mary's University of Minnesota.

Editors' Acknowledgments

The camaraderie that exists among consultants to the nonprofit sector is extraordinary. Few other industries can say the same for a group that, on a daily basis, exists as competitors.

This book came to fruition precisely because of that camaraderie. We cannot thank enough our colleagues who have so openly shared what makes their businesses successful. All of them have been in practice for a decade or more and have given graciously of their time and wisdom to this project. Their dedication to this book is a reminder of the generosity of our sector.

We also owe profound thanks to the editors' editor, Ellen Bristol, and our publisher, Stephen Nill, whose enthusiasm for this project was endless. Given the size of this project, that was no small feat.

And we especially want to thank Linda's husband Marty and Susan's family—Rob, Nathan, and Jake—who not only live with consultants who work round the clock but have also patiently endured the writing and editing process.

Publisher's Acknowledgments

This book was produced by a team dedicated to excellence; please send us your feedback to editors@charitychannel.com.

We first wish to acknowledge the tens of thousands of peers who call charitychannel.com their online professional home. Your enthusiastic support for the **In the Trenches™** series is the wind in our sails.

Members of the team who produced this book include:

Editors

Acquisitions Editor: Linda Lysakowski

Comprehensive Editor: Ellen Bristol

Copy Editor: Stephen Nill

Production

In the Trenches Series Design: Deborah Perdue

Layout Editor: Jill McLain

Proofreaders: Ellen Bristol, Linda Lysakowski, Jill McLain, Stephen Nill, Susan Schaefer

Administrative

CharityChannel LLC: Stephen C. Nill, CEO

Marketing and Public Relations: John Millen

Contents

Summary of Chapters

Part One: Getting Started

Chapter One: I Did It My Way

Not everyone starts a consulting practice in the same way. Some do part-time consulting while still employed full-time or part-time and ease into it. Others cut the cord and jump right in full steam ahead. We are not saying either is the right way to go, but we will hear from various consultants about how and why they started their consulting practices.

Chapter Two: So. . . What Exactly Do You Do?

Determining what services you want to provide is a crucial starting point for your business. Do you want to be a full-service firm or focus on just one service? Or will you create a marketable product? Are you qualified to offer the services needed by your prospective clients? What steps can you take to ensure that there is room for your firm in the marketplace?

Chapter Three: Home? Suite? Home?

Do you rent an office, or do you work from home? There are pros and cons of each. Hear from those who have tried it both ways and why they chose the option they did. We'll explore the professional, personal, and financial factors involved when making a decision on where to operate your business.

Chapter Four: What's in a Name?

Should you operate under your own name or a company name? Is there an advantage to using one over the other? How do you select a name that mirrors your vision of your consulting practice? What's involved in changing your company name after you've been in business awhile?

Chapter Five: It Takes Money to Make Money

How will you finance your business? How will you set your fees? Developing a budget is a big priority, but there are many other factors you need to consider to arrive at that point.

Chapter Six: Marketing Your Business

Your website, social media, word-of-mouth, teaching, and writing. All are great ways to market. Which methods work best? How much can you afford to spend? And how much time does it take? Balancing marketing time with client time is a critical element of success.

Chapter Seven: Closing the Deal

Now that you have interested clients, how do you get them to sign on the dotted line? What makes for a successful first impression? What are the best ways to sell your services? How do you position yourself ahead of the competition?

Part Two: Finding Your Groove

Chapter Eight: Playing the Part

Now that you're working with clients, what will be your leadership style? How often should you communicate with clients? What is the best way to establish a solid relationship with them? What kind of reputation will you create through your actions or inactions? How do you achieve maximum impact?

Chapter Nine: . . . and Associates

Who is going to do the work—you, employees, those nebulous "associates" most consultants attach to their corporate names? When is it time to hire, collaborate, or form a partnership? There comes a time when, in order to grow your business, you have to add more people. What are the pros and cons of each strategy, what is the real expense, and how do you find the best people?

Chapter Ten: Preparing for the Unexpected

At some point you will face an obstacle you didn't expect: an angry client, an impossible project timetable, a subcontractor who promised more than can be delivered. Hear first-person accounts of what to expect in the trenches. Learn how to preserve your sanity and your reputation in the process.

Part Three: Sticking It Out

Chapter Eleven: Reinventing Yourself

After you've been in business a while, you will probably decide it is time to reinvent your business. We'll hear from several consultants who did just that. What changes might be needed? Is it time to expand or shrink your business?

Chapter Twelve: Where Have All the Clients Gone?

Consulting is filled with ups and downs. Sometimes you'll find yourself in a real slump—the economy turns sour, your services are no longer needed, there is more competition, you've lost your biggest client. So, what now? How do you jump-start your practice?

Chapter Thirteen: Giving Back

How do you give back to your professional community and your local nonprofit community? Teaching, mentoring, writing, coaching, and pro bono work are all things on which veteran consultants tend to focus. How much of your time can you devote to these activities and still maintain a successful consulting practice?

Chapter Fourteen: Winding Down

Some consultants transition from consulting to staff work at several points during their careers. Others remain business owners until they retire. Whatever your reason for slowing down, there are many details to consider. Do you want to turn your business over to family members, partners, or associates? Is your business marketable when you decide to sell?

Part Four: Consultants' Survival Kit

Chapter Fifteen: Building Blocks for Success

No matter at what stage of your business you find yourself, some tools are essential for success. This chapter includes resources that help solidify your decision to consult, create short- and long-term plans, and master business structures.

Chapter Sixteen: Details, Details

No matter how long you're in business, you will need to pay attention to the little things. From contracts to state registration, it always pays to thoroughly understand your business' legal affairs. After you read about those two essential topics, you will be rewarded with some consulting humor—about the details that you can only learn with on-the-job experience.

Foreword

Darn you, Linda and Susan! Why didn't you organize this book twenty-five years ago when I first established Arnoult & Associates Inc.?

When I began my full-time consultancy in 1987, there were not many independent or small firms in the field, and there was certainly no comprehensive guide such as *The Nonprofit Consulting Playbook*! I was one of only a few fundraising and strategic planning consultants in the Mid-South. Today there are at least a dozen in this region alone. Most of the consultants in the mid-1980s represented the larger national firms. Today there are thousands of one-person and small consultancies across the country and around the world.

The number of people considering or entering nonprofit consulting mushroomed throughout the first decade of the twenty-first century, as did the nonprofit sector itself. While little data exists to track our collective numbers, our industry's growth reveals itself in the ballooning size of the Association of Fundraising Professionals (AFP) Consultants Directory.

Starting any type of business is a challenge. With The Great Recession of 2008, scores of nonprofits closed their doors, and many consultants could not stay in business through those turbulent times. Who knows how many consultants might have survived, and consequently how many nonprofits might have gotten the help they needed, had this book been available. *The Nonprofit Consulting Playbook* covers a myriad of practical "how-tos" and offers sage advice on both the mundane and strategic dimensions of growing a thriving consulting practice.

This very useful book, edited by Linda Lysakowski, ACFRE and Susan Schaefer, CFRE, covers the waterfront for anyone considering or already pursuing nonprofit consulting. It will help those brave souls considering launching their own practices, those who are well underway, the mid-career consultants, and even those winding down their work and trying to determine if they have a transferable business to sell.

Linda and Susan have assembled a seasoned group of veteran consultants with a wide variety of expertise and experiences. The contributing writers bring a wealth of knowledge to this comprehensive volume of practical and inspirational articles.

No matter the size of your firm, you'll likely learn the hard way to navigate the founding and growth of your business, making large and small mistakes along the way. *The Nonprofit Consulting Playbook* won't obviate the need for that rite of passage, but it should smooth out some of the bumps and help you avoid a fatal mistake. It will certainly flatten the learning curve as you discover the many useful tips in each chapter. As such it is indispensable!

Leo P. Arnoult, CFRE
President
Arnoult & Associates Inc.

Introduction

A man walks into a pet store looking to buy a monkey. The proprietor takes him to the back of the store and shows him three identical, happy monkeys, each housed in spacious, animal-friendly environments.

"This one costs $600," says the owner. "Why so much?" asks the customer. "Because it can sing and play the banjo," answers the owner.

The customer asks about the next monkey and is told, "That one costs $1,200, because it can talk, translate twenty languages, and mix cocktails." The man is astonished and asks about the third monkey.

"That one costs $4,000," answers the proprietor. "Wow, $4,000!" exclaims the man. "What can that one do?" To which the owner replies, "I've never seen it do anything, but it calls itself a consultant."

There are plenty of jokes made at consultants' expense. But is this how consultants to *nonprofits* are viewed? After all, it wasn't long ago that we were industriously working alongside our nonprofit peers. We, too, took home less-than-stellar salaries from our under-resourced organizations and worked more hours than we could reasonably track.

Now that we've gone the consulting route, do our nonprofit colleagues really think that we have abandoned our values? Anyone who has been in this field knows that consulting to the nonprofit sector requires a strong work ethic. And it's not exactly a career that will make you rich. But you have to remember that you're now running a business *to make a profit*.

When the two of us transitioned from nonprofit staff to "the other side," the learning curve was steep. As new consultants, were we fluent in fundraising, strategic planning, and board development? Yes. What about the business acumen, legal know-how, marketing, and client-relationship skills needed to launch and sustain a successful practice? That was another story. And as the years went by, did we know how best to steer our businesses toward growth? Not always.

We quickly learned that business-building is both a science and an art. *The Nonprofit Consulting Playbook* reveals how some of our field's most capable professionals have succeeded at integrating the two. It provides a first-person glimpse into our contributors' diverse achievements, heartfelt disappointments, and lessons learned. Collectively, the entrepreneurs represented in this collection reveal the nuances that have led to success.

Why We Wrote this Book

This is the book we yearned for during key points in our own consulting careers. During each stage of our businesses' maturity, our peers' insights have been the single best resource. Each of us relished the advice and honesty of our consulting confidants.

You know the scenario: As a new or evolving businessperson, you invite a fellow consultant to coffee or lunch. You ask the detailed questions that are hard to find in print. Those first-hand insights blend practical information with the honesty of hard-won successes and lessons learned. The takeaways—other than free therapy—are new strategies and techniques, new ways of thinking. We learned things as simple as the need to set up a business bank account and as complex as multistate consultant registration. We also learned such challenging things as how to set prices that gave us adequate compensation without blowing the client's budget.

It has been the diversity of those insights that we have valued most. The more people you talk to, the more nuanced an approach you develop for your own business.

We wondered, "What if we could gather some of our field's leading consultants and ask them about the keys to starting up, growing, or winding down their practices?" They might tell us how they narrowly avoided closing shop in their first years, or the interview tactics that land them big jobs. They might surprise us with advice like, "Bring a change of clothes to client meetings!" and, "Don't give away your consulting advice in the proposal!" Since so many consultants have generously shared their time and ideas with us individually, we hoped that spirit would follow to this project. Well, the response to our *Playbook* invitations was overwhelming. Our peers' generosity has given birth to a book full of big and small ideas about what makes a successful practice.

We consider *The Nonprofit Consulting Playbook* to be a window into what your exchanges would look like if you had the time—and wherewithal—to take twenty-five different veterans to lunch. The book's contents are certainly not meant to replace your own one-on-one conversations but to broaden your knowledge base, and perhaps serve as a springboard for discussion at your own peer-to-peer meetings.

Our Approach

Whether you're new to the field or a seasoned consultant yourself, the articles in *The Nonprofit Consulting Playbook* will provide practical, down-to-earth advice. We sought out contributing authors who would represent various-sized firms with different corporate structures and different areas of emphasis. All have ten or more years of consulting experience.

We did not provide many guidelines for our contributors, so you will find the book's format to be very organic. You'll see a variety of perspectives. Some will suit your personality and business structure; others will not. Some contributors completely contradict each other. Even when they agree, don't let that be an indicator of the path you should take for your own business. Let your values and your intuition guide you.

What Will You Learn from These Pages?

There are few hard rules.

There is no one formula for being a successful consultant. These articles prove that there are many paths to longevity in our field. While some themes emerge in these pages, the sample here is too small to draw many large-scale conclusions.

What you will find are many practical tips. Try some. Adapt those that work for you. Reject the others. In the spirit of our field, share your achievements *and* your failures with other consultants.

Collectively, the two of us have been consulting for over thirty years, but we still regularly seek the input of our peers. Many of those voices are represented in these pages. We couldn't be more grateful to them, especially since they share much of their sage advice again, here, with you.

Our Format

The book's first three sections reflect the phases of a business: start-up, growth, and maturity. Within each section, our contributors have written about some of the most talked-about subjects. You will find conventional topics, such as how to price your services and navigate the many marketing options. You will also read about how some leading consultants began their practices, how to reinvent yourself and your company, what to do when it's not working, and how to plan for your own succession.

The chapters are not designed to be comprehensive but to demonstrate the variety of strategies, tactics, and values that have enabled these particular consultants to remain successful for so many years.

The Playbook, as we affectionately call it, is designed so that you don't have to read it in sequence. If you are new to consulting or thinking about hanging out your shingle, start at the beginning. Veterans may prefer to start somewhere in the middle. Feel free to skip around if that best suits your needs.

important

Part Four includes some valuable resources that will get you started or keep you on your toes if you've been consulting for a while. Among them, you'll find legal, contractual, and consultant registration tools. You will find a suggested reading list that will guide you to many of the principles and practices in these pages.

We hope that this book will help you decipher the many choices ahead, no matter at what stage of your consulting career you currently find yourself. At a minimum, we hope it makes you feel better about the choices you do make—there are so many paths to success.

We'd love your feedback. You can contact us jointly at Lysakowski-schaefer@charitychannel.com.

Linda Lysakowski, ACFRE
Boulder City, NV
LindaLysakowski.com

Susan Schaefer, CFRE
Bethesda, MD
ResourcePartnersOnline.com

"How do we know it's not full of consultants?"

Part One

Getting Started

When you enter the start-up phase of your business, you're likely to encounter the most conflicting advice. That's probably because there are so many possible paths to entrepreneurship. Will you create a simple business card with your name on it and work happily out of your home for the next twenty years? Or will you quickly staff up, find a downtown office, and prepare to take on the big national firms? If you're like most of us, you'll end up somewhere in between.

This book begins with just a few of the paths that successful consultants have taken to launch their businesses. Some pursue consulting deliberately, others ease in gradually. The remainder of this section gets at the many decisions and actions that will lead you to your first client. You'll first have to figure out exactly what kind of work you'd like to do—there are more choices than ever if you want to serve nonprofits. Then engage your creative side: selecting your office location, naming your business, and marketing your services. You'll find some basics about making wise financial decisions too. Finally, some sage words about how to get prospective clients to say "yes."

Chapter One

I Did It My Way

There is no one way to start your consulting practice, and no one way to succeed. We all measure success differently. In this chapter, you will hear from three consultants about how they got started and why they're still going strong.

Margaret Holman shows us some simple steps to getting started. This sage advice should help you determine if consulting is for you and what you need know in order to get started.

Deb Ward "warns" you to get ready for ride of your life and offers some tips for how to get out there and make it happen.

Finally, Mary Hiland talks about going from a staff position to consultant and the pros and cons of consulting.

Starting a Consulting Business: Simple Steps to Success

By Margaret M. Holman

So you're thinking of starting your own consulting firm? I wasn't.

It was 1991 and I'd been happily employed by a large national animal welfare agency as the senior vice president for development and communications. I'd successfully navigated the challenging worlds of keeping the board happy, managing a staff of twenty-two, and working with a couple of really good consultants to help with our direct mail and planned gift programs. I'd never really considered "going to the dark side," as some of my friends and colleagues referred to consulting.

But after five years, my boss and I realized it was time for me to make a change, and I thought it would be the perfect opportunity to change careers for the fourth time. I wanted to take some time off as well.

The Consultant's Call

The day I resigned, I had already scheduled a dinner with one of my now-former employer's consultants with whom I had enjoyed a successful working relationship. I surprised him over dinner when I mentioned that I'd left my job. He naturally asked what was next for me, and I blithely said, "Dog-walking looks really appealing to me right now." We laughed and finished our dinner.

Several days later, he called and asked if I had thought about working as a consultant. I was busy checking *The New York Times* for jobs, calling executive recruiting firms, and checking out the local professional fundraising association's newsletters for ads (these were the days before the Internet, email, and cell phones). It never entered my mind that, with only fifteen years of fundraising experience, I could become a consultant.

We had several more conversations in the ensuing months—all while I was trudging from one interview to another, unable to find an appealing-enough cause or a job that matched or exceeded my last senior position.

The next call with the consultant turned into an offer to work with his firm as an independent contractor, until I found the "perfect" job. Since the job search was proving more difficult than I'd expected and dog-walking was more complicated than I thought, I jumped at the offer.

The consulting firm was headquartered in another state, so I was suddenly faced with setting up an office from which to work. It included the all-important telephone, crucial fax line (remember when having a fax was crucial?), and a computer.

So I cleared out the spare bedroom, bought a desk, called the phone company for new telephone and fax numbers and spent a miserable afternoon at the local computer store trying to find a desktop I could afford. Then it struck me, I should find myself a small business mentor.

The Importance of a Mentor

I called a woman who ran a small business managing associations from her apartment and begged her for some time to ask questions. She agreed to see me, and we spent several hours together. I jotted down the names of banks, accountants, lawyers, supply outlets, and other critical pieces of information that I'd need to move forward. And I found out that I would have to register with my state as a fundraising consultant. Apparently, I'd also need to set myself up with a business tax ID number. My head was spinning!

Few things are more important to consulting success than the advice of a good mentor.

important

Wasn't becoming a consultant as simple as calling a few colleagues, getting some business cards, and writing up a sample proposal? All of a sudden I was awash in filing for corporate status, setting up a business banking account, applying for a business credit card, hiring an accountant, and finding a lawyer to do all of the paperwork.

Consulting is as much about being a good businessperson as it is about being an expert in your field.

food for thought

When panic really hit, about two weeks into the process of reinventing myself, I called my business mentor who made me the best offer of all: I could come sit in her office for two weeks to watch what happened, to see how she set things up, and to see how she dealt with the most important thing of all—working from home.

We all have visions of working in our pajamas with a cat on our lap, the luxury of our clients not needing us often. But what about taking that early morning call or the late afternoon or evening call, the one that starts to eat into your personal life? My accountant also reminded me that to be able to expense the spare bedroom as an office, it had to *be* an office, *not* a spare bedroom. I needed to know more about what it means to set up shop at home.

Ask to shadow a respected colleague as you enter or consider entering the field.

practical tip

So I set out to apprentice myself to a savvy businesswoman for two short weeks. I took a rapidly-filling notebook with me every day, sat in on business meetings (having agreed in advance to keep everything confidential), and generally followed her every move. I then successfully made the transition to full-time consultant. My first client was the consulting firm that I represented earlier. I then began to build my own client base—that was twenty years ago!

Fundraisers by inclination are social folks. We thrive on company and love to work out problems collaboratively. Creating a network of colleagues and experts when you are a solo consultant goes a long way toward ensuring you stay current with the latest trends, have a safe atmosphere for trying out ideas, and have a place to get feedback. I don't know what I would have done without my group, informally called the Chicks in Charge.

stories from the real world

Even though I hadn't planned to become a consultant, after a year, I realized that many of my skills were perfectly suited to the consulting world. I had a solid understanding of and experience with nonprofits, I was a generalist fundraiser with experience in a variety of fundraising sub-specialties, I was a good listener, I had a lot of ideas grounded in working for a variety of nonprofits, and I'd learned how to effectively work with a mentor. I'd also spent years in my city getting to know a variety of people in the nonprofit world who helped me immensely to establish a business.

What I didn't know was the business side of things. Learning how to establish and manage a business is equally important to being an expert in your field. No matter how long you've been in the business, what positions you've held, or how many people you've supervised, consulting will be a new world for you. Don't skip the basics of running a business.

Get Ready for the Ride of Your Life

By Deborah Ward, MA, CFRE

Never in a million years did I dream that I would become a consultant. I had never thought about having a business of my own, traveling the world, or getting published. What I did know was that, in my long career as a fundraiser, I had always enjoyed writing grants.

I was enjoying my grants development job at an education agency and was lucky enough to attend professional conferences in the field. At one of them, I met an assistant superintendent who casually asked me my job title and what kind of doctoral degree I had. I stammered that I had a bachelor's degree in psychology and lots of experience writing grants as a fundraising professional. He then asked if I had a desire to get an advanced degree and if my employer had a tuition reimbursement program. My first answer was "yes," my second was "I'm not sure." He had planted a seed.

As soon as I got home, I looked into tuition reimbursement (my employer had a great policy!) and started researching graduate programs.

Get the Education You Need

I decided that the program offered at Saint Mary's University of Minnesota (SMU) was perfect for me. It was affordable, and the three-summer program would allow me to keep my job, spend only a little time away from my daughter, and give me an advanced degree in a field that I truly loved: philanthropy and development. I applied, was accepted, and graduated in 1998.

At SMU, I met amazing fundraisers from all over the world, and several of them said to me, "You should consider going into consulting." In 1996, one of my instructors asked me to teach the grants portion of his general development class "because I knew so much." I was flattered. When I completed this little teaching stint, I knew that if I did become a consultant I would definitely want to do as many workshops as my schedule would allow. And, while I was at SMU, I met one of the country's top-notch education grant writers of the time. We became friends, and she later agreed to be my mentor when I started my consulting business.

Do Your Research

I learned so much from veteran consultants. An education technology consultant I knew was a consummate businessman. He educated me about making a living as a solo practitioner, learning how to put a price on my intellectual property, and negotiating contracts with potential clients. He suggested that we conduct a joint workshop. He spoke with several contacts. The next thing I knew we were asked to do a one-day session for a large firm. The firm was willing to pay us an

A few of my colleagues at graduate school were already doing consulting work in the fundraising field, so I started picking their brains. I collected as much information as I could about how they got started, set their fees, decided what services to offer, and marketed their companies. I continued this little research project on my own back in Pennsylvania, and in fact, this is how I got to know one of this book's co-editors, Linda Lysakowski! Clearly, the networking you do as a new consultant can take you down many different paths.

stories from the real world

astonishing amount of money. (It was an astonishing amount for me, anyway!) We did the workshop, got paid, and at that point I decided that I was comfortable leaving my job and devoting myself to becoming a top-notch grants consultant.

One of my colleagues from graduate school recommended a book called *Working Solo*, by Terri Lonier. I purchased a copy and devoured the book, which was full of practical information about starting a business. I still have the copy of that book on my shelf with key ideas highlighted. Reading became a staple of my small business preparation.

Find a Mentor

The grant writer-turned-mentor I met at graduate school was critical to my success. She gave me three pieces of advice that I believe helped me shape my consulting business into a viable source of income. She suggested that I should:

◆ offer proposal writing services as the main thrust of my business;

◆ publish books and articles in industry publications; and

◆ be willing to present proposal writing workshops around the country to get my name and my face "out there."

At the time she gave me this advice, she had twenty-years under her belt as an education grants consultant. She was recognized in the field, had numerous books published, and knew every federal education department and education foundation program officer in the United States on a first-name basis. So I figured I couldn't go wrong following her suggestions. I was right.

Getting Published

My mentor played a key role in getting me published. She had been writing a regular column for an education funding newsletter and decided she didn't want to do it anymore. Lucky for me, she gave her editor my name and contact information and highly recommended me. The editor called, offered me the new assignment, and the publishing arm of my business began.

My mentor suggested to the same publisher that he talk to me about writing a book. He did, and I signed a contract and started working on my manuscript. In the meantime, the publisher was bought by a new publishing company, and my book slipped between the cracks. So, I put my manuscript away and hoped that someday I would be approached to write a book again. In the early 2000s, a publisher contacted me and asked me to write an updated edition of an already published book. The original author wasn't interested in doing this updated edition, and I jumped at the chance to finally make my dream come true. This led to my first published book in 2005, my second in 2010, and an updated version of the first book in late 2011.

As I sit back now and reflect upon my consulting business and how it began, it is clear that it was *individuals*—mostly consultants themselves—who played key roles in shaping my identity as a consultant. I was lucky enough to meet the right people at the right time. They shared the key lessons they had learned, and I was eager to follow their sage advice. I have worked hard to create a network of consultants around the country that I can go to for insight and assistance. For me, learning from individuals who knew consulting from the business side was a huge benefit, because I had no business background whatsoever.

There is one consultant whom I call any time one of my proposals is rejected. She understands exactly how I feel and tells me that I'm still a good proposal writer even when a funder doesn't necessarily think so!

The Ride of Your Life

For anyone who is considering a consulting business, prepare for a roller coaster ride, especially during the early years. It took me a while to create a steady income. Sometimes I wondered how I was going to pay my bills. Don't even get me started on the exorbitant cost of medical insurance when you can't be on someone else's insurance plan! But it always worked out, and I was lucky to always have clients.

Consulting is both fun and frustrating, and, in my humble opinion, well worth the effort it takes to launch a business.

From Nonprofit Executive to Consultant: One Journey and Lessons Learned

By Mary Hiland, PhD

I grew up in the nonprofit sector. I started as a caseworker in a mental health agency, soon became a program manager, then assistant executive director, and eventually executive director. As a result of leading two mergers while in that role, I found myself the CEO of a much larger nonprofit—overseeing 530 staff. But that's not the journey I am writing about here; it's the backdrop.

After about four years leading the large organization, I felt drawn to do something different. It was a subtle, nagging feeling. I loved my job. I had a great board (in case you were wondering). My positioning as a nonprofit leader in the community was pretty solid after twenty-five years as an executive, serving on state and local boards in my field, and even receiving a few awards. The feeling that something needed to change persisted. I asked myself: What is going on?

I was being called to something, but what?

Gregg Levoy, in *Callings: Finding and Following an Authentic Life*, says that our lives are made up of calls and responses. "Saying yes to the calls tends to place you on a path that half of yourself thinks doesn't make a bit of sense, but the other half knows your life won't make sense without."

This was true for me. Months of soul-searching (and some help from a great coach) led me to decide to leave my CEO position. I realized that the demands of that role were not giving me the space I needed to figure out my next steps. Believe me, this was a scary decision since I didn't have another job to go to and no clarity about what I could or should be doing.

At the time, I certainly didn't know that I was being called to be a consultant to nonprofits. I didn't advertise or offer myself as a coach or consultant during this time of transition. Even so, it didn't take long for my executive director colleagues to understand that I wasn't retiring, so I got a few inquiries asking if I could help them. I did some executive coaching, mentoring, and consulting within the nonprofit community I knew so well. That seemed like a logical way to keep some money flowing in while I figured out what I was really going to be "when I grew up." My first client tapped into my merger experience and asked me to help her and her board understand what was involved in seeking a merger partner. That led to my helping them through a strategic partner assessment, search, and selection. Another executive called and asked if I would be her coach—really a sounding board for her since I "had been there." Thus it began.

Lesson One: Establish and Maintain a Spiritual Practice

Once I opened up to the possibility of change, and then set my intention to change, new information and opportunities came to me. It felt as if these things came out of the blue, but I know better now. I learned the power of intention. During my transition period, I learned the importance of having and sustaining some spiritual practices (not religious, particularly). As we quiet our minds and open up, we can receive—we make space for new things to present themselves.

While this held true for my first unsolicited client calls, my open-mindedness also led me to a unique educational opportunity. Part of the pull away from my job was the desire to learn—to reflect on my career and read all those books sitting on my shelves that I never had time to read. I knew that some structure for pursuing learning would be helpful to me, but having a couple of degrees already, I did not have the patience for sitting in classrooms and following a prescribed curriculum. I knew what I wanted to study, but I wasn't looking for school.

All of a sudden, though, people and information were coming at me from several different sources. All this led me to an accredited graduate school offering an independent study doctoral program in organizational development. I found that I could focus my studies on nonprofits and nonprofit leadership and do it at my own pace. I was excited. I enrolled and began pursuing this learning path.

Six months after leaving my job, I was in graduate school and I had a few more clients. It was still my view that I was doing this as a placeholder until I figured out what I was *really* being called to do. Since I was reinventing myself, I realized that I needed to become clear about my own strengths and gifts. What did I have to offer anyway? What was I passionate about now? What did I really want to do? The nonprofit sector was the big container for my passion but I knew I needed more focus than that. I decided that I needed to get to know myself all over again, through a new lens. I was not an executive director anymore. I knew I was good at that. What else was I good at?

> Consulting is as much about being a good businessperson as it is about being an expert in your field.
>
>

I reached out to four or five of my friends and colleagues and asked them: What are my gifts? My strengths? There was a theme among all their answers that was a total surprise to me. It wasn't about a skill set; it was about how people experienced me. This feedback didn't lead me to consulting, but it helped me recognize that I did have something to offer that could contribute to others' growth. It also created a shift in my thinking: Didn't I have an obligation to bring to others the gifts I have been given?

Lesson Two: Know Yourself as Others Know You

This lesson builds on spiritual practice but it is a different dimension. I learned that it is important to evaluate how others experience me. This was invaluable during my transition period and it has remained invaluable. I believe we have an obligation to bring our gifts to others—this is not bravado or self-promotion. It is authentic service. How can we do that if we don't know what our gifts are?

If you are beginning your practice, ask others about your gifts. If you are in an ongoing practice, ask clients how you have added value. Keep asking and learning about yourself. Use what you learn.

By this time, I had spent one year exploring my calling. Business was growing and my studies were enriching my work. I was meeting monthly with a few trusted colleagues.

My friends challenged me to commit. "Make the commitment and see where it leads you! Stop putting your toe in the water—jump in!" they chided me. I have to admit that I made the commitment to consulting in part because I didn't want to have to come back to our next meeting and explain why I hadn't! Whatever the reason, I chose to commit.

Commitment for me at that time meant getting business cards, stationery, a website, a tagline, and even an email stationery signature. More than these marketing tools, though, commitment meant changing the way I was thinking and speaking about myself: I am a consultant and I am in business!

Lesson Three: Commit

I'll say it again: I am a consultant. Note that I did not say, I do consulting or I consult. I realized that if my thinking about this work was tentative, it had to influence how clients experienced me. I didn't test that but I believe it. I knew I would be different if I wholeheartedly dedicated myself to being the best consultant I could be. That commitment influenced my learning, what I studied, and how I dedicated my time. I was no longer biding my time, waiting for the lightning bolt to hit and the voice to say, "This is it!" I decided to trust the small voice I heard inside and go for it. I would know soon enough, I figured, if this was not the right calling for me.

For the next two years, I worked and continued school. I found that my own executive experience and board service were invaluable—clients felt that I had lived what they were living.

What is your commitment? What actions have you taken to make and reflect that commitment? What kind of consultant do you want to become? What does that mean for you?

Business was steady. Just when I thought the phone had stopped ringing for good, it would ring. Really! I wanted to grow my practice but I had to get clear about how I really wanted to do that. How could I grow business while I was completing my doctoral work? I tried working with a couple of associates during that time, so that I would have someone on tap in case I had so much work it interfered with my education. I found my needs for that help were few and brief. I ultimately decided that using subcontractors wasn't for me. I made the choice not to grow a *big* business and not to have associates or staff. I had run a large nonprofit. I knew I did not want to manage a large staff again.

I was doing a lot of different types of consulting work: strategic planning, board development, leadership development, coaching, strategic alliances, and some other odds and ends. Because of my experience and my education, I had the ability to help clients in a lot of ways. To be totally honest, I was afraid that if I narrowed my scope of practice I would have fewer opportunities, and thus less income and all that implied. I was wrong.

My school journey led me to do some research on nonprofit boards. That required a lot of study on a narrow subject. As I shared my learning and research with my nonprofit clients, I was invited to do some workshops on governance. The ultimate result was that I began to be viewed as an expert in nonprofit boards. I had heard that it was a good idea for consultants to focus, to be known for something. Being too generic was not necessarily an asset. I resisted this but by the time I received my PhD, I again committed, this time to a narrower consulting focus: nonprofit governance and the board-executive partnership.

> What is your expertise? What is your special message? What kind of work should you say no to? What do you want to be known for?
>
>

Lesson Four: Focus

I learned to stop being all things. I learned to say no. I again drew on self-reflection and self-knowledge and began telling clients what I am good at, what I know best, and referring them to others who are the best in their areas of expertise. I stopped being afraid of focusing my practice. It worked. My business continues to grow as does my reputation—for the good, thank goodness.

Lesson Five: Establishing Roles

I have many roles. My business coach and my training as a therapist taught me to value the distinctions between coaching, mentoring, and therapy early in my practice. That lesson led me to become aware of other roles I am called to play as a consultant: facilitator, expert, teacher, presenter, and writer. I continuously develop my skills in each of these roles. Each plays an important part in my ability to effectively contract, negotiate, and serve clients.

Lesson Six: Service Versus Servant

Customer service is an important value for any business, especially consulting. When I began my practice, I felt this keenly but I have since realized that my early approach to customer service was somewhat off track. I felt at the time that I needed to be responsive to clients' requests so I didn't question their assessment of their own needs.

> What roles do you play? What roles do you want to play? What roles are the best matches for your gifts? What roles do you need to develop?
>
> **food for thought**

For example, an executive director engaged me to facilitate a board retreat. Normally, I would have requested that a few board members, or at least the board chair, participate in creating the agenda. The executive director insisted that she was in tune with the board and that was not necessary. I did not insist. In fact, I did not even feel that strongly about it. I felt that my job was to be responsive to both what she wanted and how she wanted to get there. She and I developed an agenda, based on what she said were the board's objectives. The morning of the retreat, I was facilitating the work we planned and about an hour into it, several board members literally said: "Why are we doing this?" I discovered in the moment that there was a real disconnect between what the board expected and the agenda as planned.

I want to be very careful here not to give the impression that nonprofit leaders don't know what they need. I am not talking about being a patronizing know-it-all! Yes, consultants have expertise. We need to keep a delicate balance, however, between prescribing solutions and processes and exploring and facilitating clients' self-discovery and co-design of how to proceed. It is a delicate dance. Now, especially when I see patterns that are familiar to me, I ask more questions and offer options for consideration. I've learned that I need to have confidence in myself, to trust my judgment without judging, and to think of myself as a student of the client. I learned to ask more questions, to probe clients' needs at a deeper level—and not assume them to be right (or wrong) at the get-go. It is my experience that clients welcome this deeper inquiry and it has led to very different paths in our work together than if I had viewed myself as their "servant" in service versus their partner.

As I have reflected on my own journey—now ten years old—to write this article, I am full of gratitude. I have learned much more than I have had space to share here. The learning never stops. I hope that what I have shared has given you food for thought or, even better, something you can use right now!

> How does customer service manifest in your practice? How do you handle yourself when you think a client is heading down the wrong path or wants something that won't work?
>
>
> **food for thought**

Chapter Two

So, What Exactly Do You Do?

You might think the answer to this questions is easy—"I consult for nonprofits," right? In this chapter, you will learn there's a lot more to consulting than you might think.

Jean Block starts off by urging you to analyze your strengths and your weaknesses before choosing what kind of services you want to offer.

Linda Lysakowski questions whether you can consult part-time or whether you need to go "all-in."

Simone Joyaux reminds you that running a consulting practice involves a lot more than just consulting with clients, a theme you will hear throughout this book.

Consultant, Know Thyself

By Jean Block

Before you begin your consulting practice, conduct an honest assessment of your skills. You can do this yourself or with the help of a coach or mentor. Ask yourself questions such as, "Do I want long- or short-term engagements? Do I like to write grants? Do I like to teach others what I have learned? What am I really good at?" When you create this personal asset inventory, you'll define your strengths and not-so-strengths. Starting out, of course, you should focus on your strengths. But I'd also encourage you to think about what you really *like* to do and what you really *don't like* to do. Nothing will make your life as a consultant less fantastic than spending time doing what doesn't inspire you.

You might also want to focus your consulting on a particular type of organization, based upon your experience and affinity for a particular sector of the nonprofit world. Specializing in a particular part of the nonprofit sector certainly helps to focus your branding and promotion. For example, your experience might brand you as an expert in issues involving health and welfare, education, environment, animals, children, substance abuse, or poverty. You might also prefer to work with organizations of a particular size, from local grassroots groups to those with global affiliates. This can help narrow your initial focus on potential clients and leverage relationships within that sector as you build your client base.

Types of Consulting

Many consultants choose to work with a smaller client base, entering into longer-term contracts to deliver an end product such as a capital campaign, a development plan, a fundraising event, a leadership transition plan, or ongoing grant proposals.

> There is more than one way to consult successfully.
>
> **principle**

This is a great approach for those of you who really enjoy taking a project from idea through implementation, getting involved in many or all aspects of the project. If this is one of the strengths you listed in your personal asset inventory, then let it guide your type of consulting. You'll find it gratifying to see a project successfully completed, and you'll probably establish long-term relationships with these clients, perhaps leading to additional work in the future.

There are other consultants who prefer to focus on only one or two client organizations at a time, serving as the interim or transitional leader of an organization that has lost a key staff person, such as the founder, executive director, or chief financial officer. This type of engagement is usually accomplished on a contract basis that gives the consultant the authority to "clean up" and realign the internal staff and structure of an organization. Again, it is extremely gratifying to turn around a struggling or failing nonprofit, or in some cases, merge it into another, stronger organization, or in extreme cases, to close the organization altogether, transitioning its programs and services to other nonprofits. For me, that is just too much like "work" and my independent streak rebels against the requirement to be on call for a client over a longer period of time. In my asset inventory, I identified that I *like* short-term engagements and I *don't like* to be embedded in any organization for any period of time.

Consultant? Trainer? Advisor?

Let's clarify some terms. Although I call myself a *consultant*, I really am more of a *trainer* or *advisor*.

I advertise myself as a nonprofit consultant providing training and consultation in nonprofit management, fundraising, board development, and social enterprise. Within that broad framework, I can offer very specific programs to fit each organization's specific needs, and I promote specialized programs for each organization with which I work.

Rather than longer term engagements, I prefer to be the advisor who comes in for a day or two at the most, trains, motivates, and inspires and then goes away. One of my consultant partners calls this the "One Day Wonder" approach. Works for me! This approach takes advantage of my skills as a trainer/teacher/mentor and lets me do what I love doing the most. Often, I can refer the next steps to other consultants who want to do the long-term work as a follow up to my training programs.

For me, the fun of my consulting work is being able to offer a variety of services to a variety of clients. It keeps me from getting stale and forces me to learn and keep current with new trends and techniques. On average, I may get the opportunity to work with as many as eight to ten vastly different types of nonprofits each month, and that's fun.

What does this client base look like for me now? It's a national mix of small to large local nonprofits, national, regional, and local chapters of professional associations and organizations with missions from arts and culture to health and welfare, to human services, to animal and environmental issues. Let's face it—fundraising is fundraising and board development is board development, regardless of mission and size.

Realistically, can I charge as much for a day's training as for a longer term engagement? Probably not. But for me it's not about the money. It's about *loving* what I am doing, believing I am making a difference in the organizations I work with, and having *fun* doing it.

The Biggest Fear Is. . .

The biggest fear I have is that if I say "no" to a certain contract, there might not be another one to replace it and I'll starve next month. I have learned that over a year, it usually balances out. A few months may be slow but then I can't find time to breathe!

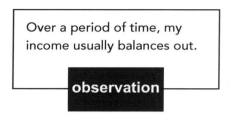

Over a period of time, my income usually balances out.

observation

The real question you have to ask and answer is how busy do you really *need* to be and *want* to be? What's the tradeoff? How will you define success? A certain goal of money earned? Or satisfaction and balance? I made a ton of money one year and was so tired that I forgot the real reasons I began consulting in the first place and began to hate life in general. Not worth the tradeoff. Everything was out of balance.

One of the joys of being a consultant is having the freedom to work with people I want to work with, doing the work I want to do...and having the ability to say "no" when I don't.

So, here's my secret. I listen to myself. When my energy is high, I go after whatever project is presented to me. When my energy is low, I stop, take a break, and forgive myself for taking a day off. I read a good book, work in the garden on a weekday instead of a weekend, have lunch with one of my consulting friends, and enjoy the freedom of my consulting lifestyle.

Options

There are many options available to us as consultants. We can develop and deliver a specific program or project. We can serve as an interim or transitional organization leader. We can coach and mentor. We can design and deliver specific training programs for a variety of organizations.

And, of course, there is the hybrid consultant who offers a variety of all these types of consulting, and that is also a viable option. The hybrid model may be more difficult to define, brand, and sell to prospective clients, but it works for many consultants.

The key is to design your business by leveraging your asset inventory of skills and likes.

Also, remember that you can modify and change your practice as you gain traction in a particular area. You might find that you started in a focused area, but your experience can now lend itself to a broader client base.

The fun of consulting is that you can design your own brand of consulting and work with whomever you choose!

Is There Such a Thing as a Part-Time Consultant?

By Linda Lysakowski, ACFRE

I've always said there is no such thing as a part-time development staff person, because anyone I know that has been in that type of position ends up working at least forty hours a week and getting paid for twenty.

When I went into consulting, I felt the same—there is no such thing as a part-time consultant.

Now, of course, I know there are plenty of consultants doing exactly that: working at a full-time job and consulting "on the side." I guess it depends a lot on what type of consulting you do.

For me, conducting capital campaigns, planning studies, and strategic plans, I cannot imagine how anyone could do this type of work on the side. You can't just say to your employer, "I am off for a week to do study interviews in Oshkosh." Well, maybe you could, but you probably wouldn't have a job to come back to.

But if your consulting work deals in research or writing, you could probably do that evenings and weekends or on your days off. That still seems challenging. Suppose a client has the same deadline as a grant you are writing for your employer? Who gets priority? And suppose your client and your organization are going after the same grant? Suppose your research uncovers a great lead that could be a prospect for your client *or* for your organization? Where does your loyalty lie?

I've always seen two major problems with consulting part-time while holding down a full-time job (which I guess explains why I've never done it!). One is the time management piece. The other is the series of ethical dilemmas you might face.

The Ethical Side

There need to be some very clear lines in the sand if you are going to consult part-time.

One consultant I know works for a consulting firm in which he is a partner while maintaining a full-time position. However, he has a clear, written agreement with his employer about what types of consulting jobs he can accept. None of his clients can have a mission that conflicts with that of his employer. Although he is a partner in the firm and ultimately shares

> I recall seeing one consultant who held down a full-time job, while consulting on the side. He was staffing a booth for the consulting firm at a national conference. I wondered who paid the consultant's way to the conference—the employer or the consulting firm? And did the employer even know that this person was consulting on the side?

stories from the real world

in its profits, he does not collect a salary for any of the consulting assignments he accepts. He gets reimbursed for travel expenses only.

This is a great way to handle the ethical dilemmas and, at the same time, build up your practice for when you are ready to consult full-time.

I jumped head-first into consulting. I didn't want to worry about such questions as: Are any of the clients' potential funders also funders of my employer? Whom do I represent when attending professional meetings, my employer or my own company? Who pays my dues to professional organizations and my expenses when I attend conferences?

Yes, the thought of being paid a salary and benefits while building your business can be tempting, but if you decide to lead a "double life," make sure you are ready to do it while upholding the highest ethical standards.

Time Management

Besides the ethical situations discussed above, I know I would never be able to handle a full-time job (often way more than forty hours a week) and still consult. Can *you*? Yes, you can work during your vacation time, but that is typically not more than about three weeks at most nonprofits, and yes, there are days off, usually six holidays and weekends.

In the United States, the Internal Revenue Service has strict guidelines that distinguish between outside contractors and employees. Employers sometimes try to hire "consultants" and treat them like employees to avoid paying benefits, unemployment taxes, and Social Security and Medicare taxes. If the person you work for exercises a certain degree of control over your work, you are *not* considered an outside contractor or consultant. Facts that provide evidence of the degree of control and independence fall into three categories:

◆ Behavioral: Does the organization control or have the right to control what you do and how you do your job? If you are a consultant, your client has the right to control only your resulting work, not the method you use to get the job done.

◆ Financial: Are the business aspects of your job controlled by the client? If you are a consultant, you should have a say in how you are paid, whether expenses are reimbursed, and who provides supplies.

◆ Type of Relationship: Are there written contracts or employee-type benefits? If you are a consultant, you should not receive benefits like a pension plan, insurance, or vacation pay. Will the relationship continue and is the work performed a key aspect of the business? If you are a consultant, you should not expect to perform for the client on a permanent basis.

Check the IRS website for more information on this at www.irs.gov.

watch out!

Of course, "days off" when you're employed at many nonprofits means time when you're not otherwise staffing events or doing other work for your employer. So how will you juggle the time?

As a part-timer, you will need to be extremely disciplined with your time. Spread out your work so that you're never running right up against a deadline. That can be hard to do if you work for a client that is disorganized. So choose your clients carefully.

If you plan to consult on the side, establish clear boundaries with your clients that do not interfere with your work life. Some of these boundaries should include not taking client calls while you are at your full-time job and not spending your employer's time and money to market your business. So you will need to establish specific times when you are working for your employer and decide if you have sufficient time during your "off hours" to market yourself and service your consulting clients.

The most realistic scenario might be an arrangement where you do very limited consulting. This might be a good way to try your hand at it if you think you might like to transition to full-time in the future. If that's the case, make sure that you create a very clear set of expectations with your client. It's ideal if you can find consulting jobs that have fairly predictable workloads and include people whom you know have reputations for being responsible. It can be a steep learning curve to be a new consultant—and hold down a full-time job—especially given all of the uncertainties associated with client reliability, information collection, and even data quality.

Are You Really a Consultant? Or Are You Between Jobs?

This field often seems to be riddled by consultants who have hung out their shingle while they are between jobs.

I once met a consultant who had worked for a large firm and then struck out on his own. Within the first year after I met him, he was working as a "contract employee" for a nonprofit. (The IRS, as we've seen, would have had issues with his arrangement, since he held himself out as a consultant while having an office, business cards, regular hours, and a boss within the organization.) Next thing I knew he was back consulting. Then, after a few months, he was working for another nonprofit. This kind of revolving-door consultant gives those of us who are serious about consulting a bad rap! Are you a consultant or just printing up business cards while you are between full-time jobs?

If you can legally, ethically, and logistically serve two masters, more power to you. But take heed—it will be a challenging position in which to find yourself. At some point you will need to make a decision: Are you a consultant or an employee? There is nothing wrong with either choice, but riding the third rail can be dangerous.

It's Not Just Consulting

By Simone P. Joyaux, ACFRE

Don't become a consultant if you just want to consult! You have to run a business, too.

You're running a small or medium or larger business. No matter the size, there's business to do.

There's marketing and administration and financial management. If you hire subcontractors or employees or both, there's personnel management. You have to fulfill government regulations, which means you have to find out about them in the first place.

You conduct interviews with prospective clients and submit proposals. You respond to requests for proposals (RFPs) and then get selected for an interview—or not.

If you work in the capacity-building business, organizations might receive foundation grants to hire you. You might have obligations to that funder. But watch out: Where does the duty of loyalty lie—to the funder or to the nonprofit? Figure that out and clarify that with the funder and the prospective client.

Billable hours are the consultant's mantra. But you have to do the business part, too. And that takes time.

How Do You Spend Your Time?

Someone once told me that consultants spend twenty-five out of forty hours doing the consulting work. The other fifteen hours are spent doing the business of consulting. Of course, it's doubtful that a viable business, or any self-employed person, is only working forty hours per week. But use the percentage: spend an estimated 37.5 percent of your time on running the business. And spend 62.5 percent of your time providing the service, e.g., consulting.

You might think that you're the exception. You might think you can spend less time doing the business part and spend more time on billable hours. But surprise—not true. You hope for more billable hours but you still have to do the business part.

I've seen consulting partnerships fail because one partner wasn't interested in the business itself. I've seen a sole practitioner go out of business because of lax business practices.

For a few years, I tracked how I spent my time.

I don't remember the results. But I do remember it was useful to track how I spent my time. Understanding how you spend your time can help you analyze your performance and make useful adjustments.

For all the years of my business, I've tracked inquiries, RFPs, and actual clients. I've always tracked my total hours per year and my average hourly or daily rate per year. I monitor the trends.

What Are You Selling?

Of course all of this business planning requires that you figure out what it is you plan to sell. Are you selling a body of knowledge, expertise, advice, and insight?

One thing you might be selling to your clients: I know more than you.

Another thing you might be selling to your clients: I have diverse experiences—perhaps more than you—and I can help you anticipate challenges and barriers, opportunities, and leverage points.

Are you selling a trust relationship that offers security and protection over the long term? Do you want to be a trusted advisor?

That second question is more complex than it might appear.

Years ago I read a great book about consulting, *The Trusted Advisor* by David H. Maister, Charles H. Green, and Robert M. Galford. Read it. Read it if you're ambitious. Read it if you want to be more than a consultant, if you want to be something really special to those you serve.

The authors define the trusted advisor as the pinnacle of consulting—where "virtually all issues, personal and professional, are open for discussion and exploration. The trusted advisor is the person the client turns to when an issue first arises, often in times of great urgency: a crisis, a change, a triumph, or a defeat."

The authors posit an evolution from subject matter expert through two intermediary steps to trusted advisor. The book includes chapters that offer tips for building trust, questions to help examine yourself, and more. I think this is an important book for all who embark on a consulting career—and all of us who currently consult but may need reminders and a challenge to our performance.

Maybe you're selling learning and change. I mean Peter Senge's learning-organization-theory kind of change, what he talks about in *The Fifth Discipline*. Individuals challenge each other's assumptions. Individuals ask the essential and cage-rattling questions to stimulate conversation. Conversation produces insights and learning and then change. And the organization's culture embraces this approach.

If you're selling learning and change, you're helping build the organization's adaptive capacity. This really works for me: Carl Sussman's adaptive capacity, Senge's learning organization theory, as well as systems-thinking theory. I guess I could say that these ideas, amongst other things, form the basis of my work and my approach.

In addition to your approach, consider your values. How do these fundamental beliefs shape your life? How will these values shape your own business and your career in consulting?

Here's another interesting question: How will all this add up to make you who you are as a consultant? Your method of work, your method of service, your approach to building and sustaining a business? How do you want to be described? You know that satisfied and dissatisfied clients will describe you to others. How do you want to be described? And realize that all of this may evolve and change over the years.

But back to what you're selling—in the sense of products. Lots of consultants sell advice and counsel, accompanied by hands-on work. I think there's a missing product line: carrying out work that is traditionally assigned to staff, but there's insufficient staff to do it.

For example, I have clients who need someone to run a special event or plan and manage a one-off program. I don't do that. I'll help plan it. But I won't do the hands-on management of it.

I know organizations that need a three-month development officer or an individual who will redesign the database and write protocols. I won't do that. I'm too expensive for that kind of hands-on work. Would you like to do that? Would you start a consulting business that provides hands-on services for special projects, or short-term absences or…?

The nonprofit sector has grant writers galore, and special event consultants, and people who serve as interim executive directors or development officers. But what about providing a permanent, typically staff-driven service? For example, can you serve as the CFO for multiple organizations, several hours per month? How about serving as the HR leader for multiple organizations?

Might you hire yourself out for one-off or short-term projects? For example, you design and run the conference, work with the volunteer committee, recruit the presenters, raise sponsorship money?

What's your niche?

Develop Yourself

That's part of what you do as a consultant.

How curious are you? Do you explore *why*, not just *how*? The really successful people—*people*, not just consultants—are curious and inquisitive, ask cage-rattling questions, and explore *why*.

Check out Carl Sussman's article, "Making Change: How to Build Adaptive Capacity" (*Nonprofit Quarterly*, Winter 2003). Then apply it to yourself, not just the organizations you consult with. Read "The Innovator's DNA," by Dyer, Gregersen, and Christensen (*Harvard Business Review*, December, 2009).

Learn new stuff. Try new things. Experiment.

I know consultants who are bored with their work. I suspect that they are rather boring—or too status quo—as consultants.

> "Adaptive capacity includes the ability to generate or initiate change—challenging the organization's external circumstances. This level of change, particularly, may require the organization to forge relationships that extend beyond its organizational borders."
>
> —Carl Sussman
>
> " "

Surely it's our job as consultants to constantly learn and to consistently try new ways of doing things. The same-old/same- old is just that. . .the same and old.

I demand critical thinking in myself. I want to challenge my own assumptions, even though I'm not always successful. I expect to explore and learn. Because only through learning can change happen.

Renew Yourself. Learn and Change.

> What is your approach to consulting? Do you see yourself as a pinch hitter or a teacher? Are you a replacement player or an outside expert?
>
> **food for thought**

Figure out how to renew yourself. Watch out because you can really get caught up in your own business and do nothing else. Especially if your office is in your home! My silly little brain regularly says, "Gee, let me just pop into the office and file all that mail. While I'm at it, send that email about that one letter. Oh, since I'm on email I may as well just finish going through my in box." Four hours later....

And those are just the days when I don't actually have weekend work scheduled with a client. I do lots of evening and weekend work because I work with boards so much.

Then there are the weekends when I have to put in eight hours per day to fulfill my client and volunteer obligations.

Be careful. This leads to burnout. Figure out how to renew yourself. Figure out how to stay out of the home office or the away-from-home office.

Just as important, develop yourself. Read. Attend conferences. Whatever.

I mean develop your knowledge base in your service areas. Then develop yourself in ancillary areas that might impact your key service areas.

Still, there's more. Develop yourself as a thinker and strategist and teacher and learner and a business owner.

Read the research in your service area(s). Read about process. Read business theory and management theory. Read about marketing and communications. Read about social media and leadership.

Everything beyond your service area(s) will help you build a business, no matter how big or small. Everything beyond your niche will make you a more interesting and insightful person, which affects your ability to connect with others and consult effectively.

My life partner—who is himself a consultant— read this curious fact: If you read one hour per day in your profession, you'll be an expert in a year. Do that for three years and you'll be a national expert.

food for thought

I'm often a bit disappointed when I realize that so many of my fellow consultants are not reading in their fields of expertise and beyond. My biggest growth in learning happened when I stopped reading in the nonprofit sector only. I'm a bit saddened when I hear that some of my fellow consultants aren't up-to-speed on research. I think it's our obligation to read and read more.

Renew Yourself Redux

Find someone to talk with, confess to, problem solve with, whine to. Any and all of those things.

Unless you work in a firm with other consultants, consulting can be pretty lonely. If you choose to be a sole practitioner, who will you talk with, complain to, confess your fears and worries to? Seek help from and give help to?

You can't talk with your clients. You might not want to talk with those you deem competitors. But find someone, more than one, if possible.

I have a long-distance relationship with a consultant and dear friend who has a practice similar to mine. Typically we talk at least once per week. We whine and complain. We strategize together. We give each other advice and problem solve together. We share sample materials and other resources. Sometimes we buy services from each other.

This began as a friendship, which is essential to each of us personally. And then it became an esteemed business association that is important to our respective consulting practices.

Foreseeing the Unforeseeable

Preparing for the unexpected. Get good at it because that's part of your job! Spend time foreseeing the unforeseeable for your clients because that's why they pay you. And foresee the unforeseeable for yourself because it will protect you.

I've fired three clients in twenty-four years in business. In all three cases, I told them I was quitting because they were not ready to participate in the consultancy.

I fired them graciously. But I made it very clear, in speech and in writing, that I was terminating the consultancy because it was apparent that the staff and board members were not ready to participate. (They didn't show up at meetings. And when they did show up, they didn't engage.)

One executive director sent me an email about a year later. In summary, she said: "We weren't ready when you were with us before. But we kept looking back at your stuff. And realized everything you said was on target and useful. And we're doing it now."

Good for them. That's great. And how delightful that the executive director let me know that.

In my twenty-third year in business, I had a client that I wanted very much to leave. I had used my good interview process and my truth-telling strategy in the interview. I was very clear about being a change agent. The organization's interview team member acted like this was all okay. I was so excited to start working with them.

But shortly into the consultancy...well, it just wasn't working. They rarely found the time to meet with me. They rarely engaged with me in telephone conversations.

None of my ideas—either gently stated or using the shock and awe approach—were received well by the executive director. Board members only vaguely listened during the rare times I met with any of them.

No matter what I did, I encountered continual resistance and avoidance and disinterest on the part of the executive director and board members. It seemed that they liked the status quo. They were proud of the organization and saw little to change, even though we talked lots about change in the interview.

I worried. I reshaped conversations. I debriefed and analyzed with two close colleagues. I grieved. I got angry and frustrated. I felt unsuccessful. I defined the consultancy as unsuccessful. If I were the organization, I would define the consultancy as unsuccessful, too.

One of my advisors said, "You can accept all the blame you want. Sure, accept that some of the responsibility is yours. Nonetheless, it is clear that the organization is not ready for change and is not interested in change. Stop this consultancy now!"

I couldn't quit. This wasn't a situation where I could tell them that they weren't ready for change. I had to get out of the consultancy, saving face for the organization and me, too.

Happily, I could claim that the work was essentially done. I had provided the products the organization wanted. I had not facilitated the process that was necessary because the organization avoided that like the proverbial plague. I didn't enable learning and change because the organization seemed so sure of its excellence that there was nothing more to excel at.

But I wrote a nice summary of progress. Said I thought the work was complete. Allowed them to save money because 50 percent of the consulting time was not used. Suggested that the contract end. And the organization agreed. Yippee.

So be prepared. Be prepared for resistance that you can overcome and resistance that you cannot overcome. Be prepared for their lack of readiness or, perhaps, your lack of realization. Be prepared that the match isn't a good match. Be prepared that someone won't pay you. Be prepared that some people won't like you.

Remember, You're Running a Business

Running a business is hard work. It may actually be harder than providing the consulting service.

You have to want to run a business, not just be a consultant. You have to do all this business stuff well. Otherwise you might not succeed over the long run. You want to be in this for the long haul.

Here are just a few unexpected or "unforeseeables" that you can expect and you can foresee:

◆ You won't like some of your clients. You'll be counting the seconds to the end of the consultancy.

◆ You'll have a few strained relationships with a few clients. It won't feel good. You'll try to fix it. It might not be fixable. It might be a bad match.

◆ Someone won't pay you. A former client (I still avoid all its board members) never paid me $3,250. Yes, I remember the exact figure. Yes, it was big money to me then. And it's important money now, too. Sometimes that happens.

◆ Then there's the readiness factor. Is the client ready for a consultancy? Is the client ready for you, whoever you are and however you define yourself?

important

Chapter Three

Home? Suite? Home?

Where will you work? In a home office or a "real" office? Or is there a happy medium?

Meri Pohutsky provides you with some of the challenges and rewards of working at home, and yes—there are both!

Martha Schumacher makes the case for renting office space and talks about the advantages of this option.

Sandy Macnab provides you with even more options—virtual office space, having a home *and* an "away from home" office.

So, what will it be for you?

Where Will You Work?

By Meri Pohutsky

When you start a consulting business, you have a lot of decisions to make. For one, do you rent an office, or do you work from home? Your choice of office location may seem simple, but it's worth thinking about in depth. In order to make the best decision, you must understand yourself, your finances, your work habits, skill sets, personal circumstances, and the relationships between them.

Understanding Yourself

Start by trying to understand who you are, what drives you, and your personality. Are you an introvert or extrovert? Are you easily distracted? Do you have good boundaries? What is it you need socially from a work environment? When do you do your best work?

For me, an extroverted night owl, not easily distracted, with poor boundaries and the need for human interaction, working from home might not seem like the ideal option, but I tried it anyway.

It *was* a challenge. I found a network of peers and mentors who I could call or meet regularly. I needed that social interaction to maintain my mental health. I had to force myself to set clear work hours so I could disconnect from home responsibilities and personal calls.

Getting dressed by the time work starts each day is vital for me. It sets a professional tone. You might laugh, but there is a seduction to the fifteen-foot commute from bedroom to home office that might tempt you to skip a shower and jump onto the computer in your jammies.

 practical tip

Flexible work hours are an advantage of having your own business. Personal circumstances and your own self-awareness will dictate when you work. For me, a single mother with three children, working while the kids were in school and after they were in bed, was ideal. In fact, I am often most creative and productive in the evening hours. Having your own business allows you to work when you work best, rather than during arbitrary office hours. You might even find you are more productive in fewer hours.

The downside of the scheduling issue is that your office is in your home, so when a client calls at six o'clock in the morning or ten o'clock at night, you will hear the call, and probably answer it, if you are home. Most consultants are available 24/7 with all of the technology available to us, but it is especially true of someone in a home-based office. Boundaries help!

Of course, not all boundary issues disappear if you work outside your home. I often hear complaints about how loud, messy, or disruptive co-located colleagues can be.

Finances

Money will determine whether your work-space preference is realistic. Renting an office means an investment of first and last months' rent, office furniture, phones, utilities, equipment, signage, and associated paraphernalia. These are important considerations, especially if you are new to consulting and do not have guaranteed contracts lined up. Of course, some of these

> When my home and office merged, my energy for household chores waned. My first splurge as a consultant was to hire a cleaning service. Highly recommended!
>
>  stories from the real world

expenses are necessary in a home office as well. In either case, those expenses with ongoing monthly payments become your overhead and the minimum you need to make each month in order to break even. Think of overhead in terms of how many hours you need to work before you start to make money.

As a new consultant, I worried about slow periods and whether I could consistently afford overhead large enough to accommodate a lease. Personally, I wanted to devote my limited resources to supplies, equipment, and increased phone costs. I wanted to keep things as simple as possible, rather than having an impressive office that would require me locking into a long-term commitment.

Of course, working out of your home also entails expenses, perhaps more of them than you think. Phone usage will increase significantly. Check with your phone company—you might be able to still use a personal account which will save you money over a more expensive business account. Consider setting up a VOIP account (such as Vonage) instead of a dedicated landline for your business; these high-tech services are very cost-effective and usually you pay a flat fee per month. You will also need all of your own office supplies and equipment. This is the thing I missed most from my employed days—all the great office supplies and toys. You will need high-quality materials reflective of your work. I wanted bright-white heavier stock paper, nice folders, and quality color print documents. Supplies can be a huge expense.

State-of-the-art equipment and software are also essential for looking professional and being able to communicate with your clients. Luckily most ink jet printers are low cost and good quality, and you can purchase inexpensive all-in-one machines that can print, copy, scan, and fax.

Whatever increases in supplies you experience with a home office, you will find decreases in other costs. I have significantly reduced the miles driven on my car, auto repairs, fuel, restaurant meals, business attire, and trips to the beauty salon.

Skills

If you plan to work from home, you need the technological skills to operate your own business.

While printers are relatively inexpensive, the cost of ink is through the roof. For major projects, check with your local office supply store or an on-line print-on-demand provider. It might be cheaper to have them do the printing for you.

For consultants, the oft-overlooked skills are those that revolve around computers, phones, and all manner of new gadgets and tools. This is when you miss having an IT department. You need to be able to hook up, troubleshoot, and effectively operate the equipment and software you need.

Take classes in programs you do not know well, like Excel, PowerPoint, Adobe PageMaker, or other skill-specific software. Become fluent in QuickBooks or whatever other accounting system you select. You also need to learn to operate meetings electronically, whether on the telephone or in a web-based environment, or find a way to outsource these tasks.

Stay abreast of technological developments and keep your software up to date. Get help if you need to. I was lucky to find a start-up company owned by two young men who built computers. They were willing to make home visits to tune up my computers and provide advice. Your new best friend, the cheap and fast computer geek, can be your best ally in determining what you need and what you need to learn.

Personal Circumstances

Factors that will influence your decision about where to work include your marital status, whether you have children, the age of your children, pets, the layout and size of your home, and the privacy available.

Find a cheap, fast computer geek.

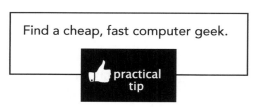

I was a single mother with a thirteen-year-old and eight-year-old twins when I started my business. They were old enough to be quiet during an important business call, but also at an age where after-school activity and what I call "background parenting" were becoming a priority. Let me explain background parenting: the thirteen-year-old was old enough to babysit during the after school hours, but not old enough to be a substitute mom. After-school activities generally happened in the middle of my work day, between two and six o'clock. It seemed critical for me to be available during these hours.

I made space in our living room for an office. I could make this space private, but it was not ideal, especially during school breaks. I recommend carving out a separate space, like a spare bedroom, basement or attic area with a door. Doors create privacy and boundaries, since you can close off your work when you are finished for the day. Nevertheless, I made it work, and my family was very cooperative, with the exception of the family dog. Without fail, the dog would notice a squirrel or bird during an important call.

Other Considerations

Another advantage to working from home is the environmental impact. It is *the* green choice. I seriously reduced my carbon footprint when I started working from home. Instead of commuting one to two hours daily, my car emitted absolutely no carbon monoxide sitting in my garage.

We've all seen office buildings with lights on well into the night and lax recycling policies. I control the environment in my home and use low-e light bulbs, recycle all manner of trash, and use a space that would otherwise be empty.

If you operate a home-based business, do not get a dog that barks.

My home-based office is also a sustainable choice in terms of my productivity. I have reclaimed the time wasted during my commute, transforming it into productive work. I accomplish more in a day, without wrestling with the stress associated with rush-hour traffic.

To Sum Up

I am a proponent of home-based consulting businesses. It is a green choice, more productive, more lucrative, and more family friendly.

Establishing a "Real" Office

By Martha H. Schumacher, ACFRE

These days, anyone can work from just about anywhere. I travel a lot for my business, and I've found that, as long as I have my smartphone and laptop, I'm good to go. Yet I'm a consultant who finds it very important to maintain both home and business offices.

Why?

There are many reasons for you to consider establishing an office outside your home. Here are five.

You Like to Work with People

If you've ever taken the Myers-Briggs or similar personality test, you know that there are introverts and extroverts, and varying levels of both. I'm an off-the-charts extrovert. I thrive on collaboration and get a lot of my energy from working with others. In my case, that means the folks down the hall at Impact Communications, the direct marketing experts who are my strategic alliance partners. They also happen to be my landlords.

You Need to Share Office Resources

As you can see in the sidebar, I have formed a strategic alliance with my landlord. This means I pay the firm rent, but it also means that in exchange for that rent, I get tech and phone support, access to a color printer and, best of all, my own parking spot. Considering the cost of parking, not to mention how challenging it can be to find downtown parking, this is a major perk.

You Want Reliable Meeting Space—for Yourself and Others.

Meeting space is often hard to come by. Sure, you can convene in a Starbucks or Panera, but depending on the meeting topic, talking over the crying baby at the next table might not be

---

Twelve years ago, I co-chaired the Association of Fundraising Professionals' Fundraising Day Conference. My co-chair and I learned quickly that we worked well together, and three years later, when I reached out to her to talk about launching my business, she kindly offered to rent me her extra office space at an extremely reasonable rate.

We quickly learned that our client services complement each other's. Her firm offers direct marketing writing, and my services target major gifts, capital campaigns, and board development. In other words, our combined services comprise the equivalent of a (nearly) full service agency. Our office arrangement has benefitted both of our businesses in more ways than we would have imagined.

stories from the real world

a productive or desirable setting. In my office, I have a conference table that comfortably seats up to six persons. I use it for my own meetings, and I've also provided the space to clients and other colleagues.

For example, one of my clients periodically spends the day on Capitol Hill. My office is just nine blocks from the Hill, so the client is able to use the space as a home base for the day and also has access to my parking spot.

You Desire Firm Boundaries between Home and Work

Working at home is sometimes more productive than working in an office. It also provides its own set of challenges and distractions, such as when you're faced with finishing a challenging client project, and somehow doing the laundry or paying your bills becomes an *urgent* priority.

If you're in a business office, there are other distractions, such as other people demanding access to you. But at least you won't succumb to the temptation of vacuuming the entire house— something I must confess is my least favorite household chore and one that I usually put off as long as possible...yet suddenly becomes of utmost importance when working from home.

You Want to Bolster Your Reputation

My office is located on Pennsylvania Avenue in Washington, DC. I may not live in the White House, but it is still an address that gets noticed. In terms of marketing to prospective clients and reinforcing my reputation with current clients, there is a certain cache attached to having a physical office on Pennsylvania Avenue.

The Bottom Line

If you do decide to rent space, here are the three questions I recommend you answer for yourself:

◆ What is my budget? I recommend that you be as conservative as possible, since you don't want your lease to eat up all of your revenue: Take what you think your office space rental budget will be and cut it in half. *Then* start looking!

◆ What does it cost to rent office space in my region? Contact real estate agents and consulting colleagues to find out what the going rate is for commercial real estate rentals. Give serious thought to which city and neighborhood is most desirable to you and why.

◆ Do I know someone who has office space right now? Until I had the discussion with the woman who would be my future landlord, I wasn't aware that she had available space. Reach out to your colleagues and find out if they have space or know of someone who does. This also goes for non-consulting colleagues who work in a building where there may be extra office space.

The most important thing you can do when deciding whether to work at home, at a business office, or both, is to consider your personal style. Are you an introvert or an extrovert? Do you have a space at home where you can set physical as well as mental boundaries? Are you someone who needs a lot of structure? Do you need meeting space on a regular basis? What other office resources are important to you? And would a business office in a certain location potentially help you to get, and keep, more business?

Each person has different needs, and one of the best things you can do for the health of your business is to perform a self-assessment that explores the answers to these questions. Who knows? You may also learn a thing or two about yourself in the process!

Your Home Base: Have It Both Ways!

By Alexander "Sandy" Macnab, FAHP, CFRE

Armed with one client and the solid promise of another, my new firm's office location didn't seem relevant until a third potential client asked where my office was located. At the time, I was using free space supplied by my former employer as part of a very generous separation package. I wasn't sure what to say, so I simply answered that from where I was sitting I could see the building from which the soon-to-be-client was calling.

"Oh good," he said, "We like to work with people who are in the Loop." I told him that technically I was just west, across the Chicago River and not literally in the small area defined by the Chicago Transit Authority's elevated train tracks that form a downtown "loop." I waited nervously for his answer and was relieved to be told, "Oh, that's okay. You're in the neighborhood!"

Until that call, I was planning to locate my office in the basement of my suburban Chicago home where I was the joint-custody dad of an eleven-year-old son and a fifteen-year-old daughter. They lived with me every other week, and they helped shape my decision about an office location as much as my own working style did.

While I was trying to work from home one day to test the waters, my daughter burst through the door one afternoon, excited with news from school, only to be disappointed to find me on a long and complex phone call with a client. She nodded and silently left the basement office I had set up. By the time the call ended, her excited wanting-to-talk moment had passed. I was painfully aware that there wasn't anyone else there for her to turn to. Those moments are special, fragile, virtually impossible to recreate, and I didn't want to miss any!

But I had to consider my working style. I'm an easily distracted, unrepentant putterer. School research assignments were an excuse to wander the stacks of books in dusty, cavernous rooms dipping into magic lands of fascinating, but often only semi-related, information. I still get that same rush today when doing online research, clicking off into Oz, Shangri-La, or Narnia with almost too much ease. I'm just not a linear thinker and I need the discipline of going to the office (preferably on a commuter train) to help me frame my day and priorities. In the same way, the return trip home leaving the office helps me let go. Without it, I could work way too much. I know that if I worked in an office in my home, I would be distracted by fix-it and "honey do" projects and would find client calls or work an annoying interruption!

When I founded my business eighteen years ago, my children were my priority. But having them with me every other week meant that on those weeks when they were with their mother, I could (and did) work early and late. Twelve-hour days were not uncommon. With help from a patient, compassionate, and understanding fundraising colleague, I ultimately found a healthy balance of work and leisure. But the time to establish my business during those non-parenting weeks—unfettered by concerns for anything but growing the practice—was a huge blessing for which I continue to be grateful.

The Costs of Renting Office Space

That call from the potential client, family demands, and the examination of my own work style pushed me to find and rent a commercial office just north of Chicago's Loop in the now-trendy River North area of the city. When I began the process, I told colleagues and friends that I was looking for space. Within weeks, a friend learned from his building's elevator operator that there was a sublet available in the building I still occupy. Initially, I found space to sublet from a tenant with an extra furnished office. The savings of this approach can be substantial. Good office furniture is expensive, heavy, and costly to move. I've had to buy most of what I have now, but by staying in the same building for eighteen years, I've been able to inherit very nice lateral files, a conference table, decent chairs, storage cabinets, counters, and even a $1,000 Herman Miller Aeron chair for free or almost free. The ten Steelcase lateral files I have, for example, were $25 each and the departing firm threw in the chair!

For those who rent, the good news is that the biggest hidden costs of commercial space are disappearing. Prior to VOIP phones and high speed Internet connections, having a commercial office meant paying the commercial cost of a phone line. In my case, two lines and the Internet were costing close to $300 per month. Coupled with a pager early on and later an answering service, my communication costs were just over $500 per month.

Parking can be another hidden cost. It's now bundled with my modest (under $400 per month) rent, but wasn't in the beginning. In major cities it's not unusual to pay $300 per month or more for an outside spot with little or no security! However, driving around looking for a parking space can be a frustrating challenge, particularly in Chicago's extreme cold or heat. Driving is the only option when client work will take me out of the downtown Chicago area into suburbs where commuter trains are either infrequent or non-existent. I quickly learned the hard way that, unlike New York, cabs to the suburbs can be a challenge, and the return trip a nightmare. So driving is the only viable option and a parking space, even if used only one or two days a week, is important. By bundling the cost with my rent, being a long-term tenant in the building and showing that I don't need a parking space every day, I was able to successfully negotiate what I consider a favorable two-year lease.

Landlords require liability insurance and some require deposits that can be financially challenging in the early years. Because I initially sublet from others, a deposit wasn't an

> Landlords are happy to have stable, consistent tenants and are willing to work to keep them.

issue, but liability insurance was. Once I began renting directly from the building owners, I found I needed to give the electric company a deposit. However, by asking if it was negotiable, I discovered that for firms with fewer than three employees, the deposit was half price. It pays to ask.

In fact, it pays to try to negotiate most ongoing costs. By letting other communication providers bid for my office phone business, I wound up with three lines, each with unlimited free local and long-distance calling throughout the U.S. and Canada (one line is now dedicated just to the fax machine), and Internet service that is triple the speed of what I used to have, all for $125 per month. This is about a third of what I had been paying for two lines and only so-so DSL Internet access. Of course the risk is that if the electric power goes out or a cable gets cut, my business will be without communication.

> No one will offer you a discount on office space, parking, phone, or utility deposits, or anything else. You have to *ask* for them. It doesn't cost anything to ask and the worst that can happen is you get told "no." Sales training 101 teaches us that a "no" really only means "not yet."

practical tip

Unlike me, there are people in my office building who do use cell phones as their primary (sometimes their only) means of communication. I'd rather have a call go to my answering service where a live person can tell the caller that I'm traveling, in a meeting, or whatever else I ask them to say, and then give the caller the option of leaving a message or being put through to my cell phone. I get a text message and an email whenever someone calls my office. This can be a big help when a response is needed quickly. In addition to audits, feasibility studies, and campaign counsel, I

> Is a telephone landline any longer necessary? They are theoretically more stable and can't get lost or stolen, but is the cost worth the peace of mind?
>
> **food for thought**

provide clients with personalized major and planned gift illustrations and, to be effective, follow-up needs to be very timely. I discovered my current answering service when calling a colleague. I liked the way my call was handled and asked who the firm used. I've been with this company for several years but went through a few before finding one that I thought would represent me well.

The Prestige of Having a "Real Office"

Probably the most significant perceived advantage of commercial office space is that some feel it differentiates a business from what was once thought of as a less professional home-based enterprise. However, as more and more firms of all sizes offer—and encourage—their employees to work from home, this difference has rapidly diminished if not disappeared completely. The perception may vary by geographic market, but I doubt that today I would be told by any potential clients that they prefer to work with consultants who are "in the neighborhood." That's particularly true in the case of the client that pushed me to a commercial office. In fact, that large organization is no longer locally-owned and does a great deal of worldwide work remotely!

So a consulting practice today can have it both ways. And a separate location can be almost virtual. If a "downtown" Madison Avenue, Michigan Avenue, or Hollywood Boulevard address is perceived to be worthwhile, it's possible to rent one at reasonable cost from office suite providers, and have your mail forwarded from them or picked up as needed. Many such firms will also answer your phone for you if you want and rent meeting and conference space as you need it, or include it as part of their monthly fee. The space is almost always furnished and comes with plenty of storage and available file space. Your company name can be listed in the building's lobby directory, and a receptionist will acknowledge that your office is there, be able to tell callers a bit about what you do, and that you are either in, out, or temporarily unavailable as you choose. If you don't need dedicated space and can live with using a different desk each time you are in the office, those arrangements can be very inexpensive.

So much now comes to us electronically that we could simultaneously have "offices" in mid-town Manhattan, the Chicago Loop, and Los Angeles without ever leaving our real work location that could vary between San Diego, San Juan, Cape Cod, or the south of France! It's probably not very practical if showing up regularly is a large part of your practice as it is for mine, but it's fun to think about.

It all means that the old notion of working from one fixed location is no longer essential or maybe even relevant. Still worth considering, however, is the number of times clients need or want to visit you in your office. That can be important for them when they just need to get away and want to meet privately. Sometimes it's to vent, and coffee shops don't work for that purpose. If you decide to have your office in your home, it's important to consider how the setting will strike your clients and the message it will convey. I have a colleague who has a very professional office on the first floor of a stunning three-story condo located in the heart of Chicago's Gold Coast. Clients can visit and be impressed by a security guard who greets them by name.

So What Do You Do?

We know that where we need to work is determined as much by how we work as it is by other factors. We can have it both ways. It doesn't have to be either/or. If I'm meeting a client in the late morning and need to drive, I'll frequently work from home rather than driving downtown and leaving from my office.

There are also some tax considerations worth thinking about. It's possible to conduct the administrative work of your business (billing, taxes, etc.) at an office in your home and produce proposals and reports or meet clients at a rental office somewhere else, if you need or want one. If the office in your home qualifies as your principal place of business, you might be able to deduct daily transportation costs between it and another work location.

While there are some practical reasons to work from home, there might be compelling reasons that some of us need to leave home and work at an office. The model that works for you is the one to choose, and you are the only one in a position to know what's best. If I were writing grants and raising small children, I would very likely work from home. I know many who do. Today we can have it both ways with a rented commercial work space and an area of our living space defined as an office. As time goes by, you might find yourself working more from one place or the other. In my case, with my children grown and gone and my wife a full-time educator, the only reason I have a rented commercial office is my own work style. That doesn't make it right. It just makes it right for me. For now.

> IRS publication 463 outlines parameters for deducting business transportation costs. So it might be possible not only to list your home office as an expense to the business, but also to deduct the entire cost of transportation to and from your commercial office. If you lease a car or depreciate an owned vehicle, the savings can be significant. Talk to your tax advisor to see if your business might be eligible.
>
> **food for thought**

Chapter Four

What's In a Name?

Decisions, decisions! Not only must you decide where to work, but now you have to choose a name for your business.

Jan Brazzell tells you why she chose not to use her own personal name as part of her company's name and how she selected that name.

Sandy Macnab says you need to "pick and stick"—choose a name and stick with it. But Linda Lysakowski offers another viewpoint—how her business survived and thrived over several name changes.

Naming Your Firm: One Size Does Not Fit All

By Jan F. Brazzell, PhD, ACFRE

Were a clever name enough, my firm should have grown by now into a large, national powerhouse, attracting thousands of inquiries and a long waiting list of clients. It hasn't. And, that's okay with me—for now.

With its melodic ring and catchy tagline, "*Helping you move your organization forward,*" I thought Advancement Consulting was poised for greatness. It topped most alphabetic listings of consulting firms. And it felt like a name to which the most discerning organizational development and fundraising clients would gravitate.

However, for all the ambition conveyed by its name, my firm remains rather small and unassuming. Becoming a large, multi-million dollar firm would entail a very different focus from the one I currently enjoy. At a minimum, I would need to create some intellectual property to sell and make huge investments in marketing so that time spent and income received weren't so directly related. Most likely, I would have to focus my time on leading and managing a team of associates rather than concentrating on my first love: providing direct services to clients. Leave it to me to enjoy most that which pays the least!

The process of naming my firm revealed to me the first of many hidden joys of owning a business: your firm becomes what you make it. It's a *creative outlet* long before you produce your first client deliverable. Everything you do for your firm, whether naming, branding, choosing a logo and tagline, equipping and furnishing, financing, marketing, setting up the books, or producing document templates, calls for creative decision making.

For me, naming my firm felt like naming a child or painting a self-portrait. The process was as intensely personal and aspirational as it was creative. I love my firm's name. It feels *right* to me. Were fame and fortune my heart's desire, the name could help carry me there. Even so, my choice actually may have proven a bit myopic. Here are some things I've learned.

Begin with Your Mission and Vision

When I started consulting eleven years ago, I was unsure about my vision for the firm. I wanted to start as a sole proprietor, yet remain open to the possibility of growing my business into a major regional, national, or international firm.

Most of my consulting friends had named their firms for themselves: Jones Development Strategies, Jones Smith LLC, the Jones Group, and Jones & Associates. Most of these were sole proprietorships or limited liability companies named to look like large partnerships or firms with multiple associates. Scratch the surface and you would find that many of the so-called associates were actually children, housekeepers, an occasional contractor, or a pet. By the way, I've learned that cats make dismal associates. But I digress.

Principals of self-named firms often begin with the vision of a small, highly-personalized firm built on the principal's reputation with, in some instances, room to grow. Some of the most common reasons I've heard for naming a firm for oneself include:

- "I'm proud to have my own firm and want it associated with my name."

- "I *am* the firm; however, I don't want prospective clients to worry about what would happen if I got run over by a truck in the middle of their campaign so I added 'associates' to the name."

- "I want people to know they are dealing with *me*."

- "It's my personal reputation I'm selling."

- "I want my clients to know that the buck stops with me.

- "I want to avoid having to trademark the name of my firm."

I find it fascinating that larger regional and national consulting firms often maintain the name of their founding principal long after the person dies or retires.

Another naming convention characterizes firms of all sizes. Owners will choose a symbolic name—a token, if you will—designed to personify their own qualities, focus, work ethic, or hobbies. For some reason, animals and landscapes seem popular: Falcon Eagle Consulting, Mountain Moon Services, Star-Bright Smith. You get the picture. I'm making all these names up to protect the guilty. I often wonder how long it takes firms such as these to explain what they actually do for a living.

Which brings me to the primary rationale behind naming my firm: my mission is to help nonprofit leaders move their organizations forward through more effective fundraising, planning, management, and governance. So, I sought a name that would convey that mission—one that emphasizes client outcomes more than my own ego. Also, I wanted a name that could grow with my firm if I chose to expand it, or that could attract buyers if eventually I decided to sell it.

Brainstorm Strategically

Yes, that's a contradiction in terms. However, once I knew what I wanted to convey, the search was on. I found some useful strategies to help me narrow the search, yet remain open to unexpected inspiration.

Peruse Membership and Consulting Directories

I began by scanning the membership and consulting directories of relevant local, regional, and national professional organizations, such as the Association of Fundraising Professionals, to see which names had been selected by firms with services similar to mine. For me, this exercise served a dual purpose: to stimulate creative thinking and to help rule out names that already had been chosen. It proved an eye-opening experience.

What's in a name? I found too much, and too little. Catchy names are a dime a dozen. And, there are literally thousands of firms that offer comparable services. I would need to find surer ways of differentiating my firm than simply naming it well.

Think Alphabetically

Most directories and rosters in the United States list people and firms alphabetically. Searching through membership and consulting directories, I learned that boredom sets in quickly (for me, as early as "E"). So, when it came time to choose a name that conveyed my firm's mission, I decided to search for "A" words first. Literally. I began with an old-fashioned dictionary. It didn't take long to find several "A words" that appealed to me. My brainstorming ended there. Interestingly, a couple of newer national firms have grabbed up the other "A" words on my original prospect list. I wonder if they wish they had gotten mine first.

Think Like the Clients You Hope to Attract

My firm's name, Advancement Consulting, spoke volumes. . .*to me*. Having been a vice president for development and university relations in an academic setting, where the term *advancement* is used routinely, I felt that it summed up my firm's mission better than any other word could find.

What I failed to consider was how the name would convey my firm's mission to the *average prospective* client. I've since learned that *advancement* means very little to most executives and board members to whom I market my services. Not knowing where to look, most people seeking the services I provide search for a fundraising consultant, campaign consultant, strategic planning consultant, management consultant, board trainer, retreat facilitator, feasibility study consultant, team building trainer, and so forth. Judging from the calls I receive, the only people who seem entranced by the term *advancement* are folks searching for career counselors and executive search capacities.

Peruse today's membership and consulting directories in our field and you will find that the savviest consultants have named their firms so that the clients they want can find them. If you're going to name your firm for yourself, make sure you create a "Cheers" world where everybody knows your name. If you're going to use something other than your personal name, pick one comprised of words that match how the clients you want would describe their consulting needs. If the name seems too common, you can always add a clever modifier or two to distinguish your firm from others doing the same thing (e.g., Vanguard Fundraising Consultants).

Experiment with Your Top Picks

With a list of exciting prospective company names in hand, i consulted a number of sources to see how well they held up to scrutiny. I began with a Google search of my favorite name. In 2001, no firm popped up with that name, or anything close. I typed in my preferred domain name, using the few suffixes available at the time. Again, nothing showed up.

Nowadays it would be much more difficult to rule out company names with only a Google search, as far more than the name you type in determines what pops up. These days, check multiple search engines and all related key words and phrases.

After my website was built, I was shocked to find that it didn't show up when I typed my firm's name into a search engine. I had to type in the complete URL in order to reach my site. Later, thanks to some excellent website coding, my firm started popping up first when someone typed "Advancement Consulting" into a search.

While I still get top billing in searches for Advancement Consulting, I find it amazing how many firms and organizations now show up on the first page that don't even have "advancement" in their name. Ad purchases, key words, and referrals from links appearing on other websites mean far more than your firm's literal name when a potential client searches for you. Also, these days, unless your firm name includes your personal name, you will have to search extensively to make sure you have uncovered all other firm names that might be the same as yours.

Increase your chances of showing up on the first page of an Internet search:

◆ When you engage a website designer, find one who knows how to make appropriate use of key words. Key words include your personal name, company name, and all common search terms your prospective clients might use. They should be scattered frequently throughout your website's underlying coding.

◆ The more times people type or click onto your firm's web address, or URL, the more prominently it will appear in subsequent searches. So make sure you take advantage of any appropriate opportunity to have your URL prominently displayed. Develop partnerships with other firms; feature one another's expertise and links on your websites; create professional accounts on social media; use social media to share your expertise and connect with others; get people to "like" your firm on Facebook; share your URL when you write articles or speak at conferences; ask your friends and family to visit your website; search yourself frequently.

◆ Customers of search companies, such as Google and Bing get top billing. If it makes sense for you, become a search company's business customer by purchasing its advertising or website optimization services.

practical tip

To get a business license in the United States, your state will require that the name you want has not already been registered there by someone else. Search all available state and federal business registration databases during the experimental stage—before you get your heart set on a name. If you want to use a business or trade name other than your own personal name and desire to have exclusive use of it, peruse the U.S. Patent and Trademark Office Trademark Electronic Search System to see if there are any possible conflicts. You will find this especially handy if you plan to work outside of the state in which you're licensed or if you want to increase the value of your business for eventual sale. Whatever the case, I would advise you to seek an attorney's assistance before making any final naming decisions.

There are lots of other ways to experiment with your top picks. You can share them with trusted friends and prospective clients and see how they react. You can re-review membership and consulting directories to see how your prospective name(s) would fit into the mix. You can practice writing a brief description of your business for your favorite consultant directory or for a consulting proposal and see how well your name corresponds to it. You can imagine yourself introducing your business at a networking event. Better yet, you can write your "elevator speech" and practice delivering it to a focus group of prospective clients. You can play with logo and tagline ideas, or enlist the help of an advertising agency or graphic designer to show you some options. You will find any of these exercises time well spent, as you most likely will have to do them as part of developing your business anyway.

Sleep on It

You've completed your research. You've found a name or two that excites you. Better yet, you know that the name you have chosen attracts the clients you hope to serve. Maybe you've already registered a couple of domain names for your website—just to make sure they don't get taken or the price doesn't escalate while you complete all the paperwork. You have consulted an attorney and, perhaps, even begun a trademarking process (which most

---

For helpful information on naming your business, as well as searchable databases of registered business names, consult:

❑ The United States Patent and Trademark Office, http://www.uspto.gov/trademarks/basics/index.jsp

❑ Your own state's trademark office, http://www.uspto.gov/trademarks/process/State_Trademark_Links.jsp

❑ Your own state's business licensing service and listings of registered businesses and corporations. Check with your state's department of licensing, department of revenue, office of the secretary of state, or office of the attorney general.

❑ There are many detailed steps involved in naming your business. It's worth some extensive reading. *Entrepreneur* has an excellent article about this subject. See the suggested reading list in **Appendix A** for details.

sources highly recommended if you wish to work outside of your own state, avoid being sued, and protect your own company from trademark infringement by others).

At this point, my best advice is to choose a name and sleep on it. If you have done all your research and you wake up feeling excited and energized by the name you have chosen, you're probably on to something. And, you will enjoy the official process of registering your name and licensing your business much more.

Naming Your Business: Pick and Stick

By Alexander "Sandy" Macnab, FAHP, CFRE

With plenty of modern-day examples around, it was pretty easy to decide that my own name needed to be the name of the consulting business I founded in Chicago in 1994. My name helped me get my initial clients and continues to help me find others by word of mouth.

When I surveyed the Chicago landscape as I was preparing to launch my business, most of the established firms such as Charles R. Feldstein, John Grenzebach, Gonser Gerber Tinker Stuhr, Don Campbell, and Jimmy Alford carried the names of their founders.

I chose to call my firm Alexander Macnab & Co. because it describes the company's organization. It's not a group, and does not have associates or partners. Potential clients know that they will be working directly with me, and the website and print promotion information says so. I thought that "& Co." was straightforward, simple, and still left room to add staff or partner with others in the future.

So what's in a name—*your* name? Well, if you have a good reputation and are not afraid to see it as the company name, I'd go for it. People know you and that will help. This is particularly true if you plan to work in the same area where you have built a reputation. The only counsel I'd offer is to pick something and stick with it. You don't want to be "and Company" this week, "and Associates" next week and a "Group" later unless it describes your firm's evolution.

> Changing your firm's name can be costly. In addition to reprinting any hard copy materials, you'll spend plenty of time reworking your electronic marketing. That's time you would otherwise devote to paid consulting services.

So whatever you do, find a name that will be comfortable now and later. Once you start advertising and people begin to know you, it will be expensive to have to re-brand yourself with a new name.

If, on the other hand, you are just starting out without a recognized name and don't think people know you, maybe an impersonal name would make sense. Or if you have a great name you've always wanted to establish and when you mention it to people, they say, "yes, that's great," maybe you should listen. Merlin Solutions, a relatively new successful firm founded by a former Association of Fundraising Professionals Chicago chapter president, Michelle Sherbun, is named for the catalyst of King Arthur's famous Round Table of peers. However, she is now considering using her own name more, particularly with other aspects of her practice. The K2 Consulting Group, founded by a former YMCA fund raiser, Kathy Kraas, has grown into a national presence. Kathy took the name from the famous mountain and also because that's what she has been called for years by colleagues and friends. Her very attractive marketing material says that the firm will help clients scale the peak to reach their goals.

There was a time when some people didn't want to have their firm's name give any indication of the ethnicity or gender of the founder or principals. Today, however, minority or female ownership is a plus when you submit applications under some requests for proposals (RFPs), particularly those from federal or state-funded organizations.

Initially, while I felt that using my name was the right thing to do, I believed it meant that the firm would have no value once my name was no longer associated with it. Lately, however, I'm getting inquiries from people who have asked if I'd be willing to consider having them join the business and gradually take over when I'm ready to retire. It's a prospect I didn't initially think possible but now believe may work one day. For a good example of how this works, see Bob Crandall's article in **Chapter Fourteen.** You'll learn how his firm, R.J. Crandall Associates based in Wabash, IN, has now become Crandall, Croft & Associates, as Robert Croft has joined the firm and is gradually taking over. It's an example for us all.

The Name Game

- ❑ Assess the power of your name and reputation.

- ❑ Consider what other firms in the area are called.

- ❑ Ask yourself what will feel right to you.

- ❑ Pick something and stick with it.

to-do lists

A Rose by Any Other Name. . .

By Linda Lysakowski, ACFRE

Naming your business is simple, right? And, if you decide you don't like it, that's simple to change too. Maybe.

My First Rodeo

When I started my business in 1993, I knew one thing. (You'll learn in another article, I thought I knew a lot of things when I was younger.) I didn't want to use my name. I had several logical reasons for this decision:

◆ nobody would be able to spell it. Not as important in 1993 as it is today when everyone finds you on the Internet, but still it was a concern.

◆ While I was pretty well known locally, no one outside of eastern Pennsylvania, where I lived at the time, would know who I was.

◆ It didn't sound very creative.

◆ And, it seemed like I had heard there could be some legal reasons not to want to use your own name for a business.

So, what would I call my company?

I thought about this question for about a month as I was putting my business plan together.

And then one day, I was sitting in church and heard the story about the "stone rejected by the builders has become the cornerstone." That resonated with me. Fundraising is often rejected by boards and executive directors as a necessary evil. We've all been rejected by donors, employers, and volunteers. But, fundraising is the cornerstone of a nonprofit organization. Without it, many would not survive. And I would be working primarily with start-up groups that needed to lay a strong foundation. So I had a name: Cornerstone Consulting, Inc. Yeah!

Well if that was the end of the story, this article would be pretty short, wouldn't it?

> I talked to mentors and people I used to work with in my former banking career and about different ideas, most of which included the word, *development*. Many of my colleagues from the banking world thought that people would immediately think I was a real estate developer, so I decided against that.

 **stories from the real world**

The Second Time Around

Ah, they say love is sweeter the second time around. I've been married to the same man for fifty-four years so I don't know about that one, but after just five years in business I found that the name Cornerstone Consulting was losing its luster. At least for me.

First, there were many people who, despite the fact that I did not use the word development in my business name, still thought cornerstone implied real estate or building. And then many people thought I only worked with Christian groups since many companies in my area used this name to indicate that they were biblically-based.

Also, in my city alone there was a Cornerstone Health Food Store, a Cornerstone Computer Consulting firm, a Cornerstone Counseling Service, and a Cornerstone Investment firm. I was constantly getting phone calls for all of these companies.

And then I found a business partner. Her company, like many, used her initials, JSM Consulting. So how did we combine those initials with Cornerstone? We decided we wouldn't. We would find a new name.

Her focus in the past had been corporate and foundation work and mine was working with start-up organizations. But in recent years, both of our companies had evolved into more capital campaign work and we wanted to emphasize that aspect of our business. After several weeks of tossing ideas around, she came up with the idea for a name, Capital Venture. I must confess that I didn't like the name. I thought we could get confused with venture capitalists. Unable to come up with anything better, we decided to go with that name. And the name has served me well.

I say *me*, because after a few years of our partnership, we decided it wasn't working out for a variety of reasons. My business partner decided she wanted to try her hand at real estate and leave the nonprofit world. So now I had another dilemma: keep the name I never liked, or change it again.

The Consequences of Changing Your Name

As we worked through the buyout process, I thought about several facts:

◆ We had spent a lot of money to develop a website for Capital Venture.

◆ After five years, we had built up a national reputation as a company.

◆ I had a lot of materials—brochures, stationery, folders, business cards—that I would have to throw away if I changed the name. (My thrifty ancestors would come back to haunt me if I wasted money like that!)

◆ Our web address had a following.

◆ I would have to train myself and others to use a new name.

So, I kept the name Capital Venture. Ironically, by this time I had moved to Las Vegas and for the first time, I did start getting calls looking for venture capital. (I still get about one of those a week.)

Another fourteen years have gone by. I have even wider name recognition, have spent a ton of money on my website, and changed my logo to include the name Capital Venture in the design.

Starting Over Yet Again

Well, someone else in the book said, "You can go home again," so guess what? I am planning another name change! This time, it is part of reinventing my company, or maybe I should call it winding down.

Over the past several years I have decided to change the focus of my work (more about this in **Chapter Eleven**). So, I went back to the drawing board and established another company, Linda Lysakowski LLC. Why did I now decide to use my name after I initially was dead-set against this idea? First, although it hasn't gotten any easier to spell, I discovered through trial and error that, when you Google or use a search engine, even if you get the spelling incorrect, the magic of technology will usually find what you're looking for.

Second, I have much stronger national and even international name recognition than I did when I started out twenty years ago. And third, I sure don't plan to change my last name at my age! (I know some people have used a family name, but my birth name, although much shorter, was just as hard to spell as Lysakowski.)

So you're among the first to hear about my recent reinvention of my company. It changed earlier this year.

Chapter Five

It Takes Money to Make Money

Money! How much will you make as a consultant? How much do you need to invest to get started?

While many consultants do not consider money the primary driving factor behind their practices, we all need to deal with it. Both in spending it and earning it.

Simone Joyaux starts this chapter off by telling you what kind of expenses you can expect to face when setting up your business. She also talks about setting fees.

Linda Lysakowski goes into more detail about how to finance your business.

And Kent Stroman talks about the importance of setting reasonable fees, making your fees equitable for you and your clients, and sticking to your guns.

Spending Money. Earning Money.

By Simone P. Joyaux, ACFRE

Starting your business really doesn't have to cost much.

When I began my business, I didn't invest much money at all.

I started out as a sole practitioner, just me. I bought my first computer because I didn't have one at home already. I printed up some letterhead.

I always intended to have a home office. I've never changed my mind. I'm still working in my home, and I deduct that square footage from my personal income tax.

How great it is to stumble into my office in my jammies. To work all day in comfy clothes.

How challenging it is to always have my office readily available. To get seduced into working more and more and more and, finally, too much.

How I Spend My Money

Since my office is in my home, I don't pay rent. Yippee! And I don't have staff. I did that for a while and didn't like it so much.

Make your office what you need it to be for comfort, focused work, and ease of work. Don't skimp here.

Of course I have my iMac—and I just love it. And my iPhone. And my iPad, although that's more personal than work-related.

Years ago, I bought a fax when the board member of a client said I needed one, "Now!" I still use it periodically, but rarely. I suppose just enough to not want it to go away yet.

I have tons of file drawers and a huge library of books. And after my computer, my favorite office equipment is probably my photocopier. I have a colleague who doesn't have a photocopier. I cannot imagine life without my photocopier.

Setting Fees: What Should I Charge?

There are lots of articles and books (and the Internet) that offer insights about price setting. I think I might have read some back when I first started. But that was twenty-four years ago and I don't remember! Apparently nothing struck me as particularly useful.

Obviously, you should think about the cost of doing business. Define the nature of your business and estimate your expenses. For example, it's more expensive if you regularly visit clients. There's the mileage, parking, and drive time. That's different from a grant writer or donor communications professional who does most work in the consultant's own office.

Think about the benefits an employee receives, such as health insurance and retirement benefits. You have to self-fund that now. You have to incorporate that into your pricing.

Think about how much someone might pay to buy your services. Be honest. What is your level of expertise and experience? How well known, respected, and admired are you in your field of service?

But mostly, think about your marketplace. For example, how many consultants are already doing what you intend to do? How many choices do your potential clients have? How will pricing affect their choosing you?

Another angle about the marketplace: What pricing will the market bear? How much are potential clients paying for various services in your area? How much do organizations in your market pay high-level employees in various fields?

More specifically, find out what nonprofits are paying for consulting services. How do you find this out? Ask around.

Back when I was starting out, I didn't ask consultants what they charged. I asked organizations what they paid for consulting services. I asked organizations that trusted and respected me.

Setting Your Fees: What's Your Price Point?

Do you want to be at the low-point or mid-point or high-point on the cost spectrum? Sure, I know, you want to make money.

When I began my business I was already well known. I was well positioned as a chief development officer in my marketplace. I gave six months' notice at my on-staff job, so I had six months to let people know that I would soon be available as a consultant.

Nonetheless, I intentionally priced myself at the low point. I figured that even though I was the new kid on the block, my reputation and a low price point would get me business.

> To learn more about other consultants—their fees and service contracts—check with the government system that collects this information. For example, many U.S. states require that fundraising consultants submit copies of contracts to a state office. And those records are mostly public. Check them out.

practical tip

I've never regretted that decision, pricing myself at the low point. Maybe I didn't need to do so. So maybe I lost some money. Who knows? Who cares? I don't. I made a decision to the best of my ability at that time.

What do you do if you're not well known? Examine the marketplace again. How will you distinguish yourself? How will you get enough business? Some of this is marketing. Read those articles in this book. Talk with other consultants about how they market their services.

But what else do you do if you're not well known? Figure out the role that pricing will play in marketing your services.

Remember, I started out at a low price point. As the years passed, I increased my rates. I continued to find out what others charged. As time passed, I asked consultants whom I respected (and considered close colleagues and friends), what they charged. We share that information.

Setting Fees: What the Client Will or Won't Pay For

Early on, I couldn't figure out how much to charge when I was doing out-of-town work—work that required hours of travel. Clients didn't seem responsive to being charged for travel time. I simply didn't know what to do.

One day I was whining with a foundation friend and she gave me the easy (and obvious) answer: charge a higher rate for work that requires extensive travel. Charge that higher rate whether you're in your own office or at the far-away site. That higher rate will compensate for the hours of travel that you cannot bill.

And so I did. And I still do.

I don't, typically, charge for mileage. Part of it is laziness. I do track my mileage, so that would be easy to do. But it just seemed like a hassle. And it began to feel like I would be nickel-and-diming clients. Since I charge a higher rate for clients that are further away geographically, I'm covered.

I treat telephone calls the same way. I don't charge the client for long-distance calls that I initiate. If we've scheduled a telephone meeting, the client initiates that call. It's the client's dime, not mine. On the other hand, I do charge expense reimbursement if I'm conducting telephone interviews on behalf of the organization.

Setting Fees: Adjusting Rates

Periodically, I review my rates. Whenever the mood strikes me. (The striking mood happens every few years; or, as the economy changes; when I feel as though I've moved up another ladder step in excellence; and so forth.)

For example, there was the day that a client told me I charged too little: "You are a great consultant, and you don't charge enough for your services." So I increased my fees.

A few years later, another client said the same thing. So I increased my fees again.

When the great recession of 2008 (and the following bad years) came along, I lowered my rates. That's the great thing about low overhead or modest cost of doing business: I'm selling my time.

I can sell my time for whatever price I want. I charge more for larger, big-budget organizations. I can lower my rates when times are tough for prospective clients. I can charge more if I suspect that the client might be problematic.

Selling my time is what matters. Having work is better than not having work.

By the way, I also make it clear that I will negotiate price. I've expressed that thought on my website. In fact, I'm impressed with an organization that wants me badly enough to say that the price is too high—and asks if I'll negotiate.

One Final Thought

Is pricing different because we're working in the nonprofit sector? I don't think so. Pricing depends upon what the market will bear. Pricing depends upon the value perceived by the prospective buyer. Pricing depends upon the quality of the service provided by the consultant.

But here are some things I notice and think about.

We consultants say that we work in the nonprofit sector. I say that, too. But what that really means is that we work *for* the nonprofit sector. And, at the same time, we are for-profit enterprises. I don't see that as a conflict.

Also, I think we are generally—but not necessarily always—stronger, better, more effective consultants if we previously worked as an employee in the nonprofit sector.

> It's worth remembering: consultants are part of the for-profit sector.
>
> **food for thought**

Sometimes when organizations contact me, they tell me that they are nonprofit. They ask for nonprofit rates. I find that somewhat curious. Curious, I guess, because it suggests that the organization didn't do any checking before contacting me. I only work for nonprofits. All my rates are for nonprofits.

Maybe the organization means that it is a small nonprofit, lacking the resources of a hospital or university or other large entity. That's a fair question and an understandable hope...do you have special rates for smaller nonprofits?

Another Final Thought

I don't want to work for organizations that are price shopping. I want to work with organizations that seek the best consultant that best matches their needs and their ambitions. I want to work with organizations that seek a trusted advisor whose approach and values match theirs.

Financing Your Business

By Linda Lysakowski, ACFRE

There is one part of consulting that no one likes to talk about or perhaps not even think about—that dirty part of our business—how do you finance it? First, you need to develop a realistic budget. Personnel expenses are usually the biggest chunk of your budget. Whether you are paying staff, subcontractors, or just yourself, you need to consider not just the salary you will be paying, but payroll taxes, health benefits, social security, etc. See an accountant to help you determine what the real costs of personnel are.

Projecting Expenses

It is important to calculate the real cost of doing business. For example, you might think that charging $100 to $250 an hour sounds pretty good compared to the salary you have been getting as an employee, but the costs to provide consulting services include such things as:

◆ Rent. Even if you are using your home as an office, there are utility and other bills that need to be considered.

◆ Technology. A consultant needs the latest technology in order to remain competitive.

◆ Marketing costs. Website, brochures, etc.

◆ Travel expenses. Transportation and meal expenses that may not be billed to the client, for instance, visiting prospective clients.

◆ State registration fees.

◆ Legal and accounting fees. And don't forget banking charges.

◆ Insurance. Health insurance, liability insurance, professional liability insurance.

◆ Taxes. Federal, state, local, payroll taxes.

◆ Salaries. Subcontractors and/or staff salaries.

◆ Communications. Phone, fax, cell phone, and Internet fees.

◆ Continuing education. For yourself, staff, and possibly even contractors.

◆ Memberships in professional organizations.

◆ Office supplies.

◆ Printing and mailing costs.

So after you create a realistic budget, figure your rates accordingly. While some consultants work on an hourly or per diem basis, others find it more valuable to the client, and more practical, to work on a project basis. One important thing to remember is that you are not an employee! A good consultant gets paid for knowledge and experience, not simply hours on the job. Even if you work primarily on a project basis, you should have an hourly figure in mind when calculating how many hours you will work on a project in order to determine the project fee.

While price fixing among consultants is prohibited by anti- trust laws, you can informally shop around and find out what other consultants are charging and how much people are willing to pay for the services you plan to offer.

When your client hires a staff person, the organization typically must allow the equivalent of about 40 percent of the staff person's salary for fees such as taxes and benefits. For example, this means that the organization pays out about $50,000 for an employee whose salary is $30,000. So, the client should understand that an outside consultant also has to pay these costs.

practical tip

A good rule of thumb for personnel expenses is that employees or subcontractors should be generating three times the amount you pay them. For example, if you pay a subcontractor $50 an hour, you will probably want to charge the client $150 an hour for the work that subcontractor is doing. One-third goes to the subcontractor, another third of the fee is for overhead, and the last third will cover your time for oversight of the project and your profit.

You also need to budget for office expenses, rent, and utilities if you are working outside your home. Even if you decide to set up a home office, there will be additional expenses for a separate telephone line, office furniture, and equipment, and the like. And don't forget marketing expenses and professional education for yourself and your staff. Those are all costs of doing business.

Paying for Start-Up and Ongoing Costs

How do you finance the start-up and continuing costs of doing business? Often small business owners use their credit cards or personal lines of credit to finance their start-up costs. You might be able to get a bank to consider a loan, but you will probably have to use your personal assets as collateral. Many consultants use their personal savings accounts to finance the start-up costs of their businesses. I know that when I left my job, I had a retirement account that I was able to tap into along with some other savings.

One thing about consulting is that there are always peaks and valleys in your income stream, and you will need some source of funding to get you through lean times. Once your business has been established for a year or two, you might consider getting a business line of credit to cover you during slow times. (You'll probably need at least three years' experience and financial statements under your belt before most banks will consider your application.)

> Pay close attention to terms of loans and lines of credit, as well as credit card charges. While these are legitimate business expenses, you need to know the real cost of financing. For example, banks can require you to "clean up" (pay off) your line of credit periodically.
>
>

The bank will want to see your financial statements, projected income, and a good business plan since a line of credit is basically an unsecured loan.

There are some less obvious options to get your business off the ground. Your local Chamber of Commerce may offer to match entrepreneurs with venture capitalists, so you might want to investigate that option. Remember, though, that venture capitalists are less likely to be impressed with your products and services, and *more* likely to respond to a business plan showing effective plans to sell the goods and services. Some chambers offer a business incubator in which small businesses receive support in the form of financial guidance, marketing advice, and human resource guidance. You might also check to see if your local university has a small business center that gives similar support for emerging businesses. And, depending on your location, there are enterprise zones in some cities that provide tax incentives for locating your business within the enterprise zone.

If you are a minority business-owner, there may be even more financing options available to you. The definition of "minority" includes woman-owned businesses, where at least fifty-one percent of the entity is owned by a woman or women. Check federal and state regulations governing the status of minority-owned businesses. The process of qualifying as a minority-owned business can be extensive, but if you plan to work with government or quasi-government entities (such as a state university) you might gain a competitive advantage by registering as a minority-owned business.

No matter what decision you make to finance your business, a good business plan is an essential first step. See Helen Arnold's article in Part Four of this book for a detailed guide to business planning.

Setting realistic fees and ensuring that your expenses are covered are essential steps to a sustainable consulting practice.

Surviving Today and Succeeding Tomorrow: Striking the Right Balance

By M. Kent Stroman, CFRE

When I hung up the phone, I was overwhelmed with gratitude. I had just completed a conversation with a board member of the organization I was leaving. Because Mary and I had worked so closely together for so many years, I felt I owed it to her to personally inform her about my plans to launch my own consulting practice.

I'm so glad I made the call.

Mary was exceptionally encouraging and uplifting with her response that day. She expressed confidence that I could succeed in my upcoming venture and extended her enthusiastic support for my decision. She even offered to help me in any way possible. Who could ask for more?

I didn't ask, but she offered. And, although I didn't realize it at the time, she provided some of the best advice I ever received for positioning myself for long-term success. Here is the nugget of wisdom Mary shared with me: "Kent, don't be afraid to charge clients what your services are worth."

This insightful, articulate friend knew me well enough to know that I could easily yield to the temptation to charge too little. For many years, my role had been to control expenditures for the organization. I had become quite proficient at this duty. I knew how to *not* spend money. And it was natural for me to come up with creative ways to reduce costs. I had unknowingly taken on a scarcity mentality. I could readily spot a glass half full. I would immediately sympathize with those in unfortunate circumstances.

And it was almost second nature for me to come up with ways to solve the other person's problems for them. She knew this would be the death of me if I carried it into the marketplace as an independent business person.

Mary went on to explain. "Any organizations needing your services can afford to pay a reasonable charge—even if it is expensive. And for those who do so, your counsel will be worth many times what they pay. Don't sell yourself short."

These few sentences gave me the confidence to set my fee schedule where it really needed to be. She was right—the fees did seem high, even to me. She was right—clients could afford it. And she was right—the value delivered far exceeds the cost charged.

Here is my advice regarding your fee structure. *You* determine an appropriate charge for *your* services. Your decision should be influenced by your own business model and cost structure. It should take into consideration what other firms charge similar clients for equivalent expertise. But, in the final analysis, the fee structure is yours. And the results will be yours also.

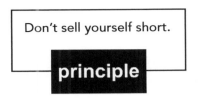

Don't sell yourself short.

principle

If the fees you charge are too high, you will have to live without the revenue you don't earn from the business you *don't* get.

If your fees are too low, you will have to live without the revenue you don't earn from the business you *do* get.

Your situation is similar to that of the Three Bears as they tried to decide which of the beds in Goldilocks' home they would sleep in. You have to make a selection that is "just right."

Avoid the urge to subsidize your client's budget by charging fees below the level that you can live with.

As a former professor of business, economics, and marketing, take it from me: if you set your fees too high, you can easily get away with lowering them, whether for just one client or for all comers. But if you begin with rates that are too low, it will be extremely difficult to increase them after the market has embraced your fee structure.

In fact, positioning is an extremely important concept to consider. Where do you want to be perceived among your competition? And don't try to kid yourself into believing that you are not in competition. You are! Failure to acknowledge this fact will create a weakness your competitors will exploit relentlessly.

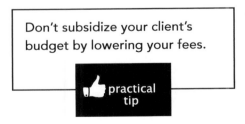

Don't subsidize your client's budget by lowering your fees.

practical tip

When I started my business, consultants with similar experience and expertise were charging between $1,000 and $3,500 per day. Since I was just starting my business I knew I couldn't justify fees at the top of the range. I also knew I didn't want to place myself at the bottom of the scale. My service model called for in-depth, high-impact, high-value consultation.

Early on, I strategically set my fees near the middle of the range. Ten years later they are significantly higher but still below the top rates.

Let me illustrate my position in the marketplace this way. At a given time, I wanted to be viewed as a $2,500 per day consultant. Although there were projects I took on at a lower rate, say $1,800 per day, I preferred to position myself as a $2,500 per day consultant who was willing to discount his fees for select projects, rather than becoming an $1,800-per-day consultant.

Think carefully about how you want to be perceived by your potential clients and then structure your fees accordingly. We may ask that our fees not be shared with other nonprofits or vendors, but this factor is ultimately beyond your control. Therefore, you must decide what messages you want your clients to relay when they do discuss your fees with others.

This topic reminds me of a saying from horse and buggy days. Roads were often muddy, and the wheel ruts became deep and nearly impossible to pull out of. Signs at intersections aptly warned, "Choose your rut wisely. You'll be in it for the next five miles."

Choose your rut wisely.

principle

When it comes to fee levels, choose wisely. You'll spend quite a bit of time in that "rut."

Another decision you have to make is how your services will be billed. Here are some of the approaches used by consultants:

◆ By the hour, day, or month

◆ By the job (project)

◆ By the amount of time on-site or on task

◆ By what you think you are worth

◆ By what you think the client can afford

◆ By a percentage of the contributions raised

The decision about how you will be compensated has far-reaching ramifications. As you contemplate the optimal arrangement for you, consider getting input from others in the field. Meet with people you look up to and get their advice. Ask what they perceive to be the risks and rewards associated with a given approach.

For example, some consultants use what they call a "sliding fee scale" based on the size of the client's budget. The smaller the budget, the lower the fee. Conversely, larger organizations are charged higher fees. Once this practice becomes known in the charitable sector—and it will—it becomes very difficult to justify to larger organizations. One of the primary

Charging clients a percentage of contributions raised is considered unethical by the Association of Fundraising Professionals, but some consultants use that method anyway.

watch out!

objections is that it requires more effort by a consultant to generate $1 million in gifts for a small organization than to do the same for a larger entity. Consequently, larger nonprofits will view their fees as subsidizing your engagement with smaller organizations.

The smaller organizations will love it! Word will spread about how affordable you are, and more and more small organizations will seek your assistance. Fewer large agencies will engage you, in an endeavor to avoid paying for their own consultancy plus a portion of the cost of the services provided to your smaller clients. This arrangement is based on noble intentions but creates a downward spiral, eventually resulting in a clientele of small organizations, paying low fees and few, if any, large clients who are really paying their own freight.

Decide what works for you, and then provide quality services for the fees you charge, without apology.

As you work to establish your fee schedule, study the regulatory climate within which you will operate. There are numerous federal and state laws governing the ways you charge for and report fundraising services. Just because another consultant uses a particular method for charging clients doesn't mean it's legal, moral, or ethical. Do your homework. You don't want to engage in practices that are contrary to the regulations and find out about it by reading the front page of *The New York Times.*

> Determine what your services are worth and don't apologize for the fees.
>
>  practical tip

An in-depth evaluation of each of the arrangements listed above is beyond the scope of this chapter. Instead, let me encourage you to:

- ◆ Educate yourself on the alternatives.

- ◆ Seek out trusted professionals.

- ◆ Learn from their experiences.

Another element to which you must be attentive is the reputation you are building. Someone once said, "Character is who you really are. It's how you act when you think nobody is watching." Reputation, however, is what people *think* you are. They may or may not be accurate in their assessment, but you are still viewed in that fashion.

I believe a consultant's most precious resource is reputation. There will be occasions when you will have to spend (or forfeit) money in order to protect your reputation. Consider it an investment in your long-term success. There truly is no substitute for a solid reputation.

The client was in a hurry. Too big a hurry as it turned out.

Staff had arranged a challenge gift with a deadline and had quickly called me to help secure the match, requesting a proposal for services. A special board meeting had been called so that I could be presented for consideration. They asked me to "fast track" the project. I did.

One day later, I was back on-site to launch the engagement. The letter of agreement for services was signed, a check for the initial fee was placed in my hands, and we jumped in with both feet.

Early the next morning, I received a troubling voice message from the charity's executive director, "Kent, we've got a problem. I got ahead of myself yesterday. I signed our agreement before obtaining the last formality. Now the chairman of the board has called with a big objection. I'm in a mess."

As Jason revealed the complex details leading to the dilemma, it became clear to me that a sizeable fee was at risk. What was I going to do?

Two alternatives began to emerge. One possibility would be for me to hold tenaciously to the legally binding contract the client had executed. I had acted in good faith. My bases were covered. His problems were his problems. He would have to work it out with his board.

The other option would potentially cost me many thousands of dollars in fees on this project. I could rescue the client and take a loss.

Drawing a deep breath I said, "Jason, let me put you at ease. Your relationship with the board and my reputation in the charitable community are too precious to jeopardize. If need be, I will simply void our contract and return your check."

The agreement never did get the formal approval required. The engagement did not move forward. Thousands of dollars of fees were not earned. The challenge was not met. The challenge gift was not received.

The good news, in my mind, overshadows the bad. The executive director's relationship with the board was untarnished. My reputation as an honorable businessman was intact. The charity could easily consider me as a provider of services in the future. The donor was receptive to revising the terms of his challenge gift.

And perhaps, most important to me, I can sleep at night with a clear conscience.

My reputation is not for sale.

stories from the real world

Considerations such as this are critically important if you sincerely desire to become a professional consultant. If you wish to be seen as a professional, you must act as a professional—always! As an independent business owner, there simply is no time when it's okay to be a jerk. There is no time when you are off duty. There is no time when someone *else* can portray the face of your business.

We are all in the business of managing expectations. In order to be successful, you will have to guide the marketplace in forming impressions and expectations about what you charge and the unique value you deliver to clients. Someone once observed, "How we sell is how we serve." Are your sales and promotional efforts honorable? If the prospects you pursue were to engage your services, thus becoming clients, would they be thrilled to be served in the same manner as they were courted?

Striking the right balance between surviving in the short-term (today) and succeeding in the long-run (tomorrow) is an ongoing challenge. As stated so eloquently by Stephen Covey, author of *The 7 Habits of Highly Effective People*, we must "begin with the end in mind." Once you have a clear vision of the destination at which you wish to arrive, you will experience remarkable clarity for the steps you need to take along the journey.

We are in the business of managing expectations.

principle

Chapter Six

Marketing Your Business

Now, here's the fun part—or is it? Maybe you are a born marketer. If so, you eagerly enjoy promoting your business. If not, maybe you just want to consult and wish some fairy godmother would come handle all your marketing tasks.

Simone Joyaux starts this chapter by asking a very challenging question: Why would anyone hire you?

Betsy Baker tackles a specific type of marketing that all consultants can and should use—LinkedIn. What you learn in this article will help all your social media efforts.

Finally, Jean Block talks about how the focus of your marketing changes over the years, so if you're in this for the long haul (and if you aren't, you probably wouldn't have invested in this book), this article is a must-read.

Why Would Anyone Hire You?

By Simone P. Joyaux, ACFRE

That's a really big question. Do you have an answer?

Here's another question: How will prospective clients know about you?

For example: What's your marketplace position before starting your business? To what degree do people and organizations already know you?

Also consider this: How would you describe the consulting marketplace in your target market? For example, how many consultants are there and what kind of work do they do? How much work is available for the existing consultant pool? Is there any gap in service that you might fill?

Be honest with yourself. Is there enough work for another consultant? Will you be good enough to get work? There may well be lots of choices in your marketplace, many different consultants. Will you get chosen frequently enough to have sufficient work to survive? There are lots of choices to select from when hiring a consultant. So are you good enough to get hired?

Have you spoken with other consultants either locally or elsewhere? How candid have these consultants been with you? What have you learned?

I ask again: Why would anyone hire you?

How Will I Market My Services?

Word-of-mouth is best. And, if you work with boards, that means all those board members can talk about you. That's many more people than just working with a few staff people.

Before we talk about marketing, you have to ask yourself what you are marketing. It's you! What do you have to offer?

I'm always stunned at people who join a consulting firm right out of university. I'm always stunned at consulting firms that hire people right out of university.

There's nothing quite like actually working in an organization. There's nothing quite like facing the real world rather than the rarified world of consulting. There's nothing quite like trying to explain something to a boss who is reluctant to hear it—and worrying that you might get fired. Or dealing with less-than-adequate resources to do your job. Or navigating the organizational culture and agency politics and individual personalities.

It's easier to consult. You give advice. You offer your important insights. And then you leave. You don't have to live with the consequences long term.

watch out!

In my early years, I periodically sent out a direct-mail letter with an offer. In the early years, I offered a free print newsletter. Today, I offer a free e-newsletter on my website and I mention it in my workshops and conference handouts.

In my early years, I periodically sent out a direct-mail letter to the key nonprofits in my state. (I live in Rhode Island; it's really small.) And there was some offer but I don't remember what.

I do remember that none of the direct-mail letters produced anything, at least anything memorable.

Writing and Presenting

What really works is the advice I got listening to some audiotapes about how to market yourself as a consultant: Present at conferences. Write articles for publications. Write books.

Presenting and writing builds your reputation far beyond your local market. Presenting and writing positions you as an expert. And, depending upon your presenting and writing style, your personality can engage and intrigue people.

For example, several years ago, I joined the international speaking circuit for fundraising and NGOs. I've spoken in Australia, New Zealand, Italy, Paris, Geneva, Brussels, and Mexico City, and all over North America. I regularly present at the International Fundraising Congress in the Netherlands. None of this would have happened had I not made a name for myself presenting in North America.

As a speaker, I'm considered a headliner. I don't have tips to give on how to do that. I didn't know I had it in me. But I sure do practice a lot. And listen to the feedback. And take risks. Some organizations hire me because they heard me speak and fell in love. Some organizations don't hire me because they heard me speak and I scared them.

I regularly get notes from people I've never met saying how much they learn from my books and articles, blogs, and columns. People say I inspire them and challenge them, and help them solve problems.

I didn't know I'd be able to write well either. Most of that is because my life partner is a journalist and accomplished writer. I learned from him. Others can learn from him and other great writers.

The thing is: just because you want to write and present doesn't mean you'll be good at it. Maybe you'll be good or great. Maybe you'll only be mediocre. Maybe you won't like presenting or writing.

By the way, you likely won't make money writing for our sector. Only a few business books (in the for-profit sector) actually make money for the authors. My two books are considered standards in the profession, well respected and in rather wide circulation. Yet, the cumulative royalties I've earned represent barely 50 percent of one of my larger consulting gigs.

> Why do I write? Because I want to. Because I think I have something to say that might be helpful to others. Because I am inspired and angry, frustrated and hopeful. Because philanthropy is my life's work and writing helps fulfill that vocation.
>
> **principle**

But writing isn't for everyone. Neither is presenting.

So what can you do?

Produce your own e-newsletter. (But don't add anyone to the newsletter list unless you get permission.) Develop good resources and make them available for free on your website.

If you're going to use presenting to market yourself, you have to be a good speaker. Good presenters deliver good content in an engaging style. Maybe you already do this well. Maybe you can develop this skill. Or maybe not.

Watch lots of presenters. Figure out what you like and dislike. Carefully distinguish between surface and substance.

Then take a risk. Start small. Present for free. Debrief with audience members to identify strengths and weaknesses. Repeat. And if organizations start inviting you to present, you're making a name for yourself.

I began my business in my geographic community. Rhode Island is a small state. I knew the community. The community knew me well enough to help me get business.

I could easily drive to clients. And, until I moved to the country—away from where organizations are—I could even go back to my home office between appointments. There was little cost in drive time, little time lost between appointments.

But then something curious happened. The inquiries expanded beyond Rhode Island. And that happened as my presenting schedule expanded. Not so curious after all.

I wasn't intentionally expanding my reach. My reach evolved because so many people all over the United States heard me speak. Word spread about my speaking so I got more and more speaking gigs. Soon I charged for my speaking, and that now represents an important part of my time and my income.

Sometimes those who heard me speak would then hire me. Sometimes. Be wary. Lots of conference hosts will tell you it's a great marketing opportunity for you to speak, so you should speak for free. Not so true. Sometimes those who hear you speak might hire you. But not always. Not necessarily in most cases.

Speak for free when you're starting out. Speak for free as you learn whether or not you are a good or great speaker. You might be a great consultant but not a great speaker. The two are not interchangeable.

Do Pro Bono Work

You can work pro bono, or do work for less money than you might normally charge. Do the work well and use the satisfied organization as a reference.

Serve on community boards to demonstrate your expertise and experience, to get your name out there.

Exhibit at Conferences

You can showcase your wares at a conference, buying a booth as a vendor.

But make sure the financial investment produces a good return. I never "do a booth" anywhere. It's not how I sell myself.

Get to Know Nearby Community Foundations

If they know your services and respect your performance, community foundations may refer you to nonprofits.

> I cannot imagine working for nonprofit organizations without serving on a board. Whether you are a consultant or a staff person, how can you work in the nonprofit sector without knowing what it's like to serve as a board member? I've served on boards for more than thirty-five years—since my start in the nonprofit sector. There's nothing quite like experiencing a different perspective.
>
> **observation**

Some community foundations host consultant databases. Participation in the database is usually free. And, typically, the community foundation neither vets nor rates the consultants in the database.

Some community foundations offer trainings. If you're a good presenter, let them know you'd like to present.

Some community foundations provide technical assistance or capacity-building grants to nonprofits. If foundation staff members know you and your work, they can refer you to their grantees.

Use the Internet

Of course, you need a website. And in this day and age, develop a good website, one that is valuable to nonprofit staff, volunteers, and their organizations.

I can remember saying years ago to clients, "If all you're going to do is put a brochure up on a website, then why bother?" I was wrong. Even if all you do is put a brochure on your website, have a website. People will look for your contact information by searching on the web. You want to be findable and found.

Make sure your website comes up high on search engines. I used a search engine optimization (SEO) specialist and professional designer for my new website, launched November 2012. I don't pay for web placement.

Use client stories and project highlights to describe the impact you have on nonprofits. Post these on your website.

Collect client testimonials and post them on your website. Include testimonials from board members and staff covering all your service areas.

Then decide if you want to do more. I made a decision to operate a very active website. My first purpose: to provide a free library for nonprofits and NGOs around the world. Honest. That was—and still remains—my first purpose.

My second purpose was for organizations to learn about me and how I might help them.

Everything is on my website now. I don't send out print marketing materials anymore.

I spend most of my website time writing my weekly blogs, writing a free e-newsletter, and updating the free resources. I give away lots of stuff. This approach reflects my concept of serving as a trusted advisor, and my commitment to philanthropy as my life's work: vocation and avocation; working and volunteering for the sector.

I choose to spend this time on my website, but not because it's great marketing. It mostly isn't. My extensive website, the choices I've made there, enhance my reputation to some degree. People find my website very useful, once they discover it through my presenting or client service.

The real purpose of my website, as extensive as it is, is a gift to the field. The website reflects my commitment to philanthropic organizations.

I made another very important decision for my website, perhaps a somewhat strange decision. My blog is called "Simone Uncensored." And some of my blogs focus on social commentary. Sure it's a risk to include social commentary in a blog on a business website—especially when the commentary is staunchly liberal and highly progressive. But it wasn't a hard decision for me.

Marketing Into the Future

What a big worry marketing was at the start. And mostly the worry doesn't go away. I always need business in the future. So will you.

As a sole practitioner, I'm typically booking work three to six months out. Sometimes more. That means I'm telling organizations that I would love to work with them but I cannot start for three months because currently I'm booked solid. Sometimes organizations will wait. Sometimes they won't. That's the challenge of the consulting business, whether you are a sole practitioner or have staff. At some point, you're full up. At another point, you're not so full.

No matter what, find new ways to put yourself out there.

I choose to comment on social issues on my business website. While it's a risky decision, I worry more about the tendency to go safe. I worry about the silent voices, which I describe as sins of omission. People can ignore my social commentary. Or not. Their choice. They can focus instead on all the free information and professional tips. I suspect that my website is part of my brand—just like my presenting style.

food for thought

Secrets of Using LinkedIn to Attract Consulting Clients

By Betsy Baker, MPA

Are you puzzled by how everyone seems to be growing their consulting business using LinkedIn—everyone, that is, except for you? There's a lot of noise out there, but I've come across some simple, surefire ways to use LinkedIn to grow my business by leaps and bounds! I've boiled down the essentials and share them here with you.

Your LinkedIn profile is your public presence. It gives you the opportunity to present your skills and expertise to potential clients. It can include your work history, your focused skill set, and others' recommendations of your work.

Your LinkedIn status allows you to post ideas, suggestions, and links. It is very similar to your Twitter status, since it can only be 140 characters or fewer. You can link your Twitter account to LinkedIn so that when you update Twitter, you will automatically update your LinkedIn status. For maximum results from your LinkedIn status updates, provide meaningful content with helpful advice and links to relevant blog post topics. Feel free to share status updates of others in your networks if you find it helpful to your potential clients.

In case you're not familiar with it, LinkedIn is a business-related social networking site. Many people use it multiple times a week. While some are there just to expand their networks, plenty participate actively, reading and engaging in discussions of very narrowly-defined topics. As a consultant, LinkedIn provides a perfect platform for you to get your expertise known far and wide.

Start With Your Profile

The whole point of putting yourself out there on LinkedIn is to become visible and credible, two very important ingredients in establishing yourself as *the* sought-after expert. When you set up your profile, be sure to include a quality photo and a detailed work history. Highlight specific jobs or volunteer roles that play up the type of work you're seeking. Update your status often. Complete all the personal and contact information fields. LinkedIn also allows space for you to list your website and social media handles. Pay attention to the details. Mass communication vehicles such as LinkedIn aren't the place for typos.

How You Choose to Connect with Others on LinkedIn is Up to You

There is no right or wrong strategy to forward invitations to connect on LinkedIn. I certainly connect with those in my field of grant writing but expand my network to include nonprofit professionals, writers, social media experts, and other small-business owners whose services I might need at some point. Some folks are very protective of their connections, but it's my opinion that LinkedIn is all about making friends of friends. Unexpected opportunities are waiting for you. When you put yourself in a position to encounter them, you will begin to harness LinkedIn's ability to drive new business.

Make Connections without Even Trying

What you have heard is true: participating in LinkedIn Groups is a must. When I first joined, I floundered along on my own and joined a few groups here and there, but I didn't know how to use them to my advantage. The big secret of making connections via Groups? Participate! Jump in and join the conversation. If you belong to a Group and don't participate, it's like standing in the corner at a party facing the wall. Be open to conversation. Pose questions, answer questions, and be visible. Your participation allows you to make connections with other Group members. You all have a shared interest by virtue of being in your particular Groups.

By making yourself known, other Group members come to recognize your name. They get to know your consulting niche. They see your expertise in action. You provide more subtle indicators of your skills as well: people will understand your commitment to the sector. They will see you giving your time to help others solve their problems. They will see your writing skills. In short, a whole new audience will come to know you, your values, and your talents.

Effectively Issue Invitations to Connect

When you find yourself interacting with Group members, you often will be asked to connect with others, or you can issue an invitation on your own. Either is an acceptable way to grow your network. When I send connection invitations within Groups, I follow a certain protocol with Group members:

- Introduce myself to the invitee as a fellow Group member.

- Provide context, such as, "Since the purpose of our Group is to network, I am extending an invitation to connect with you."

- Add a value statement of some kind suggesting how I might help them.

- Thank them and include my full name.

My invitations overwhelmingly result in positive responses with many new connections. Why? Because people are open to connecting when there is common ground. People are looking to build their own networks, and membership in the same Group establishes a baseline of credibility.

Give Meaning to Your Posts

Only post content that is meaningful to your Groups. Do you have a great blog post with helpful tips you'd like to share with your Group? Insert that link into the discussions tab. That's a great way to drive traffic to your website. Want to begin a conversation and get Group members involved? Ask a question pertaining to your expert subject matter. Remember, LinkedIn is seen as a method of sharing meaningful content and conversation and shouldn't be used only as a platform to hawk your wares. When you contribute good, solid, and helpful information, your credibility skyrockets, and people will seek you out if they want what you're selling. Play it cool.

LinkedIn in Just Fifteen Minutes a Day

With your busy schedule, you might not think you can add one more thing to your regimen. But dedication to LinkedIn pays off with big results. Here are four quick things to do in just fifteen minutes to grow your results:

❑ Update your status.

❑ Check your in box for pending invitations and messages.

❑ Check Groups for activity that will enable your meaningful comments.

❑ Search for three to five people to connect with and send invitations.

See how easy growing your business on LinkedIn can be? Learn the basics at first and then move on to more complicated measures to grow your network and to expand your opportunities.

I would definitely suggest these groups if you're not already a member. They offer support as well as potential clients:

❑ The Chronicle of Philanthropy

❑ Non Profit Professionals

❑ Nonprofit Consultants Forum

❑ The Association of Fundraising Professionals

❑ CharityChannel

Did you know that someone has to hear your message between seven and twelve times before buying anything from you? LinkedIn presents the perfect opportunity for folks to hear from you, on the topic of your choosing, and begin the process of getting to know, like, and trust you. Only after these steps have been completed will you find clients beating down your door!

> LinkedIn has dramatically increased my consulting business. It happened quite by accident since I had heard of LinkedIn but didn't participate actively until a couple of years ago. It didn't take me too long to gain a steady presence because I dedicated myself to regularly issuing connection invitations, participating in Groups, and posting meaningful content.

stories from the real world

Your Marketing Focus Changes as Your Business Matures

By Jean Block

When I started out, I spent hours and hours doing research to create a database of potential client agencies and organizations. I submitted proposals to speak at regional and national conferences. I sent letters of introduction. I asked everyone I knew in a local nonprofit to recommend me to their national office as a potential speaker. It paid off, and the referrals came in quickly.

I still submit proposals to speak, but now most of my speaking engagements are repeat performances or come from referrals. At first, you will find that you must spend a considerable amount of time letting your target audience know who you are and what you can do for them, but over time, this will change. Your reputation can precede you, and you will find yourself responding to offers to speak and consult that have come from others with whom you have worked. It's great when your clients do your promotion for you!

Target Your Potential Clients

Clearly, you'll have to narrow your initial outreach efforts to focus on those potential clients that appear to be matched most closely to the skills you have to offer. This is important so that you don't spend valuable resources on those potential clients and opportunities that aren't likely to pay off.

Ask yourself:

Who Are My Target Clients?

Large or small nonprofits? Individuals or groups? Personally, I target small to medium nonprofit organizations for individual training programs and large organizations and associations for presentations. Those presentations might evolve into other work from the participants who have attended the larger conference.

Where Are My Target Clients?

My client base has developed over time to represent nearly every state. The current environment allows in-person training as well as live Internet training (webinars), both of which I can use to best serve the particular client or group. I present my own webinars and regularly present webinars for other nonprofits, nonprofit consulting businesses, and for-profit companies serving nonprofits.

Know Your Competition

It is also important to know and understand your competition so you can define and promote your competitive advantage. Attend webinars offered by others who provide similar services and learn from them. Looking for ideas? Search the Internet for other consultants' websites and evaluate them. Which ones "work" and which don't? Which ones look like you or how you want to look? What can you tell about your competition from their collateral materials? Are there opportunities to collaborate?

Critical Promotional Materials

You should focus your promotional materials just as you do on your outreach efforts to potential clients. And, you've got to use a variety of promotional methods to generate the highest return. You will want to take advantage of current opportunities for Internet, social media, writing for publication, and even old-fashioned print.

Your Website

A professional website makes you real. Keep it current, keep it vibrant, keep it useful. Keep it in sync with your brand. I want my site to look like me: professional but relaxed and fun, useful and easy to navigate, current and snappy. I interviewed several designers before choosing the one that "got me" and created the sites to match. I was willing to spend a few thousand dollars to get it right the first time. This isn't the place to scrimp and save. If you want to be recognized as a professional, you've got to project a professional image.

I capture rave reviews and post them on my two websites, and include them in proposals and other collateral materials. Besides my business name brand, I brand myself as the "high energy, entertaining presenter who gives practical tips and ideas you can put to work immediately." The reviews support this branding.

I post free, useful forms and fundraising ideas for download on my website—again, creating value and reinforcing my brand and my expertise.

Include a listing of representative clients on your website, since this helps a prospective client see who you've worked with. Include an abbreviated version of your resume, including that information that adds credibility, such as related professional experience and education.

Prospective clients who look at your website will form an immediate opinion about whether you are a match for them—or not.

Collateral Materials

Printed materials are also important. I haven't ever used a brochure, because it is out of date as soon as it's printed. But I want something to leave behind when I speak, so I developed one-page highlights for my main topics and give them out as take-home promotions.

I have also had buttons made with one of my favorite slogans, which I give to all participants.

It's critical to stay in front of current and prospective clients. I used to print and mail a newsletter to several thousand nonprofit names in my database. You remember how it worked, don't you? You designed the format, wrote the newsletter, got it printed, labeled the newsletters, sorted them for business rate bulk mail. Thank goodness we don't have to do that anymore!

Now I send a monthly e-newsletter. Sometimes I capture hot news from sources such as BoardSource, CharityChannel, GuideStar, *The Chronicle of Philanthropy*, and others. Sometimes I write short original articles that promote my knowledge and specific services. Sometimes I give other consultants in my referral network the opportunity to write an article. I might include a limited-time offer on my self-published books. Or I promote upcoming national or regional conferences where I am speaking. The key is to make your newsletter timely and useful for the reader but also serve as a sales tool and reminder that I am here and ready to consult.

Sending an e-newsletter requires an easy-to-manage database (an Excel spreadsheet will work), and a subscription to an email service such as Constant Contact. Not rocket science, but if you aren't reminding people that you exist and giving them useful and digestible information on a regular basis, you'll get lost in the clutter.

Use the social media avenues available to you that will reach your target client base. My clients don't use Twitter. Neither do I. I haven't found a blog to be useful, so I don't do it. I post and answer questions on LinkedIn groups that target nonprofit professionals and referral sources.

Don't forget to put your website and email address on everything. Encourage people to contact you and be responsive when they do. I don't charge for email and phone advice. It adds to my credibility and my brand of being useful and practical.

A professional website makes you real.

Writing for Publication

If you want to share your expertise and brand yourself as an expert in a particular field of consulting, then writing an article or book can add instant credibility.

Start out by writing articles for publication that will reach your target client base. Some quick Internet research will reveal how and when to submit articles to professional journals and magazines. Although you are not likely to be paid for these articles, any printed articles add credibility as you promote your consulting practice.

I submit articles to newsletters and magazines that appeal to my target client group, including professional associations. I get regular requests to reprint in professional trade journals and publications, which extends my reach even farther.

My first two books were self-published. There are advantages to this route. First, you get to keep all the profit from every sale. And the cost of producing the book (printing, graphic design) is tax deductible. Self-publishing isn't difficult to do.

As easy as it is to self-publish, the disadvantages include storing, shipping, selling, and promoting the book. I offer books as "prizes" when I speak in exchange for business cards, the contents of which I add to my database. I offer copies of the books at conferences for a silent auction prize.

My buttons are showing up all over the country now!

And I regularly promote books in my e-newsletter at a limited time discount. I have even sold them in bulk at a 20 percent discount to organizations that mark them up to full price, making a profit. If you've got a huge database, then you can promote fairly well, but if not, then you'd best submit your manuscript to a professional publisher.

Although my first two books were published in hard copy, I now avoid the hassles and cost of shipping and storing by making them available as download only, giving away the remaining hard copies as promotions. You might make reprints of articles you've written that show your knowledge and expertise. Amazingly, merely saying you have written a book can give instant credibility!

Joining Things

In addition to the other ways to promote yourself, you'll want to join some professional associations. You *could* join dozens of organizations and associations and add the list of memberships to your website. However, I'd suggest you target only those organizations that will allow you to reach your targeted client base. But joining isn't enough. You've got to be active and visible to take full advantage of memberships. Local chapters of national associations work well. Network. Mentor. Write. Present webinars and workshops. Lead.

Put your website and email address on everything!

important

When I was starting out, I promoted my business in conversations with new people, by handing out tons of business cards and talking to anyone who would talk to me! As my business grew, I discovered that people began coming to me for advice, for mentoring, for relationship building. The key here is to realize that your consulting business will go through phases. When you start out, you'll be *pushing* yourself out there, but one day, you'll find that you have become an asset that others want to take advantage of and learn from.

Chapter Seven

Closing the Deal

Well, if there's anything you might dread more than marketing, it's probably selling—closing the deal. In this chapter, three consultants reveal everything you need to know about selling your services.

Marti Fischer reminds you that your work is not charity—you need to set reasonable prices for your work.

Ellen Bristol helps you develop sales strategies that work—and debunks five myths that will change the way you think about sales—we promise!

And Simone Joyaux tells you how to get the clients to pick you—or does she? Maybe it's as much about *you* doing the picking. . . .

You Might Work for Nonprofits, But Your Work Is Not Charity!

By Marti Fischer

Closing the deal is the sales component of the nonprofit consultant's job. Just as many nonprofit board members are uncomfortable asking for money, many consultants are uncomfortable articulating their fee structure and asking for a contract. Before I became a nonprofit consultant, I spent fifteen years in the advertising and network television industry. My primary responsibility was closing deals for advertising time between television advertisers and the network—I love asking for money.

The following steps will help create the framework for a mutually successful negotiation. Every successful client interaction helps to build your business, solidify your reputation, and create the most important selling tool of all: word-of-mouth referrals.

> Closing the deal is 20 percent about your contract, and 80 percent about your client's satisfaction with how you have presented yourself.
>
> **observation**

Know Yourself

Before entering into a relationship with a client, it is important to have a firm grasp on the values that define how you conduct your business. Define these traits for yourself to identify the parameters of your business. Before entering into a contract with a new client, ask these questions: "Would I be happy as an employee of this organization? Do I believe in what this organization is doing?" If the answer is "no" or "not really," don't take the job!

Determine Your Value

Ask around about the market rate in your area for nonprofit consultants. Factor in your prior business experience and determine the rate you will charge. Will you charge a flat fee, an hourly rate, or a hybrid? When structuring a contract, do you treat a start-up differently than an established organization? Decide all of these things in advance so you will have a clear answer when asked.

Create Trust

Creating trust is the secret sauce that makes any relationship successful. Just as people give donations to people based upon trust, clients give business to consultants based upon trust. Clients are revealing the details of their business to you and must trust your judgment and discretion. You cannot close a deal if you have not created this foundational relationship. Period. Here are some ways in which to create trust.

Do Your Homework

Know your client's business and needs. Do not rely only on what a client says to you in meetings. Read everything you can about your client's organization, talk to others in the sector, track movement among board and staff members, and do your best to understand the issues for which your help is required. Be prepared with intelligent and insightful questions that indicate you are engaged in your client's business.

Articulate Your Philosophy

Just as you have done your homework about your client's business, assume that your client has done homework about your business. Be prepared to talk about your philosophy and tell your story about how you became a consultant. *Always integrate how your philosophy and experience can help your client meet the specific needs at hand.* Tell related stories from your personal experience.

Talk About Your Failures

Surprise! Everyone fails, but not everyone views failure as an opportunity. Relate a business failure with emphasis on how the issue was resolved, what you learned, and why applying this learning can help your prospective client. Everyone fails. It's how you rebound that matters.

Articulate Your Return on Investment

Determine statistics about your business that are important to articulate to a client. For example, amount of funds raised in a campaign or at an event compared with the previous year, or percentage of grant dollars awarded compared with previous year and national averages. It is important to recognize and relate any trending in your business since the economic downturn of 2008. Talk with your client about how your business has addressed the new economic landscape.

Don't Be Afraid to Mention Money

You might be in the nonprofit sector, but your business is not charity. Determine your value and know your market as discussed earlier. Decide before going to the closing meeting how you want to structure the contract. Think about contingency plans and be prepared for client feedback.

Expect that the Client Will Ask You to Lower Your Rate

I have never met a client who hasn't asked me to lower my rate. I have never lowered my rate, yet have never been turned down by a client because of price. I will add here that the bulk of my business comes through word-of-mouth. Prospective clients come to me from other clients and business associates, so in a way, they are predisposed to working with me. I do ask prospective clients to interview at least two other candidates for the consultant position. After all, you wouldn't hire the first person you interviewed for a staff position. Hiring a consultant is no different. However, you should be prepared to articulate a clear and succinct reason for your rate structure. Explain that lowering your rate would be a disservice to your existing client base. If you want to work with the client, change the terms but don't lower your rate.

Be Flexible and Nimble in Your Discussions

Always know what you will accept and what you won't accept. Take notes about any new terms. If you are not sure how the new terms will look on paper, it is okay to say that you want to rework the plan and look at the new configuration, and that you will get back to the client shortly. Remember that this is a business arrangement that must be mutually beneficial.

The First Ninety Days

> If you are meeting in person to discuss terms, be aware of your body language. You do not want to appear anxious or nervous. Maintain good eye contact.
>
>  practical tip

My favorite device to close a deal: outline for your client what you would like to accomplish for the organization in the first ninety days. Be optimistic and realistic. Providing an outline will give your client a clear sense of the value you bring to the organization and the change you can effect. If you are meeting in person, provide your prospective client with a brief project list that you can discuss and tweak during the course of the meeting. An outline indicates that you are proactive about the prospective client's needs and interested in helping the organization.

The Close

Initiate the close. Thank your prospective client for the time spent and indicate that you would like to work with this organization.

Use phrases such as, "I would be happy to draw up a contract of the terms we discussed for your review."

Create an Action Step

"I will send you a contract by Wednesday and follow up with a phone call on Friday to discuss moving forward."

Follow Up

Keep the conversation alive and be attentive to your client's comments and needs.

If the Prospective Client Turns You Down

Consider the turn-down conversation as an exit interview and get as much information as you can. Ask why the organization is turning you down and if there may be an opportunity to work with this organization in the future. Keep the door open by sending interesting news articles or research that applies to the client's business.

The manner in which you conduct yourself when closing a deal speaks volumes about your level of confidence in your business and your abilities. Always consider contingency plans and practice what you want to say out loud before the meeting. Listen and react to what your client is saying.

> Remember—a "no" today can be a "yes" tomorrow.
>
> **principle**

It is a privilege for consultants to provide a needed service to help a nonprofit. Once the deal is closed, it is up to you to provide a positive customer experience. Building a satisfied client base and creating a positive reputation as a problem solver will lead to word-of-mouth referrals and an increased presence for your work.

Selling Your Nonprofit Consulting Services: Five Sales Myths that Slow Success

By Ellen Bristol

Hooray for you, you've decided to be a consultant! Now comes the fun part: selling your services. Yes, I said the four-letter word—sell. You have now moved proudly into the world of pure, unfettered capitalism, where you offer services and clients offer cold, hard cash. If you've spent your career working in the nonprofit sector, you may be experiencing a little brain freeze. But in due course, you'll get over it.

I was one of the lucky ones. I worked in corporate sales for over twenty years before I started my consulting practice, and I consulted with for-profit companies (still do, in fact) before I started to concentrate on nonprofit clients. So let me share some of the things I learned, usually the hard way, to make it easier for you to get up to speed.

There are five myths you need to be aware of if you want to succeed in selling your services to nonprofit clients.

Myth #1: Everybody is Your Customer.

Everybody is *not* your customer, or even your prospect. The awful truth is that when you act as if anybody is your prospect, you are throwing money down the drain. Your time is too scarce, and too expensive, to waste blundering about approaching any old nonprofit executive. What you absolutely positively must do instead is to figure out which prospects and customers are right for you, and concentrate on them. And *only* them.

Mythbuster #1: The Right Prospects Seek the Value You Add.

Selling is simple, really. Find out what you do well, and offer it to the people who want it. Replacing the "anybody who'll buy from me" habit requires some effort on your part. Analyze the things you do particularly well, including your product, service, price point, and personal charm. Yes, decide what your price point is before you make the sale. You can always negotiate the details later.

Now, once you know what you offer and how valuable it is, think about the nonprofits you know, or to whom you have already sold. Describe the characteristics of your ideal nonprofit client. Be sure to think about the following points:

◆ Location. Is your ideal client within driving distance, or are you willing to fly?

◆ Type of nonprofit. Do you only want to work with arts organizations, or healthcare, or social services? Or doesn't the sector matter?

◆ Annual budget. How big should the client be to be right for your services and your prices?

◆ Experience with your offerings. Has your ideal client ever hired a consultant to do similar work? What did staff and trustees like or not like about those other consultants?

◆ Available funding. Does the agency have enough discretionary budget or grant money to pay for your services?

Remember, if prospective clients don't need (or want) the kind of service you're offering, don't have the money to pay you, or don't like you or your approach, they are probably not going to buy. And therefore you should not spend too much time attempting to sell to them.

Myth #2: Every Sale is a Good Sale.

Watch out for this one. Just because you think you can land the client, do you want to? Will winning the deal advance your reputation? Will it help you get better at doing what you do best? Will it fulfill your own personal or corporate objectives? If you take any and every sale that comes your way, you are letting your customers run your business. If that's the case, you'll find it extremely difficult to market yourself.

Mythbuster #2: Good Sales Bring Profit to the Seller and Satisfaction to the Buyer.

It's genuinely easier to sell your services if your buyers know what you're good at. You've already defined your ideal customer; now define your ideal sale. Describe not only the activities you'll perform but the results you'll get for the client. Write down the amount you need to earn to make the sale profitable and don't violate it. Think about other desirable attributes of the ideal sale.

I like to say that you can make a profit at least three different ways. You can make a financial profit; you can learn something new; and you can have fun. In more pragmatic terms, every time you have an opportunity to win a sale, ask yourself:

◆ Will I make more money than it costs me to do this contract?

◆ Will I be able to use this client as a testimonial, case study, or referral?

◆ Will the client and I both enjoy this experience?

◆ Will I learn something new that I can apply to future opportunities?

If you get at least three "yes" answers, then make every possible effort to land the client.

Myth #3: Never Take "No" for an Answer.

Refusing to take "no" goes hand-in-hand with "everybody is our customer" and "every sale is a good sale." Always remember that a sale is not a one-way transaction. If it isn't right for one of the parties, then it is probably wrong for both.

Mythbuster #3: Don't Beat a Dead Horse.

Ask the right questions early in the cycle, to learn if the prospect (a) is a reasonable match to your ideal customer, and (b) if the sale is going to give you three out of four "yes" answers to the questions above. If so, keep on trying, but if not, walk away. Your selling time is too costly to blow it on a prospect that can't afford you, doesn't like you, doesn't want what you offer, or is too difficult to deal with.

Give yourself a break. You can't win them all; you don't even want to win them all. You're doing yourself a favor if you walk away and a disservice if you keep on beating that dead horse.

Myth #4: There's Always Time to Make More Sales Calls.

Well, there isn't, not really. A sales call is any kind of direct interaction with a prospect, whether it's by phone or in person. If you're just going into the consulting business, then you've got to invest many hours in figuring out what your products and services are, marketing them, delivering services and fulfilling contracts, managing your books, and cleaning the bathroom. In fact, rather than thinking there's always more time to make more sales calls, you might actually want to schedule blocks of time on your calendar for making sales calls in the first place!

Now maybe you are one of those people blessed with unlimited reserves of stamina. (I'm not, unfortunately.) If so, you might be able to do your administrative and marketing work outside of business hours. But even if that's possible for you, there are only so many useful hours during which you can connect with prospects and cultivate them into clients.

Mythbuster #4: Make Scarce Sales Time Count.

Learn to make your limited sales time work for you. Put a lot of time and energy, up front, into figuring out what you do best, how you want to price your services, and how you're going to get the message out to prospects. If you do this strategic work first, you'll find yourself with more time to attract prospects, connect with them, and offer them enticing proposals. Also, reserve a few hours every month to analyze your sales results and think about how to improve them.

Here are a few suggestions for making your scarce sales time count:

◆ Define your unique selling proposition. Figure out what you do exceptionally well, and learn how to say it in a sentence or two. What I often say about myself and my consulting firm is this: "We're experts in sustainable fund development. We bring you the science that makes the art of fundraising possible."

◆ Put together your sales kit. Get testimonials or endorsements from clients or former employers, and write them up on your letterhead. Describe your services, emphasizing the results of what you do, going light on the step-by-step how-to and heavy on the benefits. If you've got credentials, include them. Every time you visit a new prospect, bring copies of these key marketing pieces.

◆ Pump up your Internet presence. If you don't have a website, set one up *now*. It's remarkably easy and cheap to do so. At least set up a page that describes your services and gives your complete contact information. You must make it easy for people to find you.

◆ Create your social media presence: Facebook, Twitter, LinkedIn, Google+, and YouTube accounts. Now. YouTube can wait until you have some video. Your website and social media presence solve the "sales kit" challenge and help you attract a following right away.

◆ Establish some performance metrics for yourself. How many sales do you need per month to meet your income goals? How many new prospects have you contacted, how many have turned into opportunities, how many have reached the proposal stage?

Myth #5: Sales and Marketing are Too Costly.

Any given selling and marketing effort should bring in more money than it costs you, but at the beginning you probably don't know how much marketing work you'll need to do. Don't forget that you're now an independent consultant. Sales and marketing now play a strategic role for you.

Mythbuster #5: Sales Pay for Everything.

Once you step away from a salaried position and go out on your own, you must recognize that it's always *the next sale* that produces your pay check. Don't make the mistake of believing that your new job is all about doing the project, or delivering the service, or whatever. You have now become an entrepreneur, and your new job means making as many sales as you can, in order to meet your corporate obligations. One of those corporate obligations is to make a financial profit, so that you can *stay* in business for yourself.

And maybe, if you get really good at it, your business can become so valuable that you can even sell it to somebody else before you retire. Imagine that.

Pick me. Pick me.

By Simone P. Joyaux, ACFRE

No one ever picked me for anything in elementary or high school.

I think that memory flashed through my mind when I chose to become a consultant.

What does it take to get picked?

Competence in the service you're selling. That includes knowing the body of knowledge and having direct experience doing what you're advising others to do.

One hour of professional reading per day per year can make you an expert. Imagine what more reading will do? So read lots. Every day. On vacation or on the weekend or in the evenings or whenever. Follow the best bloggers and the best authors. Read research in the field.

Bring all that knowledge and expertise, all that practical experience, to the client.

But there's more. There's trust.

Consultant—or Trusted Advisor?

I don't just want to be an organization's knowledge expert. I don't want to be an organization's "extra hands to do the job."

I want to be an organization's trusted advisor.

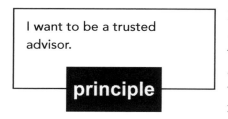

I want board members and staff to turn to me when they are anxious or scared–about anything, not just this consultancy. I want board members and staff to come to me with their worries about this consultancy, and other stuff, too. I want to share their success and failure, whether related to this consultancy or not.

I expect them to call me after hours. I've had executive directors and board chairs break down with me, angry or sad or frustrated. I expect to joke and celebrate together.

I want to be a trusted advisor.

Taking a Risk and Telling the Whole Truth

I know consultants who don't exactly tell the truth.

I'm not saying these consultants lie or misrepresent. Absolutely not. The consultants I know are highly ethical and committed to good service and making a difference for their clients.

I'm talking about truth in the sense of facts. Avoiding the facts is, at best, a delay of game and at the worst, harmful.

I'm talking about truth in the sense of how hard some of this work is. How important it is to learn and change.

Sometimes it's just so hard to push the envelope, to tell the whole truth. Sometimes it seems easier and wiser to go along with the organization for a while and slowly tell the client the facts, gently let the client see the difficulties as the project goes along.

If we believe that customer centrism is key, and I suspect that most of us do, then that means meeting the customer's expectations. But sometimes the customer's expectations are somewhat inappropriate or flat-out wrong.

Is it the consultant's job to explain that "wrongness" graciously? Is it the consultant's job to dispel inappropriate expectations and explain what the truth is? Are we purveyors of the body of knowledge and truth tellers?

For me, I decided the answer to those questions is "yes." I am described by my clients as a "truth teller."

For example, consider fundraising consulting. There's so much misunderstanding of what fund development is and what it is not. There are lots of myths and impracticalities, and lack of knowledge.

I believe that those misunderstandings compromise an organization's ability to raise charitable gifts. I believe that those misunderstandings inhibit learning and the change necessary to raise more money for so many valuable organizations.

So I choose to let them know in the interview—kindly and graciously—more of the truth. I inform them of their misunderstandings and explain some of the fundamentals. I show them a bit of the body of knowledge and explain how it applies to them. I describe how this body of knowledge can help them achieve their goals.

I choose to be a truth teller. I show them that I cannot provide good customer service unless they accept the reality of the body of knowledge. I let them know that if they aren't ready for change, the consultancy won't work.

I highlight typical challenges and barriers. I explain, very clearly, what it takes to overcome these obstacles and how difficult it can be. I describe my role as their consultant. I

Are you a truth teller?

food for thought

talk about how I will help them learn and change. Then together we can move the organization forward.

I tell them a good consulting process should involve challenging assumptions, exploring essential and cage-rattling questions, and deep conversation. I tell them that I see the consulting process as a process of learning and change, that I see myself as a change agent. And if they haven't run fleeing yet, then maybe we'll be a good match.

When to Reveal the "Real" You

I've asked other consultants if they do this. If they intentionally show the prospective client where they are "unreasonable" or "wrong" in an initial interview. I've asked my peers if they talk about the consulting process (and its pluses and minuses) and learning and change.

Many do not choose this approach. Many consultants get the job first and then, over the course of the consultancy, explain the truth.

I used to take that approach in the early days of my business. I needed the work and chose not to explain reality and share truths in an interview.

But eventually, that approach just didn't work for me. I'd get the job, and the organization and I would go off together. And pretty soon, conflicts would begin. I'd move into reality and truth mode. The organization would balk.

The organization's leadership—from staff to board—wasn't ready to be questioned or to challenge its own assumptions. The organization wanted to produce money (in the case of a fundraising consultancy). Even if the organization understood that there was no silver bullet or quick fix, the organization wasn't sufficiently prepared to learn and change.

So early in my consulting practice, I began using the interview to screen prospective clients in and out. I moved into "Real Simone Mode."

Real Simone Mode evolved over the years into a personal brand. I dislike the use of the term "brand," often finding that people think it means logo or tagline. But I came to realize that I *have* a brand—and I like it. It isn't for everyone or every organization. But for those that choose that brand, our partnership produces success.

I Pick Them

In all my years of business, only a few organizations have ever asked me what I look for in a client. Those are really smart leaders. It's a joint interview, you know. They're interviewing me and I'm interviewing them.

I use the interview as a screening device to see if the organization will like working with me and if I will like working with it. I explain to my interviewers that I am interviewing them just as they are interviewing me. It comes as a shock to many organizations that the consultant is deciding whether or not to work with the organization.

Choose your clients as carefully as they choose you.

!
important

In the interview, I share some challenges that typically arise with the proposed work. I explain that my goal as a consultant is to help the organization learn and change. Right there, that screens some organizations out. They don't think they have anything to learn. They see the proposed consultancy as a transaction to achieve a goal, not a change process to help move the organization forward to a new, stronger place.

In the interview, I am purposefully, although somewhat mildly, provocative. I use the interview to demonstrate how I work during the consultancy. If they aren't comfortable with me in an interview, they won't be comfortable with me during a consultancy. And the reverse is true: I won't be comfortable with them.

The Ultimate Job Requirement

The match between organization and consultant is *not* about expertise and experience.

I remember an executive director telling me how much she wanted to work with me. "But you scared the hell out of my board, and so we won't pick you." My response was, "Good for you to help your board *not* pick me. If your board isn't comfortable with me, this consultancy won't work."

stories from the real world

The match is about personality alignment. I hate to use the words "personality" or "style," but I suspect those are the appropriate words. The organization, at least most of its staff and board members, has to feel comfortable with the consultant. We are trying to create a relationship of comfort and trust. I want to be the organization's trusted advisor, as described by David Maister, et al in *The Trusted Advisor*.

I figure that most organizations are smart enough to select a consultant with the body of knowledge. My experience shows this is usually true.

But lots of organizations are not comfortable with truth-tellers, challengers, and provocateurs. You know the old phrase "different strokes for different folks."

I'm looking for the match. And I explain to organizations that they're looking for the match, too.

I don't want them to pick me if I'm not picking them. I don't want them to request a proposal if I think it's a bad match. I don't want to waste my time or theirs.

Get the Board on Board

By the way, I don't usually submit proposals without a preliminary conversation with the prospective client. I never take on work that relates to the board—whether its fund development, governance, or planning—without interviewing with a few board members, too.

Moreover, I never plan board-related consulting engagements or work sessions without board members participating in the planning. I learned that one early on. An executive director and I planned the board's session—without my having a conversation with any board members. Wow. How dumb could I have been?

Another never: I never accept a consulting job in any area that involves the board and its members unless the board has officially agreed to the consulting process. I require that the board formally approve the consultancy and board member role in the process. I'm willing to use the consultancy to convince board members to engage more. But I'm unwilling to take on a consultancy when the board hasn't agreed to participate.

And I do remind any prospective client that if the board votes in favor of moving forward, even those who voted "no" have to participate. That's a basic concept of governance: the board—the collective—decides and all individual board members support, and that means participate in, the decision made.

Good Clients and Bad Ones

There's a saying in the consulting world–or at least in my office building: vendor trash. Yes. That's the way some clients treat their consultants. Sure, the clients don't actually call consultants that. But the behaviors are rather clear. You'll find a few in the sidebar.

I'm not a vendor. Usually I can tell if an organization thinks of consultants as vendors. And I then make myself unavailable. I fix it so I'm not invited to submit a proposal. In fact, I use my proposals, as well as the interview, as a strategy to get them *not* to pick me if I don't want to be picked.

Usually organizations don't invite me to submit a proposal if I've scared them enough during the interview. That's the point! Why waste my time and theirs with a proposal.

When I do submit a proposal, I'm candid there, too. Given my experience, I've identified several non-negotiable tenets for a consultancy. I explain those in the proposal. Usually I've explained those in the interview, too. But I typically reinforce those in writing in the proposal.

For example, I expect the full board—yes, all board members—to participate in all fund development and governance work sessions. Not just a board committee. Certainly not just the staff. And if there's an argument about that expectation during the proposal process, we resolve it then. Or we aren't a good match.

My proposals also include a few remarks about negotiation. I explain that this is a proposal based on my understanding of the organization's need. Perhaps I have not understood adequately. Perhaps there is more to know. And assuredly, if we were to work together, things might change as we go along. A consultancy is a process and, together, we might adjust during the process.

Signs of Less-than-stellar Clients

"Hey you, Ms. Consultant, I need this right now. What? You cannot do it right now? But I need it. I demand it."

"Hey you, Mr. Consulting Guy. How much do you charge? I'm comparison shopping and maybe you'll win."

"Hey, Missy. I want this. What do you mean I might not be ready for it? What do you mean you can't produce it for me? What do you mean I have to work for it?"

"Hey there, I bought your services. I bought two silver bullets and five quick fixes. Start producing. And don't expect me to learn or struggle. You're bought and paid for and I get what I want. Quit examining and questioning. I'm not interested in your advice or counsel. I want results."

"Look, all you consultants out there: you're a dime a dozen. You really aren't any different, one from the other."

watch out!

For me, the interview and the proposal are both screening and sales devices. I always assume that the organization has interviewed multiple consultants. I also assume that the organization is requesting proposals from multiple consultants. I proceed accordingly.

Part Two

Finding Your Groove

Once you've landed your first client, or two, or three, your business begins to take on its own personality. Of course much of that persona is determined by you, the owner. Your values, your vision, and your preparation for life as a consultant can steer your practice in many different directions. From the moment you have that first signed contract until the day you close your business, everything you do will be a reflection on your company.

This section examines the decisions you make that affect the way your clients and community view you as a businessperson. What kind of consultant are you in the eyes of your clients? How do you keep your skills and your presentation fresh? What kind of staff team, if any, will you create? The answers to these questions will define you in the eyes of your clients and potential clients. But you can't anticipate everything. You'll see here how some consultants have gone to great lengths to ensure that, no matter what natural or other disasters life throws at them, they are always prepared to put their best foot forward.

Why does all of this matter so much? Your reputation depends on it. If you want to be a successful consultant over the long run, your reputation is really all you've got.

Chapter Eight

Playing the Part

What does it really mean to be a consultant—are you a vendor, an advisor, a leader in the nonprofit world?

Marti Fischer challenges you to think about your leadership style and how you will use it in your client relationships.

Susan Schaefer asks if the best consultant style is to be the dutiful, inquiring type, or the heroic savior of failing organizations.

Pam Cook probes further into the client/consultant relationship by asking you to be open and honest in your communications and to carefully prepare the work plan with each client.

Your Leadership Style: It's Time to Walk the Talk

By Marti Fischer

Congratulations! You have a new client. Now is your time to shine and use your experience to help an organization move toward a sustainable future. Defining and articulating your leadership style will help clarify the skills and practical applications you bring to the relationship. Delivering on your promises will establish your position as an effective leader. As you progress through the project, self-assess your work by asking the following questions:

◆ What promises have I made?

◆ Am I keeping those promises?

◆ Is my client having a positive experience?

Keeping your promises and creating a positive experience will build trust with your client. As you refine and nurture your consultant persona, continue to consider your leadership style, how you communicate, how you build relationships, and the impact your work has on your client's organization.

> "Creating without claiming,
> Doing without taking credit,
> Guiding without interfering,
> This is Primal Virtue."
>
> —Lao Tzu

What Is Your Leadership Style?

Leadership style has a lot to do with your individual approach to a client's issues. Create a two- to three-sentence philosophy about your business. Past business experience and your ability to address problems from a unique vantage point will influence the development and tenor of this philosophy.

Your stated philosophy will help shape your role as a consultant and communicate the specific skills you bring to an organization. Your role is to provide the guidance, creativity, processes, and internal continuity for solving the issue at hand. When you are crafting your philosophy, be clear and concise. Here is my philosophy: I help the organization develop the founding principles and messaging necessary to identify its core purpose and communicate its potential. I am also really good at finding money.

Here is an example of what can happen when you say one thing and a client hears something else. I was hired by a start-up to help it through the process of developing mission, vision, and values statements, and a marketing plan. I articulated my philosophy to the organization's founder and explained that I prefer to work collaboratively with board, staff, clients, or potential clients. After a few months it became clear that the founder really wanted me to work solely with the board president and present the organizing principles and marketing plan to the board for approval. This was not a good match for either of us, and we eventually—but amicably—parted company. What I learned from this situation is the importance of asking many follow-up questions of the client to make sure that all involved understand how my philosophy will translate into practice.

So, how best to avoid the situation described above? When you agree to work with a client, try to determine the character of the organization. Ask staff and board members open-ended questions like these to gauge how the organization approaches issues: Does it react quickly to issues, or is it deliberative? Do the staff members collaborate, or do employees operate in silos? Understanding the relationship among the organization's component parts will help tailor your approach to the staff.

Answers to these questions will help you understand how best to lead the organization and work productively within its existing framework:

◆ "This has been my experience with the issue you are currently facing. [Explain your experience.] We approached the subject in this manner and it took us [timeframe] to reach a conclusion. Knowing your board and staff, how do you think your organization would react to this approach?"

◆ "I have recent experience in this area. We worked collaboratively across departments to identify solutions for an issue similar to this. Is your organization comfortable with brainstorming across departments?"

◆ "Do you find the staff and board to be proactive or reactive when it comes to solving problems? Why?"

◆ "Has your staff worked with consultants in the past? Was it a positive or negative experience? Why?"

How Do You Communicate With Your Clients?

Change the conversation to promote change. Recently, I was speaking with the president of a big healthcare foundation. The foundation had come to an advanced stage of its development and was poised for growth. So, how did its stakeholders decide if growth is the right path? This is what we discussed. We did *not* talk about department-by-department goings-on to determine what each group had accomplished since our last meeting and what each would do next. Instead I suggested gathering all staff in a room with one open-ended question written on a big piece of paper. I asked them

"We can't solve problems by using the same kind of thinking we used when we created them."

—Albert Einstein

to choose a question such as, "What is our organization's purpose?" or "How can we better serve our clients?" As opinion-based questions, these are catalysts for conversation. They also level the playing field between junior and senior staff because there are no wrong answers. If you use this exercise, your job is to write down the salient points and keep the conversation moving in a positive direction.

When the initial session is over, it is your responsibility to keep the conversation going. Put an internal communication plan in place that includes all relevant parties, identifies the issues to be solved, clarifies expectations, and discusses any progress. Once a month, continue the open-forum meeting and address issues one at a time. Focus on the future and what will be effective. Do not get mired down in the actions of the past. Consider some of these steps when building internal communication:

◆ Assemble a list of contacts that you will interact with during your project. Set up initial meetings, introduce yourself, and get feedback about the issue at hand.

◆ Ask your contacts how they prefer to communicate. By phone or email?

◆ Schedule a weekly conference call with stakeholders. Stakeholders are the principal players in your work, e.g., board members, senior staff.

◆ Follow up each conference call or meeting with an email recap and a next-steps section.

◆ Compile a clearly written accountability calendar so that each of the stakeholders knows what is expected and the milestones that need to be reached (more on this later).

◆ Survey your stakeholders at least once during the project to determine what is working and what is not working. Revise your planning based on this information.

During your weekly client calls, you might introduce a new topic for discussion or report on the status of projects. Provide an agenda in advance of the call so that participants have an opportunity to consider and submit questions. Keep the call on-topic and limit its time. If a topic requires additional discussion, an in-person meeting can be arranged. End each call with an action step to be addressed before the next scheduled meeting. If some staff members are part-time, work from home, or if you want to create a more inclusive atmosphere, consider using video chat instruments like Skype for the weekly calls.

practical tip

If you engage with all of the relevant parties and create a team that thrives on inclusive dialogue, you will discover each person's strengths and capabilities. Capitalize on these traits by encouraging proactive conversations that will generate action plans to effectively address the issues.

Have You Built a Solid Relationship with Your Client?

The most successful consultant-client relationships are those in which the consultant's advice and recommendations are successfully implemented and utilized long after the consultant has left the organization. Your task is not to dictate to a client, but to analyze the strengths and weaknesses of the organization, and help the client reach a solution that works best given the organization's needs and capabilities. Trust is the most important element in every consultant-client relationship. Creating trust is based upon an open dialogue and attention to client needs.

"Tell me and I'll forget. Show me and I may not remember.

Involve me and I'll understand."

—Native American Proverb

◆ Listen to your client's needs. As you listen, factor in the capabilities and capacity of the organization to resolve the issue. Offer creative solutions that will not overextend an already-overworked staff.

◆ Understand not only the issue at hand, but also how it fits into the overall picture of services offered to the organization's clients. There are two groups of stakeholders who are most directly affected by your work: (1) board and staff, and (2) the clients who benefit from the organization's services. When you articulate how your services will help the client base, you demonstrate an understanding of the organization's mission.

◆ Engage all of the stakeholders in the planning process. Meet with your client contacts and hold a brainstorming session about the most efficient ways to achieve their goals. Staff members have the most realistic handle on the capabilities of the organization and can be very helpful in the planning process. The results of this session will be factored into tactics and action plans, and the staff will feel included and proactive.

◆ Prioritize issues according to your client's timeframe, not yours. To ensure that expectations are clear and that milestones are met, develop an accountability calendar to be reviewed, discussed, and accepted by all relevant parties. When structuring the calendar, be mindful of the time commitments for daily activities and once-a-year projects like the annual campaign or an event. Discussion and acceptance of the calendar by all parties will create an inclusive atmosphere.

◆ Establish deadlines and stick to them. Create deadlines as a group. Being inclusive in the planning stages will help all parties embrace the tasks at hand. Establishing and adhering to deadlines will also help you establish credibility as a consultant.

◆ Answer requests and questions promptly. Be respectful of your client's time and respond in a concise manner. Part of your responsibility is to keep the momentum and conversation moving toward resolution.

◆ Move the project forward. You may find that midway through the project, it begins to lose steam. It is your job to reinvigorate the staff to keep the ball rolling. This is a good time to survey the staff about what is and is not working.

◆ Celebrate success. In our zeal to complete a project, we sometimes forget to celebrate the progress we have made along the way. Pick a date midway through the project to stop, regroup, and celebrate.

> "Unless someone like you cares a whole awful lot, nothing is going to get better. It's not."
>
> —Dr. Seuss

When you understand the capabilities of the organization, you will succeed in guiding your client. Your attention to detail and to the needs of your client will help build a foundation of trust and provide a positive client experience.

Is Your Work Having An Impact?

The goal of your work is to have lasting impact for the organization and its clients. How do you determine if your work has real impact? Set up short- and long-term frameworks to articulate the promises you have made to your client. Sit down with the client and analyze your progress at defined points during the course of the project.

Short-Term

Create and document goals for "The First Ninety Days" and show them to your client before embarking on the project. This creates a tool that your client can use to assess your short-term impact. It also indicates that you are proactive about your client's needs.

Midway through your ninety-day goals, review with your client the progress that has been made and make any necessary revisions to the balance of the project list. Of the work that has been done to date, determine the following:

◆ What progress has been made?

◆ Has staff or board behavior changed (if relevant)?

◆ Can progress from this work be seen in the programs delivered to the organization's clients?

Long-Term

Create an accountability calendar with benchmarks, milestones, and goals. The calendar establishes the long- and short-term goals of the project and the tasks to be undertaken to reach those goals. Embedded within the calendar are assignments and deadlines for you and the staff, which create accountability and transparency among the stakeholders. Have your client discuss and agree to the timetables, deadlines, and assignments.

"You can either take action or hang back and hope for a miracle.

Miracles are great, but they are also unpredictable."

—Peter Drucker

At the conclusion of the project, ask the three questions above again and quantify the change. The answers will determine the impact of your work.

How Effective Are You?

To be truly effective you should have a real interest in helping your client achieve the organization's vision and mission. If you are not personally interested in the organization's work, I believe you cannot be effective in guiding the organization to identify and achieve its goals. To quantify how successful your contribution has been, consider developing an exit survey. When the project is complete, ask your client to review your work on paper. This will give the client the opportunity to be candid and offer constructive criticism. Try a written format such as a short survey with room for comments.

"We must remember that one determined person can make a significant difference, and that a small group of determined people can change the course of history."

—Sonia Johnson

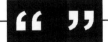

Your reputation will be formed and sustained by the quality of your work, your insight, your ability to galvanize the staff and board around articulated goals, and your capability to deliver on your promises.

Your Consulting Persona: Clark Kent or Superman?

By Susan Schaefer, CFRE

You're hired.

You might breathe a sigh of relief once you and your new client sign on the dotted line, but some of the trickier waters still lie ahead. It's time to set the tone for the rest of your relationship.

After all, you are "the expert," the person charged with taking your client's organization to new heights. The interview period was a time for you to introduce the client to your personality, your approach, and your ideas. Once you're under contract, small talk quickly gives way to high expectations.

It's understandable. New clients are nervous. It's easy for us to forget the professional risks clients take when they hire us. Executives are often under extreme scrutiny from their boards, who might consider consultants a luxury in this back-to-basics economy. Our clients risk hiring someone who produces less than stellar outcomes or has a personality that doesn't jibe with other stakeholders. Sometimes different factions of the hiring organization are at odds about which consultant they want to hire. So it's imperative that you make those first few weeks an impeccable show of your professionalism. You have some important work to do:

◆ Establish a trusting relationship.

◆ Communicate well, directly and indirectly, with multiple stakeholders.

◆ Convey high ethical standards.

It's no small feat to achieve these goals. The skills required go beyond consultants' knowledge of nonprofit management or even running a business. They get to the psychology involved in a client-consultant relationship. I never studied psychology in school but wish I had. It would be a great prerequisite to a consulting career. Nonetheless, I have now read and practiced enough of it to have developed my own approach.

Leading Through Listening

Clients often expect that we will enter a new job as a superhero: strong and ready for action. While some might appreciate a consultant who immediately goes into problem-solving mode, a more measured approach is more likely to engender long-term trust.

The people who hire us are professionals, many with years of experience. If we problem-solve too much in those early meetings, we may not grasp all of the nuances behind what we're being told. What a client is *not* telling us can be as revealing as what *is* being said. We build trust by taking a sincere interest in what others say and doing our best to interpret what they don't.

> When meeting with a new client, content is a given. Trust is not.
>
> **observation**

We also build trust by asking questions. Good ones. Ask about the organization, its culture, and even your client's past experiences with consultants. What went right and what went wrong? When I asked one client about prior consulting engagements, my contact confided that the nonprofit's last two consultants bungled the deliverables. So I redoubled my usual efforts to get that client's buy-in as we created a development plan. When I was later rehired to work on another project, I realized how valuable those details about my predecessors had been to the project's success.

Clients will assume that you are well-versed in the area for which you've been hired. But it's the way in which you convey your expertise that matters most in your initial meetings. I tend to do more listening than talking. And my learning mode goes into overdrive: "Why is that?" and "Can you say more?" make up a good part of my vocabulary.

At the beginning of the relationship, you are Clark Kent: mild-mannered journalist focused on getting the scoop.

The Communications Conundrum

You're always communicating with a few audiences, either directly or indirectly. It's easy to feel overwhelmed by the competing desires of each. When you begin a new job, try to get ahead of the game by creating some simple communication strategies that allow you to take the first steps toward building trust.

> New-Client Etiquette:
>
> ❑ Listen.
>
> ❑ Ask probing questions.
>
> ❑ Listen some more.
>
> **to-do lists**

Your Primary Contact

This is the point person you work with on a regular basis. The frequency and tone of your communication will provide the first indications of your leadership style. I strive for open, honest communication and by modeling it, hope that my client will reciprocate. I also check in regularly to ask how I'm doing and what I might do differently. I once helped design a major program for a large university and asked my contact, the dean, what he thought of our progress so far. He said that things were going well, so well that he decided to step aside and let me lead the project without his involvement. Suddenly my duties increased about three-fold. I led a large faculty team to develop a capital project, wrote the funding proposal, and otherwise ended up with a much broader contract. I've often wondered if that added responsibility—and fee—would have come about if I hadn't asked how things were going.

I do like to establish communication protocols. They give clients reliable means of hearing from me and create additional ways to establish my commitment to their projects. I meet with clients regularly, create project calendars, write up short weekly updates, and speak with them by phone whenever they like. Most clients like that system, but some propose their own. That suits me fine, so long as we're regularly in touch.

The Boss

When the CEO, or board members for that matter, don't see your face regularly, it's easy for them to think of you as an impersonal service provider and cut your contract during budget season. So if the nature of your work doesn't inherently get you face time with those who hold the purse strings, work with your primary contact to ensure that it happens. It will benefit both you and the person who hired you.

A client update can be as simple as a bulleted email message that lists tasks completed and activities that are "on deck" for the period to come. It builds a good measure of trust in a new relationship.

 practical tip

On an ongoing basis, ask your primary contact what you can do to help keep the boss up to speed. Should you copy the CEO on your weekly updates? Can you contribute to an internal status report or meeting? Can you provide your contact with some talking points for that person's own one-on-one meetings with the boss? I've had clients choose all variations of these options.

The ultimate communication vehicle doesn't really matter, although meeting face-to-face is ideal when possible. What does matter is that the organization's leader understands the value of your work and the subordinate's impeccable taste in consultants!

The Board

Even if your work isn't directly board related, ask to spend some time in front of the board. Thank the group and reiterate the importance of the project you were hired to do. Make yourself available for questions or just to chat. Then just observe the meeting. The quality of your work will benefit from a deeper look at organizational dynamics in action, and you'll have begun to build ties with an important constituency.

While I'm no fan of attending clients' special events, mostly because there can be so many of them cumulatively, the occasional event can provide a great opportunity to get to know board members one-on-one. It's great to forge relationships with individual board members, especially for clients you'd like to retain for the long run.

Funders

Then there's the case when a funder has enabled your consultancy. The dynamics can certainly get complicated the more stakeholders you add to the mix. Things can get especially sticky if the funder has strong opinions about the direction your project should take. Sometimes those preferences can differ from those of your client's staff and board. I've found it best to be honest with the funder if you are juggling competing demands. While honesty is not a panacea, it does often enable a little more understanding and leeway as you move forward.

Values-Laden Consulting

In the end, the consultant you become is all about your values. We all strive to be knowledgeable, professional, and fun to work with. But the way you demonstrate higher-order values engenders the best kind of working relationship—and the best reputation. And on the occasion when you make a mistake of some kind, your clients will be much more forgiving if they have seen a consistent pattern of integrity in your behavior to date.

> Your reputation is grounded as much in your ethics as it is in the quality of your work.

Reliability

Your reputation for reliability is based on things as small as showing up promptly for meetings and as significant as pulling together a complex long-term project. It also includes less-tangible actions like keeping your word—and getting out in front of opportunities and threats. In each case, you're reassuring clients that you've got their backs.

I create a lot of deliverables, such as funding proposals and case statements, many of which are deadline driven. In nearly every case, my documents are completed well before the due dates. That reliability creates a sense of comfort for clients. If you do fall behind schedule, be honest about the reasons and convey your recovery plan.

Honesty

Be honest. About everything. Acts of omission are dishonest when you're getting paid to provide insights, even if it stands to cost you a job. When a client of mine was about to receive its first million-dollar grant, we celebrated. Soon after, I had to dampen the celebration with words of warning. As I saw it, the funder was pushing this organization away from its signature work. The client accepted the gift anyway, but my honesty at the outset enabled us to have an ongoing dialogue about the inevitable strain on core activities and on the relationship with the donor. While there were times when I wondered if my job would be jeopardized because of my candor, I'd like to think that it helped us plan to mitigate what became a tumultuous grant period.

A corollary is to be honest even when you don't know the way forward. There's no better way to ruin your reputation than to lead clients on. Most people understand that our sector changes quickly these days. So if you don't have an answer, say so, do your research, and respond as soon as you can.

Honesty also comes into play when we sign our contracts: don't overpromise. If you do commit to more than you can handle, you'd better find a way to get the work done. Delegate, subcontract, stay up all night. Deliver what you promise.

Quality

Don't get lazy. Or greedy. It's always better to take on fewer projects and do them well than to cut corners. Know and track your own capacity and that of your employees or subcontractors so that you know your firm's limits.

I still feel a healthy anxiety just before I deliver completed projects. I read them repeatedly, making minute changes right up until I hit the "send" button. I may drive myself crazy, but my clients are consistently happy. When I wrote my first case statement for a client, I obsessed about it. Same thing when I wrote my first development plan many years ago. I remember these "firsts" because the thrill of sharing—or maybe just finishing—what I considered a good product was so tangible. When you begin to lower your standards, regroup. Learn a new skill, restructure your business, or consider closing shop.

> Many consultants will tell you that you should never turn down a job. I think the opposite is true. If you are picky about the work you take, the perception of your worth increases and people *want* to work with you more.
>
> **observation**

At the end of the day, what do you want to be known for? Spend some time defining how you'd most like clients to define you, even years after you've finished a job. I'd like to be defined as having performed with integrity. For me, integrity leads to the honesty, reliability, and just plain good results that clients want.

If you've played your cards right, by the end of the consulting period, your client has witnessed your transformation from Clark Kent to Superman: your curious, trusting demeanor has led you to save the world—at least your client's world.

Making the Client/Consultant Relationship Work

By Pamela A. Cook, ACFRE

All consulting relationships are not equal. Some work well, others are challenging. Almost every long-time consultant can cite an experience where the expectations of the client did not match what the consultant provided. While changes in personnel or board leadership often lead to less-than-optimal outcomes, there are steps a consultant can take to improve the chances of success.

The most successful engagements have clear expectations regarding everything from fees to timing. If you do not believe that your services will meet the client's needs, it is better to walk away than make an arrangement that you will not be able to complete successfully.

Assess the Match

Potential clients can come from many sources, including referrals, requests for proposals, or your own direct outreach. You might meet potential clients at conferences or seminars. They might contact you by phone, email, or through Facebook. However you are contacted, respond quickly and professionally.

If I know the name of an organization that contacted me (sometimes I do not because all I have is a phone message with a number and a name with which I am unfamiliar), I will do a little research before I contact the caller. I will review the website and look at mission, staff, budget size, and board. Since I do executive searches, I will look to see if there is a job description or open position listed on the website.

Once I have done my initial research, I quickly get back in touch with the prospective client and have a phone conversation about relevant needs and history. Usually we will discuss what my business could provide and the fee structure. If it appears that the organization's needs and my services could be a match, we arrange to meet in person.

When we meet, I take the time to understand the services and role of the nonprofit. I ask what the client is seeking in a consulting relationship. We discuss the timing, fees, and who will be involved in the search in more detail. We talk about the challenges and opportunities for an individual in the position I will be seeking to fill and the involvement of staff and board in the process. I try to understand the physical environment and corporate culture. We talk about both what I can provide and what I will need from the organization to meet our goals.

I also make sure that I know the decision-maker and that person's contact information. It will be important that both parties have the ability to contact each other quickly when we are working together. We will need one decision-maker from each side who can approve the next steps in the process.

If any of these steps raises doubts about whether the project could come to a successful outcome, I take one of two steps: (1) ask very pointed questions of the prospective client to clarify any sticking points, or (2) remove myself from the process before it goes too far. Remember, your reputation is your best marketing vehicle, so don't take on jobs unless you're reasonably sure you can complete them successfully.

Use the Proposal to Guide Your Work Plan

The next step in the process involves the submission of a proposal. The proposal should clearly outline what you can accomplish and in what timeframe. It should state deliverables, deadlines, and payment schedule. The client might also ask for references of past clients.

The client might have additional questions at this time, and you may need to negotiate aspects of the contract. Do not make changes in your contract unless they are actually acceptable to you.

Get the Signed Contract

Do not begin work until you have the signed contract in hand.

Sometimes clients tell you that they are ready to get started, but they have not yet sent you back a signed contract. Do not initiate your work until they do so. When the signed contract has not come back, you might find later that a situation has changed at the organization—anything from a staff change to a budget limitation—and you will not be able to bill for any work that you have done before the deal was inked.

Communicate Regularly

Continually check in with your clients and be prepared to make mid-course corrections. Once you sign the contract, discuss the format for the final product and how your contacts prefer to communicate over the course of the engagement. Clients might want to receive information by email, by phone, in oral or written report, or in a particular format. Some might want to establish regular conference calls or check-in points while others might want to communicate when there are action items. The key is developing communication systems that work for you both so that you can stay on target with the clients' goals and adjust course if needed.

Make sure that you communicate with clients and stay on course with their expectations. If you encounter delays or run into obstacles, let your clients know right away.

Presenting Your Findings

Present your findings when and how they will be most helpful to your client. Be honest in your findings. The client hired you because you bring specialized knowledge of the issues at hand. While it is helpful if you and your client assess the challenges from the same perspective, you have to be forthright if you do not agree.

Sometimes findings should be presented to your client's leadership first and later to other staff, board members, or both. Learn who will see your findings and make recommendations on who should be included. You can advise the client on issues of best practice and confidentiality.

Leaving a Legacy

Consulting reports and results can last long after your engagement. Make sure that the product that you leave behind is clear, honest, and appropriately preserves confidentiality. While your client owns the materials that you produce while under contract, you can discuss what will be done with your reports. Nonetheless, keep in mind that your report may be shared with others who do not know you or who may be unfamiliar with the nature of the work you performed.

Clients: Your Best Source of Referrals

Consultants love to get referrals. Clients who are pleased with the work that you have done can refer other organizations to you. When you finish your consulting project, ask your client how the relationship worked and how you could improve. Ask if your contact would be willing to serve as a reference. And then stay in touch and continue to check in with the client in the months or years ahead. You never know when the organization might need your services again, and the very best new client is a satisfied past client.

On occasion, things might not go as you hoped. If you cannot meet client expectations, make sure that there is a way for all parties to discontinue the relationship without ill-will. Including a standard cancellation clause in your contract can save face.

Like any relationship, you need to work hard to make your client relationship succeed.

Maintaining Your Mojo

By Susan Schaefer, CFRE

I've been consulting for a long time now, but I still wake up excited about what each workday will bring. It would be easy to slip into monotony, even the doldrums. After all, I work from home, alone, with one regular subcontractor who lives a thousand miles away. Some days I see clients, but there are many days when hours of computer work awaits. Is it a challenge to keep up my enthusiasm? Not at all.

Work in our field is what you make of it. I like to work for nonprofits with missions that are new to me, so the subject matter is fresh. And I've learned that it's good to be picky about the people I work with, too. Good people make good clients. And I love the work itself. The work, the people, and their organizations—that's more than half the battle right there. So I've been selective. I've figured out my preferences. I've made job interviews a two-way street.

But sometimes I need more than the work itself to keep myself going. I bet you're no different. Here's how to infuse your workday with something inspiring and out of the ordinary.

Mix things up a bit.

Once we've been at this consulting thing for a while, we default to nurturing our businesses. Most of us spend ample time marketing, acquiring human and other resources, and cultivating clients. What about ourselves? What activities induce new thinking, promote strong relationships and foster your best self? After all, we are our businesses' best assets.

Broaden Your Scope

Most consultants are naturally inquisitive. That's good, because it's so important for us to be conversant across a range of subjects. We're at such an advantage if we can walk into a client interview with some basic knowledge about Alzheimer's disease, constitutional law, or whatever else a nonprofit's mission might deliver.

I've decided that expanding my knowledge base is so beneficial that it's worth my while to spend some of my work week learning more—about almost anything.

I belong to a group of about 150 women that brings speakers to a local church each week. Recent topics have ranged from easy weeknight cooking to writing as trauma therapy. Wouldn't you know it? The latter was directly related to the mission of a new client of mine. I invited the executive director to attend the session. We both learned something and got to know each other better.

You can also learn so much from those in your everyday life. Unlike the early days in my home office, my neighborhood is now bustling with other remote workers. On occasion, I invite one of them for a walk to learn more about mutual interests. Last week I walked with a woman who works for a publishing house. It was perfect timing, as I was putting the finishing touches on this book. That's my kind of multitasking: exercise for the heart *and* the brain.

Those outside of the nonprofit sector can provide some of the best insights into your work. Take an architect to lunch and delve into the world of design and construction; your capital campaign clients will thank you. An estate-planning attorney friend and I are putting together a workshop about current fundraising trends. He will talk about individual giving, and I'll tackle institutional giving. The options are endless. Get to know those in your community, and good things can come from most any new relationship.

Last year I started working with a client dedicated to bringing more women into elected political positions. I knew little about the details of that field, except that I was passionate about helping the client achieve its vision.

As I began to write a case statement and funding proposals for the group, I read book-length studies about why women have traditionally shied away from politics. I attended lectures and listened to podcasts on the subject. I met people from industry circles who answered my questions.

I was quickly able to "talk the talk." Not only was I personally fascinated, but my work was stronger for it. In the end, my interest in the subject made my work, and my daily grind, more fulfilling.

stories from the real world

Peer Power

I meet quarterly with a peer of mine. These aren't consultant meetings of the mentor or mentee sort. In this case, I meet someone who is a peer in age, stage (of our businesses), and consulting type. What a treat it is!

We keep each other updated about new projects and challenges. Mostly, we support each other. I've noticed that we have complementary skill sets, which helps. My colleague has great business sense, so if I'm about to configure a contract poorly, she gives me sound advice. I'm more the bookworm, so I might know of a research study that backs up a point she's making to a client.

Travel, museums, articles, blogs, lectures. People. All are resources for the wide-ranging work consultants do.

observation

But mostly, we go back and forth about the next stages in our businesses' development. We're often encountering the same opportunities and challenges at about the same time. So when one of us talks about the struggles of taking on a few new clients at once, for instance, the other can relate to what that's like for a similarly-sized business and offer insights. She encouraged me to hire my first subcontractor, and I talked her into attending a recent cross-country conference, where she made some great new contacts. And so it goes.

The Next Big Thing

I also like to keep people in my life who are big thinkers. We push each other to take the next big leap. I have a longtime friend and colleague who serves this purpose. I met him years ago, when he served as executive director of a local nonprofit and I was his board chair. Yes, we're still talking to each other!

What will be your next big thing?

Will you learn a new skill? Create a new product? Work toward a credential? Attempt to secure your ideal client?

Will you present at a new venue? Write articles? A blog? A book?

If you can find someone who will listen to and pragmatically encourage your next reinvention, hold on to that person. It's great to have someone to dream with…and bring you back down to earth when you've gone too far.

As your consulting career steadies, don't lose sight of ambitious goal-setting. This friend and I have thrown out many career trial balloons over the years. I've brought home many ideas from our meetings, including the seed for this book. At that point in the process, my husband Rob patiently nods and says, "Go for it." It helps to have a life partner who's a big thinker too.

All A-board

Most of us agree that volunteerism is a given in our field, but it's worth being strategic about where you spend your limited time. While personal passions often drive volunteer service, it's good to ensure that the endeavors we choose provide balance and new insights. I don't want to serve on any two boards that are remotely similar. The redundancy would make that volunteer work feel too much like *work*. It's quite a perk when we can learn extensively from our volunteerism.

I'm serving on two boards right now, and they couldn't be more different. One is a $16 million regional agency that strengthens the lives of children and families. Meetings take place in a designated board room where trustees wear their business suits late into the night. There I've honed my knowledge of multi-state child welfare laws, complex real estate deals, and quality assurance procedures. The organization has grown quickly during my tenure, so conversations about scope and scale are frequent.

My other board raises tens of thousands of dollars annually for a local school's capital needs. Our meetings take place in jeans and T-shirts around board members' kitchen tables. The topics there keep me grounded in grassroots issues and the workings of our large local school system. There is no staff, so we're constantly in the weeds, a good reminder of the issues my smallest clients face daily.

A range of other committees, award panels, and grant-review boards can take on added relevance to our work. On a committee that crowned our region's best nonprofit leader, I got to philosophize about leadership with local nonprofit standouts and then interview some incredible executives. When my small neighborhood raised money for a legal fund to battle an encroaching hospital, I went door-to-door and was reminded of grassroots fundraising in its most basic form.

Professional Development

Then there are the more formal vehicles for continuing education. The options are endless these days.

Reading

When friends ask what I'm reading, I can often rattle off a good history or foreign affairs book, or even a few novels over the summer. But admittedly, I spend a great deal of my reading time pouring over the growing number of studies, analyses, and ideas from the burgeoning nonprofit research and think-tank scene.

I find reading the most productive way to learn. Unlike webinars and workshops, books and articles allow me to advance at my own pace. If the content is too basic, I just put the thing down. If it's not, I can revisit the details as many times as I'd like.

Not too long ago there was a dearth of nonprofit information. Colleagues and I would sit around debating issues that would have obvious answers in other industries. We still do that on occasion, but the volume of information I now receive electronically, and even in my old fashioned mailbox, is stunning.

These are just a few of the resources I suggest reading regularly.

- ❑ *Advancing Philanthropy* (Association of Fundraising Professionals)
- ❑ Bridgestar reports
- ❑ *The Chronicle of Philanthropy*
- ❑ Grantmakers for Effective Organizations studies
- ❑ CompassPoint publications
- ❑ *Harvard Business Review*
- ❑ *Nonprofit Quarterly*
- ❑ *Stanford Social Innovation Review*
- ❑ Urban Institute reports

to-do lists

Don't limit yourself to reading within the sector. Business, public policy, and many other topics can provide great insights into our field.

Professional Associations

Many of us have grown up on our professional associations' meetings, networking events, and conferences. Those are still excellent ways to learn and expand our circles. New and narrower groups are forming all the time. The competing market for credentialing and continuing education hours benefits us all. It means that we can all find more detailed information in the fields that interest us most.

Some associations cater to particular sectors of nonprofit management or fundraising, while others focus on consulting. The Giving Institute and the Association of Philanthropic Counsel provide opportunities for those in our field to formally connect and learn about best practices in nonprofit consulting. Whether you own a small shop or a growing one, the training and support offered by these organizations can be invaluable.

Of course, when you join an association, the networking can be as big a boon as the education.

Plugged-in

There is also an incredible number of interactive resources, such as CharityChannel and LinkedIn Groups, geared toward reading and responding to nonprofit interests. (See **Chapter Six** for more information about LinkedIn Groups.) These are great when you have specific questions you'd like answered, want to network, or help a colleague by responding to a post.

And webinars are fantastic, especially for consultants in smaller cities and rural areas, where there are fewer face-to-face workshops available. If you're like me, you receive several invitations to webinars every day in your in box, many of them free. So if there is a third-sector topic you would like to learn more about, there are dozens of opportunities waiting for you. Admittedly, some of these webinars are sales presentations, but you can always "walk out" of a webinar by simply closing your computer's window.

Don't overlook the value of podcasts. I download them onto my computer or iPod and listen to interviews with experts in our field and others while I'm doing my bills, driving, or walking downtown. Search iTunes or your favorite websites—nonprofit or otherwise—for topics of interest.

Unplugged

Despite some very good electronic resources, remember to unplug regularly. Our minds really are too cluttered these days. After many frustrating moments, it never fails that I go for a walk or a leisurely bike ride—with no electronics in tow—only to emerge with some of the best ideas I've had since my last mind-clearing activity.

During a recent unplugged moment, I decided how I would approach a client's development plan. It was a much more creative strategy than I'd had previously. While walking to the store a few weeks ago, I mentally refined an article I'd been working on. These are minor improvements to everyday issues, but I've also had some of my more "aha" moments during an unusually quiet state.

The beauty of being your own boss is that you can make time for these quiet activities. You must. They make room for new solutions and put our busy lives into perspective.

Carpe Diem

You're the boss.

No one else is watching.

How you decide to spend your day is up to you.

Be creative and have fun with the range of professional development opportunities out there. Even when business is at its busiest, continue to pursue the people, events, and resources that keep you sharp. Don't let up. If you do, your skills, networks, and future business will dry up.

Self-employment allows you to seamlessly toggle between client work, volunteerism, networking, and continuing education all within a typical day. It's the art of managing those endless options that consultants must find.

Chapter Nine

. . . And Associates

When you own your own business, you will inevitably dream about how large you might like it to grow. Your human resource options are nearly endless—from subcontractors to employees to formal business partners.

Sandra Migani Wall is a proponent of subcontractors, and she proposes "be one, use one" as the two-sided coin optimizing the benefits of associates.

Jean Block, on the other hand, provides you with some valid reasons for going solo.

Martha Schumacher explains how you can achieve the spirit of teamwork and interaction using multi-faceted arrangements with associates of different kinds.

Michelle Cramer leaves you with practical advice about what may be the hardest part of hiring associates: finding and retaining the best people.

Associates: Be One, Use One

By Sandra Migani Wall, PhD

I have worked as an associate, or subcontractor, and hired them too. Doing so is a fantastic opportunity for both parties.

You might wonder, "Why the heck should I work for the competition?" Or, "Why should I hire a subcontractor whom I have to pay? That impacts my income." Here is some food for thought.

The Advantages of Being an Associate

Working as an associate has enriched me personally and professionally. I have developed relationships with smart, extremely capable, and generous experts who have taught me well. Being an associate has enabled me to work on a wide variety of projects and thus gain experience outside of my original direct area of expertise. It has also enabled me to work with a much more diverse group of clients in terms of size, mission, and geographic location.

Being an associate for several firms helps when your own client pool temporarily dries up. Without being able to pick up work as a subcontractor during the downtimes, survival would be much tougher.

How Do You Become an Associate?

By networking. Ask your local community foundation for a list of consultants that it shares with local nonprofits. Contact those firms. Go to the meetings of professional associations and introduce yourself to other consultants. Find out what kind of work these consultants do. Visit their websites and see who their clients are. See if the quality and content align with your standards. If you don't know them by reputation, ask around to see how they are perceived. Call them up and invite them to coffee to explore mutually

---

One time I had lined up two lucrative projects to cover a three- to four-month period. One contract had been signed and the other had gone to the vice president to be signed. Both were to start in three months. Pretty convinced that I had these contracts in the bag, I had not accepted any other work for that time period, stopped networking, and planned some downtime. Well, the vice president who "hired" me left the institution before signing the contract, and this person's replacement did not want to commit to any project without reexamining priorities. The other nonprofit's revenue stream was severely reduced in the economic downturn, so it also indefinitely put the project on hold. My rosy economic forecast disintegrated.

Luckily, a colleague happened to call, overloaded and needing help with a few projects. While my subcontracting income did not replace the lost income from my anticipated contracts, the fees did buy me some time to regroup.

 stories from the real world

beneficial opportunities. Ask if they hire subcontractors, and if they do, whether they would be interested in seeing some samples of your work. (Come prepared with a portfolio to share.) You might also request samples of their work and ask if they'd be willing to subcontract with you.

What Fee Should You Expect as an Associate?

Your fee depends on the part you will play in the process. As a subcontractor, I do not get paid the same rate that my own consulting firm charges when I expend the time, resources, and energy to obtain the client and win the contract. If the consultant hiring me will do all or most of the work in getting a client and job, then I expect a lower hourly rate or project fee. This assumes that the consulting firm hiring me takes a leadership role and bids for the job, writes the proposal, does the initial meetings with the prospective client, sends the client invoices (and pays me whether it gets paid or not), takes the final responsibility on submitted reports, and sends me a 1099 form to keep the IRS happy.

On occasion, as a subcontractor, I have been asked to join the consultant in meeting with prospective clients and to help review, revise, and present the proposal. For this I usually get more compensation if we get the job. However, be careful and deliberate. You can spend a lot of time with someone else's potential clients without compensation for your time. And you might not even land the client. However, if you are new to consulting, this can be a great opportunity for you to learn from a more experienced consultant.

> Be careful with whom you align yourself. If your research of the hiring consulting firm indicates any red flags, back away graciously. Say that you would love to work with this firm but you're overcommitted, you'll be on vacation, you're sick. Why? Your reputation is on the line. If the quality of the firm's work is substandard compared to yours, then you and your reputation might be tainted by association.
>
> Use the same standard of care to evaluate the nonprofit client of the consulting firm hiring you, as you would if your firm was being hired directly by that client. Is the nonprofit reputable and well managed? Does it have a strong, committed, and supportive board? What are its chances for success in getting the grant or completing a capital campaign? Again, your reputation is on the line.
>
> **watch out!**

How Does One Juggle Being an Associate for Multiple Firms?

Be honest and upfront. I always let the firm for which I am an associate know that I also work as a subcontractor with other consulting firms. I never accept any work with one firm that might pose a conflict of interest for my or another firm for which I am working.

How Do You Present Yourself As an Associate to a Client?

Some consulting firms that have hired me as an associate have provided me with their business cards stating my name and contact information, listing my title as "associate." This is probably the least confusing for the client. Other consulting firms have allowed me to use my own business cards and indicate that, while I have my own firm, for this project I am working as a subcontractor under someone else.

In both cases my role and communication lines are made clear to the client: I am part of the hired consulting firm's team.

The Advantages of Having Associates

On the flip side, having associates to work with you on your projects also has multiple benefits.

When You Have Too Much Work

While consultants sometimes face a paucity of work, we sometimes find ourselves with *too much business*! When you're a sole proprietor and you've been networking and planting seeds, you may suddenly find yourself deluged with work. All your marketing efforts stand to go down the drain if you turn down the client and it hires another firm. What if it really likes the other consultant? Horrors! You might have just thrown away *future* opportunities as well.

You could buckle down and try to do all the work by yourself. This approach may cause other problems. For example, you probably won't have time to continue the necessary ongoing networking and marketing efforts that line up future clients. This "solution" will cause cash flow problems down the road. Also, the quality of your work may decline if you find yourself over-tired and over-stressed. You may then end up disappointing a potential repeat client or losing out on referrals.

So, what might you do? Consider calling in one of the associates whom you have previously vetted and cultivated. It's a win-win for everyone involved, and you'll be able to sleep at night, preserve your reputation, and have time to line up work for the future.

Improving Outcomes and Energizing Influences

It always helps to bounce ideas off a colleague, so contact associates for advice. Sometimes, they can spur you on to go the extra mile—especially useful if you are overworked and dragging. Trustworthy relationships with subcontractors can help you maintain standards and stay focused and on task.

Minimizing Clients' Concerns

How do you handle a client who asks during your interview, "What happens if I hire you and you have an accident and can't complete the project?" This is really only a problem if you're a sole practitioner. Tell the client that you will bring in an associate to work with you on this project, someone who will be very capable of taking it over, if necessary. You might include the associate's name and resume in your work proposal and be willing to set up a meeting with the associate and the client, if the client so desires. Foster preexisting working relationships with several subcontractors to make this scenario viable.

☐ Become a subcontractor.

☐ Vet and cultivate a group of associates who can collaborate with you as needed.

☐ Watch your business grow.

to-do lists

Minimizing Overhead

It's usually cheaper to use subcontractors than to hire full-time staff. As an independent contractor, your associate is responsible for payroll taxes, and you might not have to pay workers' compensation fees or benefits like health insurance and retirement funds. (See **Chapter Two** for more information about how the IRS defines independent contractors.) However, make sure your subcontractors carry their own workers' compensation insurance or you might be required to cover them on your policy. Using an associate also precludes you from providing office space and the accompanying overhead, in the form of furniture, technology, and utilities. Subcontractors eliminate the stress of having to generate enough work to cover the substantial cost of staff or the necessity of establishing a line of credit to cover overhead when cash flow becomes a problem.

Preventing Problems with Associates

How do you ensure that your subcontractors will deliver a high quality of work? How do you make sure they will follow through on all aspects of a project? How can you prevent them from promising more than they can deliver? Luckily, I have had limited problems with my subcontractors. Even so, I now take precautions.

Vet Candidates

Carefully screen and evaluate your prospects for the specific skills you're seeking. Ask potential subcontractors for samples of their work. Check with previous employers and other references.

Communicate

When working with new people, set up frequent meetings for both of you to touch base. The associate should report on progress made and provide ongoing drafts of expected deliverables.

Use a Contract

Having a contract or written agreement signed by you and the associate is essential. It simply prevents misunderstandings, corrects faulty memories, and thus minimizes the potential for problems. Good contracts also preserve valuable relationships.

Everyone forgets. It never ceases to amaze me how often I have had to refer to a contract to remind myself what both parties agreed to do. Especially if the project lasts a few months or more, I review the contract to be sure that we're both still on the same page and headed in the right direction.

Cover Your Bases

So what are some of the basics that an associate's contract might include?

- ◆ A statement listing the nonprofit for whom the work will be done and a general descriptive term for the work, e.g., special event, feasibility study.

- ◆ A list of the specific duties and deliverables for which the subcontractor is responsible. Be as explicit as possible. Include the universal "other duties as discussed and agreed upon by both parties."

- ◆ If known, the deadlines should be included by which the duties and deliverables should be completed. (Always allow ample time to compensate for problems and delays that may occur.) Mention the expected frequency of updates by the associate.

- ◆ An addendum, if any significant changes are made in any aspect of the agreement. The addendum should state what has been added by mutual consent (e.g., responsibilities and concomitant fees) and signed by both parties.

- ◆ The compensation structure, whether an invoice must be submitted and by when, and when it will be paid. If paid in installments, then the dates and conditions must be clearly spelled out.

- ◆ An expectation that the associate will be paid on time as long as all assignments are satisfactorily completed, independent of when the client pays your consulting firm.

- ◆ An expectation that the subcontractor will perform all job-related tasks diligently, in good faith, and with a mindset of advancing the best interests and benefits of the firm for whom the subcontractor is working.

- ◆ An expectation that the subcontractor will at all times perform as a member of the hiring firm's team.

- ◆ A non-compete clause, usually in effect for a year after the agreement is signed. The subcontractor should agree not to directly or indirectly provide consulting services to the client unless such services are directly related to the project for which you are hiring that person. The only exception would be if the associate solicited and received written permission from your firm to provide services directly to the client.

◆ A confidentiality statement declaring that the subcontractor will keep private any and all client information encountered during the contract.

◆ A statement indicating that both parties have the right to terminate the agreement by providing a written notice to the other party within a certain time period (usually thirty days).

◆ A stipulation that the written contract represents the entire agreement between both parties and may only be revised through a written statement signed by both parties.

Final Words

Whether you're an associate or hiring an associate, it is definitely smart to have a contract. To be honest, with people whom I have previously had positive working relationships, I am not as rigidly careful to have every change written up as an addendum and signed. Instead, I might jot off a quick email delineating my understanding of the change and asking them to suggest any corrections if their perceptions are different. However, it does pay to be careful.

Why I Chose to Go Solo (And My Experiment with a Co-Pilot)

By Jean Block

It's just me. No one else, and I like it that way. Staff meetings are easy and can happen anywhere and anytime. I don't have to check in or out with anyone, although at times I would like to fire my scheduling secretary (me) since she thinks I can travel way more than I'd like to! I have developed the discipline to prioritize and get the work done on time.

I do have professionals to advise me in areas where I lack experience or expertise, such as a corporate and tax attorney and an accountant. And I have an exceptionally talented graphic designer who built my brand and logo, and created the design for the two books I self-published.

I have defined and refined the type of consulting I want to provide and narrowed my focus by creating two identities and companies. Through Jean Block Consulting, Inc., I provide consulting and training in nonprofit management, fundraising, board development, and strategic planning. The other business, Social Enterprise Ventures, LLC, focuses entirely on developing earned-income ventures. In spite of these two entities, I occasionally get requests to do the types of consulting I don't want to do or don't do as well as my core services. While it is tempting to take on ancillary work, I resist the temptation to dilute my services and provide less than my best effort.

The Virtual Consulting Experiment

Here is how I solved this dilemma. I built an informal network of other consultants who do what I don't want to do. They are people I know and trust to serve my clients as well as I would, only they offer different services. Some are local and some reside in different parts of the country. My intention was to create a network of practitioners who specialize in the full array of services that any nonprofit would need, from board and staff training to consulting in finance, human resources, coaching, grant writing, fundraising, events, and more.

> Partnerships? Virtual consulting groups? One of these might work for you.
>
>
> 👍 practical tip

At one point, we formalized the relationships with written referral agreements and regular business meetings, and we developed a virtual consulting group with a name, website, promotional materials, and all the other bells and whistles. We divvied up the business responsibilities and agreed to share a percentage of all work we generated with one of us for handling the administrative duties. We did not share office space but worked from our home offices, using a post office address so we looked from the outside as if we were a traditional partnership.

But then it wasn't fun anymore, so we relaxed and kept the informal arrangement that still works well for all of us. It is an arrangement built upon trust and a firm belief that we ought to do what is best for the client and that we will all come out ahead in the long run.

We refer business to each other. We keep it simple with no referral fees or payments. What goes around comes around. We use each other as sounding boards and as supporters. We share the rave reviews and commiserate with each other when we get that occasional nasty comment. We leverage contacts for each other. And we celebrate each other's successes.

The Formal Partnership Experiment

I tried a formal partnership once. It seemed like a good idea at the time. I would have someone to share in the expenses of the business, someone to serve as a springboard for new ideas, someone to share in decision-making, someone whose contacts I could leverage to generate new business, and perhaps someone to pass the business to when I was finally ready to retire. The partnership would focus the business model on providing just social enterprise training, separate from each of our other nonprofit consulting firms, which we would continue to operate separately.

We did all the legal stuff you need to do when forming a partnership. We invested equally in the cost to set up the partnership. We wrote the business plan and named the business. We paid professional advisors to write contracts for the partnership and to develop our accounting system. We had the graphic designer create the logo and the necessary collateral materials. We developed a website and promoted the partnership to our contacts nationally.

As part of our business model, we wanted to encourage other consultants nationwide to join the business as senior consultants and trainers. They could identify and manage a geographic territory and earn a percentage of the net profit of every training program they provided. Of course, that meant more contracts and more collateral materials and more time recruiting and managing this team of collaborators.

We tried it for two years. At the end of the second year, my partner and I agreed to dissolve the partnership while we were still friends, because our friendship was more valuable than the partnership.

Why didn't it work for us? Our basic working styles weren't compatible. I think we knew that going in but didn't listen to our inner voices. I make decisions quickly and my partner was more into process. We traveled at different paces—literally. He wanted to reinvent our business while I wanted to be sure it was viable

> If your working styles aren't compatible, a partnership is likely to fail eventually.

important

before changing it. I became impatient waiting for decisions to be made and responses to come. I was carrying more of the business load but sharing revenue equally and becoming resentful.

So now I am back to the informal virtual relationships with both of my businesses. I merged the second business into my primary consulting business, but kept the separate identities because the focus is different for each. I streamlined accounting processes and reduced the amount of time I spend on administrative duties. I still use a formal annual contract for senior consultants to protect copyrighted materials and clients. Life is good.

Lessons learned? I learned that I am a sole practitioner at heart and was unhappy trying to fit my way of working into a form that didn't work for me or for my partner! I learned that, for me, a simple referral system built on trust and a client-focused approach serves me and my client base best.

To Grow or Not to Grow—That Is the Question. Or Is It?

By Martha H. Schumacher, ACFRE

As your business matures, there are many ways to acquire the extra hands you might need. In my years as a consultant, I have collaborated (formally and informally) with other consultants in every fundraising specialty. I have formed a strategic alliance with a direct marketing consultancy. I have hired staff and contractors.

In my experience, you will not succeed if you're focusing on growth for growth's sake. Your top priority should be delivering high quality services in a cost-efficient manner (for your clients) and doing so in a time-efficient manner (for your business).

How Important Is the Bottom Line?

While we live in a country that often places the highest value on companies that make the most money, I believe that success is best measured by more than just the dollar figure on your balance sheet. So I am growing my business based on the opportunities available and of interest to me, not according to a monetary goal.

Maintaining a work/personal life balance is a high priority and driver for me. Perhaps not surprisingly, my revenues tend to be more robust when I am achieving an optimal quality-of-life balance. These are the times when I tend to utilize additional staff and contractors the most.

For me, another top priority is working with great people. Because I am energized by people who do their jobs well, motivated by strong collaborations, and understand the power of bringing talented people to the client's table, my firm partners with a number of key players.

My business serves a variety of nonprofit types and sizes, and I have found that being able to offer a wide range of services has given me a "leg up" in the market.

That's why my team includes a:

- ◆ Strategic alliance with a direct marketing consultancy

- ◆ Contracted foundation grant writer

- ◆ Contracted donor researcher

- ◆ Various consultants with specialties ranging from major gifts and capital campaigns to corporate partnerships to development generalists to direct marketing production

◆ Part-time project and administrative support

◆ Marketing and research intern

Working backwards, the last position listed is unpaid. Because this person devotes so much time stepping up my marketing efforts (i.e., tweeting regularly, updating my LinkedIn profile, and researching market trends), I spend significant time overseeing this position. There is a bonus: it is extremely fulfilling for me personally and professionally to mentor a new student each semester.

Regarding project and administrative support, I recently made the decision to change this position to contract work, as opposed to part-time employment. A contributing factor in my decision was based on the costs associated with payroll, payroll tax, and unemployment insurance. The deciding factor was a bright and trusted recent graduate who was interested in providing her services contractually.

Referring Business

Meanwhile, on the referral front, I have been particularly picky about whom I refer a potential new client to when I can't take on a new project. There are just a handful of folks in my pool of referrals and they represent the best in the industry (in my humble opinion). Not only is it crucial to refer top-notch consultants to prospective clients, but your reputation is riding on it.

This is also true of your collaborating partners. If you have a client who needs a particular expertise that you either do not have or that you don't have time to provide, it is imperative that you bring in someone who holds to the same high standards you possess.

While expertise is critical, it is equally important that the people to whom you refer business know how to effectively manage client relationships because you trust them to represent you and your consulting business. Again, the priority must be to maintain, reinforce, and build your consultancy's reputation for excellence.

The Benefits of Strategic Alliances

Last but certainly not least, before I hung out my shingle, I approached a long-time friend and colleague about working together. I was still at my old job and frankly, I was focused on finding office space. She had a spare office and was thrilled to receive $400 per month from me for rent.

Needless to say, the rent has gone up considerably in the past decade, but it has been well worth it. We are now strategic

> Some of my contractors have full-time jobs. I am therefore very selective about how I use their time, as they provide very high quality but not quantity.

 stories from the real world

partners, which means that we work together on numerous projects—sometimes from the get-go, but often after one of us has developed a client relationship over time and we recognize the need to bring the other in to provide enhanced services.

My marketing partners provide storytelling services to nonprofits, which includes annual reports, campaign case statements, and direct mail copywriting. This provides an excellent complement to my major gift, capital campaign, and board development services.

These conversations with potential partners often involve highly confidential information, which brings us back to trust: if you aren't comfortable having this type of discussion because you're not sure you can trust the person on the other end of the line to keep the information confidential, you probably shouldn't be partnering with that person!

For my company, high quality service delivery is always our number one goal. Is it yours? If not, it may be time to take a look at your business plan and make sure that, if you are promoting growth, you're doing it because it will best serve your clients and there is a clear need in the marketplace—not just growth for growth's sake.

Hiring the Right Team and Keeping It

By Michelle Cramer, CFRE

I am often asked by clients, friends, and peers, "How do you find such great staff members? How do you keep them working with you for so long?" Often, those same people proceed to tell me how well my team and I work together, support one another, and respect one another.

Many consulting firms struggle with hiring and retention, regardless of whether they use staff or subcontractors to get the job done.

My ability to assemble a team of professionals who will go to the ends of the earth for clients with a smile did not simply emerge overnight. I have founded two successful consulting firms in the past twenty-five years, so building a team of talented professionals has been a priority for me over much of my career. While many consultants prefer to remain sole practitioners, I thrive and feed off the energy that comes with building a strong and dynamic team.

It all starts with finding individuals with potential, cultivating the relationships over a period of time, then asking the candidates to join my firm. That is just the beginning. Once on board, it is critical to thank and steward the relationship... hmm, sound familiar?

What to Look for When Hiring

No matter where I go, I keep my eyes open for people who stand out to me and possess that "wow" factor. That can sometimes be intangible. But think about someone you have met whose personality just draws you in. Maybe you sensed that person's passion for life, work, or just doing a good job. After someone like this has caught my attention, I typically don't forget that person.

I guess you could compare me to a talent scout or agent, always on the prowl for exceptional people. Many times, those individuals are in jobs where they are undervalued and have a hard time seeing themselves in leadership positions. Perhaps for several years, they have been doing the same jobs and have gotten into ruts where they are no longer excited about the work they do. Often, there is no one in an organization who is encouraging or recognizing these "underdogs." These are the individuals who, if given a chance, a pat on the back, or a word of encouragement, will knock your socks off. They will give 110 percent and exceed your expectations if *you believe in them and in their abilities.*

When I am looking for someone to join my team—notice how I use the term "team" rather than "staff"—I ask myself these questions:

❑ Is this person positive and uplifting?

❑ Does this person make me feel good?

   ❑ Is this person a team player?

   ❑ Is this someone who will help take my entire team (and me as well) to the next level with passion and a zeal for life?

Of course, I look at the candidate's experience and track record. But I first look to answer "yes" to the questions above and *then* I consider relevant experience. You see, I can teach someone how to lead a capital campaign or conduct a feasibility study. What I can't teach someone is how to bring a positive approach to each day's challenges; to be friendly, caring, and optimistic. These are the sorts of traits you cannot teach. These traits come naturally from within.

Personality Can *Trump Experience*

Several years ago, while working with a client on a capital campaign, I was meeting with the marketing director to develop our campaign materials. As I sat in this meeting, I marveled at the director's vivacious and engaging personality. She left a lasting impression on me. I knew she had those core personality traits that could make her an outstanding consultant.

A couple of years later, I ran into the same woman at a conference. She told me that she had left the organization and taken another marketing position with a for-profit company, but she missed working in the nonprofit world. I immediately invited her to lunch.

During that lunch, I asked if she had ever thought about becoming a fundraising consultant. My question caught her off-guard. She had never thought about this career move and didn't believe she had the necessary experience. She pointed out that she had never asked for money; she just developed the messaging, brochures, and other materials to support campaigns. I told her that the first time I had met her, I saw a special something in her, a spark that convinced me she had what it takes to be an outstanding consultant. Before long, she joined my firm and became an incredible consultant for over eight years, until she needed to relocate to care for her ailing father.

Today, she is a successful motivational speaker. In her opening comments, she often mentions that my belief in her helped her to believe in herself.

Cultivation is the Key

Two years ago, a highly respected community foundation executive and expert in planned giving called me and said he was planning to retire in one year. He said he had always been impressed with the team I had assembled. He went on to say that he did not want to retire completely and was considering consulting on a part-time basis. He was also scheduling meetings with several regional and national consulting firms.

I invited him to lunch. During that lunch I made the decision that he had what it takes to be an outstanding consultant, and I was going to recruit him very actively. So I spent the next year inviting him to numerous lunches where I would share my vision for the firm and tell him what a tremendous impact his expertise in planned giving could bring to our clients. I cultivated him in much the same way as you would cultivate a new donor prospect.

> By taking my time to cultivate relationships before I hire, I have found that my chances of making a great hire, one who will be with me for many years, skyrocket.

My competition was stiff, as I knew that other respected firms were vying for this man's services. After a year of breakfasts, lunches, dinners, and special events, he called me one day and said he had made his decision and had chosen to join my firm. I was thrilled.

My cultivation worked. Today, he has more than tripled our book of planned-giving clients.

Look for That "Twinkle"

Several years ago, I was looking for a new team member, a junior consultant who would also assist with marketing. My best friend, then the national marketing director for the largest carpet-cleaning company in the United States, was looking to hire an assistant marketing director. She called me one day and said, "I interviewed this guy today who really impressed me, but he just doesn't have the experience I'm looking for. I think you should interview him."

Two days later I had the candidate come to my office for an interview. He was just out of college and had very little experience. But during my interview with him, I noticed a twinkle in his eye—*something special*. He was witty, engaging, and confident, and he left me feeling like I had known him my whole life. While he had no fundraising experience, I decided to go ahead, take a chance, and hire him.

That was nineteen years ago. He is now a partner with my firm. Today, not only is he exceeding his clients' expectations and goals, but also helping lead and build our consulting practice. His clients love him and have a hard time letting go of him even after reaching their campaign goal. This is a perfect example of finding those intangible, ingrained traits, and then teaching the art of development, or whatever content area is your specialty. Hiring that young man—the one without any development experience—was one of the best decisions I have ever made.

Keeping Them!

It's one thing to find and hire good people, and quite another to keep them. I believe there are two key elements critical to retention. First, show praise and gratitude for their efforts and accomplishments. Second, encourage them to grow, take chances and get out of their comfort zone.

I truly believe that while money is an important factor to each associate, more important yet is how you openly, regularly demonstrate and communicate your appreciation for efforts and accomplishments. I do my best not to let a day go by without finding something positive to say to each and every one of my team members. I might leave a voice message, send a quick email or, what's even more powerful, verbalize how grateful I am to have that person as a part of the team.

I thank my team members constantly for the job they are doing and the commitment they make to their clients and our firm. I do not say these things just to say them, but the sentiments come from my heart. I truly believe without each of their contributions, our firm would not be as highly respected and sought after as we have become.

> I have found that I can get the very best out of a staffer or subcontractor if he or she feels highly valued.
>
> **observation**

Celebrating the little things can make a huge difference in developing a positive culture within your organization. Little things such as knowing the names of your associates' children and pets, birthdays, or the way they take their coffee make a difference. Celebrating each team member's victories, such as a client securing a lead gift for a campaign, are ways to build unity and a strong culture within your organization.

Show Discomfort with Comfort Zones

I recruited a team member who had worked for ten years as an administrative assistant for another nonprofit consulting firm. After a couple of weeks of working with her, I saw a great deal of potential above and beyond her clerical and administrative skills. I saw a person with a great deal of talent, knowledge, and desire to help but who had always seen herself as a "behind the scenes" person. She had never been encouraged nor given the opportunity to interact with clients.

I began bringing her with me to client meetings and helping develop strategies for various campaigns and projects. I then asked her to be part of educational training sessions, and later, asked her to develop our firm's social media platform, something she knew nothing about at the time.

I will never forget taking her to meet with one of my clients. The executive director was asking questions about various topics. Before I knew it, she had the client thoroughly engaged—it was a beautiful thing! After we got in the car to leave, I said to her, "You know what you were doing back there?" She said, "No. What do you mean?" I said, "You were consulting. You are no longer going to be working behind the scenes. You are now officially a consultant."

> Encourage your team members to get out of their comfort zones and take chances.
>
> **practical tip**

She thought a while and then said, "Wow, I think you are right. All I was doing was offering some advice that I had seen and heard before. I guess you are right... I *am* a consultant."

Over the course of about a year, I saw this young woman, who previously would rarely leave her desk even for lunch, now leading efforts inside and outside our office.

By seeing her potential, encouraging her, and providing the support she needed to believe in herself and her abilities, today she is a senior consultant who leads one of our firm's most highly visible client campaigns. Also, as a result of her efforts, our firm is recognized as a national leader in social media networking and engagement. All of this talent rested within her for all of those years. It wasn't until she was given the opportunity that she blossomed.

I now tease her after we leave meetings where she runs the show that, "It's a good thing I don't have an ego!" because she really does excel in our field.

I recently received a holiday card from her which read, "Michelle, I cannot say thank you enough for such an incredible year! I feel like I have grown by leaps and bounds in my career this year, and I owe it all to you for inspiring me to reach for the stars!!!"

Sense of Team

In addition to the importance of building individual capital and potential, my firm has built a culture based on camaraderie. We support one another when things are good, and when one of our team members is down or struggling, we are there to help out. That closeness permeates our firm and then spills over to our clients. They sense our team spirit and know that when they hire our firm they are getting a close-knit team that will do what it takes to be successful!

Recently one of our clients, a vice president for development, was preparing to make a major presentation, not to a prospective donor but to her boss, who had extremely high expectations. The VP called our office and said she did not feel she was getting adequate support from her development staff; she needed our help urgently, as the presentation was the next day. Within two hours, two of my team members were in her office, first reassuring her, and then diving into preparation for this important presentation.

> Once you have built your ideal team, they will rise to all sorts of challenges—together.
>
> **observation**

The Cramer team was able to step in at a critical point and act as members of her staff to prepare a superb presentation. The next day, the VP for development sent my team an email reading, "I cannot thank the two of you enough for coming to my rescue at a time I needed it the most. The way you worked together, complementing one another, is remarkable given the short turn-around time on this project. Thank you for having my back and for being there when I needed your help and guidance most!"

Easy Come, Easy Go? Not So Much.

We have all heard the phrase "easy come, easy go." But in consulting, or any business, it is not easy to find dynamic team members, and it's certainly hard on you and your clients when they go.

Taking the time and making the effort to find individuals with strong core values is critical to the success of your business. And once you have those special individuals on board, make it a priority to thank them and acknowledge their efforts on a consistent basis. These steps help ensure that you gain their commitment and loyalty and retain it over time.

With the commitment and loyalty of each member of the team, you build upon the infectious passion and enthusiasm that your clients are searching for when hiring consultants. Once you can deliver what prospective clients are searching for, *you win*!

Chapter Ten

Preparing for the Unexpected

This chapter title might sound a bit perplexing. You might ask, "If it's an unexpected event, how can I be prepared for it?" And, true, none of us was prepared for something like September 11, 2001. But consultants dealt with it because we had the right mindset, a crisis plan, or just plain resilience.

Sandra Migani Wall reminds you of life's "banana peels," and offers some unexpected events that you can actually learn to predict after a while.

Kent Stroman talks about the importance of margins—those safety nets we all need.

And, Mary Hiland writes about how she handled the one problem all consultants dread: an angry client!

Avoiding Consulting's "Banana Peels"

By Sandra Migani Wall, PhD

My husband's motto about life is, "We all have one foot on a banana peel."

How apt. No matter how well prepared or experienced you think you are, sometime or another you'll come face-to-face with an unexpected obstacle. Your job is to prepare yourself as much as possible, so that the unforeseeable becomes a little more foreseeable. I have been very fortunate in that my clients and colleagues have been wonderful! They have taught me so much. But one thing *is* predictable: we all run into some of these "banana peels" with our clients.

Problem: An Angry Client

Clients may become angry for many reasons. Sometimes their expectations exceed what you can deliver. Other times you can't provide the deliverable on time because you lacked information that the client's staff was supposed to submit to you weeks ago.

Once I did a feasibility study that indicated that some of those interviewed had complaints about the executive director. We provided what we thought was a balanced, carefully worded report indicating the nature and percentage of respondents who had complaints. The executive director and some board members were offended.

Solution: Have a contract that clearly specifies the expectations and responsibilities on both sides. Refer to it throughout the project. If there are any changes in the scope of the work or fees, draw up a written addendum that both the client and consultant sign. Within the contract, specify required meetings between you and the point person (and the executive director, if not the point person). This is especially critical in the beginning when you're developing a relationship with the client. As the work progresses, continue to require meetings at strategic points. Use the meetings to make sure expectations and underlying conditions have not changed and to remove potential or existing obstacles to success.

> To minimize client anger:
>
> ❑ Never promise what you can't deliver.
>
> ❑ Don't take on work outside your area of expertise.
>
> ❑ Use a contract that clearly delineates the work to be done and everyone's responsibilities.
>
> ❑ Communicate clearly and frequently.

 **to-do lists**

A contract should always include an opt-out clause for you and for your client. That way you can terminate the relationship before a situation gets ugly.

Once the contract is signed, ask a few questions in the first meeting to further clarify expectations. For example: Why did you choose my firm? What's the bottom line that must be achieved in order for this venture to be a success? What will constitute a home run for you?

Regarding the feasibility study mentioned above, we decided not to change the report. We felt strongly that we had to accurately and honestly reflect everything we discovered. Unsurprisingly, we were not asked to do any further work with that client. Sometimes if there is an ethical issue, there may not be an easy or palatable solution and you will just have to live with the consequences.

Problem: A Dishonest Client

One executive director removed unfavorable material from the consultant's feasibility report before delivering it to the board. The consultant felt obligated to be a true voice of those interviewed. What to do?

Solution: Seems obvious, but hindsight always is. Send even your draft reports as PDF files. You can still solicit feedback from the executive director and make the changes yourself.

Another option might be to confer with a respected colleague when you encounter an ethical situation. If you don't know one in your area of expertise, contact your professional association.

Problem: An Impossible Timetable

Consultants regularly encounter problems with inadequate staff cooperation, data availability, and other assorted delays. I contracted to help a well-established and respected nonprofit write a very complicated proposal for federal funds. As with many projects, the seemingly ample two-and-a-half-month window came down to the wire.

If you're being contracted to do a feasibility study, development audit, or other report with potentially negative feedback, be proactive:

❑ Address the possibility of negative findings in your preliminary meetings with the executive director and board president.

❑ Obtain the client's agreement to report all findings, whether positive or negative.

❑ Stress that finding out the true perceptions of those interviewed—even if disapproving or erroneously off-center— allows the nonprofit to handle the issues and misperceptions, thus removing obstacles to future growth.

to-do lists

Solution: There are many things you can do to get out in front of time constraints:

◆ Be careful about which jobs you will accept. Don't take on a project unless you have adequate lead-time and can be reasonably sure of success.

◆ In your contract, identify a point person who has clout and with whom you will interact. This person should be the one who will reap the praise or censure for the project's outcome. Keep this contact up to date on whether deadlines are being met. Discuss with the executive director and point person—ahead of time—how staff will be encouraged to meet deadlines and what will happen if material is not provided to you in a timely manner. Make sure the staff knows the details of this conversation.

◆ Communicate proactively. In fairness to the staff, you need to be proactive, polite but forceful, and on top of deadlines. Send out emails periodically and copy the point person. The emails can subtly remind staff of the deadline, ask if the staff has questions or problems, and share what colleagues have found helpful in completing the assignment. Depending on the working environment, heap praise on those who have successfully completed the assignment (thus indirectly identifying who is holding up the process).

◆ Build extra time into your timetable. Establish due dates that are reasonable but that also provide ample cushion for you and the staff to handle unforeseen problems.

◆ Include "cover yourself" clauses in the contract. For example, "The client recognizes that progress in any of the above activities strongly depends on (a) the amount of information already compiled by the client on specific projects; (b) the rapidity with which the client shares this information with the consultant; (c) whether the client meets mutually agreed upon deadlines; and (d) whether the client fulfills its responsibilities as listed above. The consultant will not be held responsible for delays in performance under this agreement covered by an Act of God or any other cause over which the consultant has no reasonable control."

◆ Charge for the stress of impossible timetables. If you're going to take on the additional pressure of meeting last-minute deadlines, charge

> While a "cover yourself" clause might not motivate a client to meet deadlines, I still point it out before the point person signs our contract. Some consultants' contracts warn that if the client does not meet critical deadlines, the consultant can terminate the contract immediately. While you stand to lose income in this case, you do save your reputation by ensuring that you are not responsible for a shoddy product.

watch out!

a heck of a lot more. Let the client know that the proposed fee is above what would normally be billed and why.

Problem: Trouble Collecting Your Fee

While I have never had a problem collecting fees, I have experienced delays in scheduled payments. Unfortunately, plenty of my consulting colleagues have suffered from true non-payment.

Solution: Require an initial significant payment *before your work begins.* I usually ask for one-third of the total fee. If the client can't come up with this amount, you might think twice about taking this client on.

You might also consider for your contract: (a) a penalty fee for payments made after thirty days, or (b) a bonus discount of 5 percent if the invoice is paid within thirty days. Of course you have to build the extra 5 percent into your billing rate, but everyone loves a discount!

> No matter the quality of your work, there are sometimes individuals within your client organization who think that consultants are an extravagant waste of valuable resources. One colleague told me that a business manager with this view kept "losing her bills" for months on end, even though the grant funds paying for her services had been received.

 stories from the real world

Smaller or newer nonprofits might have problems with cash flow, making timely payments less certain. Ask around and find out what kind of reputation your prospective clients have before you pursue their business.

Finally, it should be obvious that you should maintain a cash reserve to tap into when your own cash flow problems arise. If you're a larger consulting firm, you probably should have a line of credit. Establish it when you're solvent and having a great year. If you have to tap it, pay it off as quickly as possible.

Problem: Founder's Syndrome

Founders can retain tight control over an organization, presenting unique challenges to consultants. They might lack the organizational and business skills necessary to grow and sustain a nonprofit. Sometimes they don't see the necessity of putting the appropriate checks and balances in place. Often they have a hard time trusting others with "their" nonprofit.

Solution: Run! Well, at least seriously evaluate the situation, because while working with founders can be uplifting and inspirational, it can also be exhausting and frustrating. So, after your initial discussion with the founder, if you're still interested, you should schedule a joint meeting with the founder and the board.

Ask pointed questions of the non-founder board members to determine:

◆ Exactly what are you being hired to do.

◆ Exactly what are the expected outcomes.

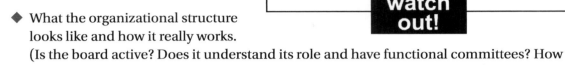

It is a definite warning sign if the founder tells you that there's no need for you to meet with the board.

watch out!

◆ What the organizational structure looks like and how it really works. (Is the board active? Does it understand its role and have functional committees? How are decisions made? What are the official and *actual* roles of the founder?)

◆ What are the parameters within which you are to work.

◆ If the agency is collaborating with like-minded organizations.

◆ What the organization has tried in the past in regard to your potential area of work, and why has it worked or failed to work.

Listen carefully. Watch who speaks and directs the conversation. If it is very clear that the board is made up of passionate community members who nevertheless do not really understand their roles as board members, they likely serve as rubber stamps to the founder. In that case, I suggest that you walk away.

If board members' answers are clear and positive and indicate that the board understands its role, uses its authority to achieve the mission, can act independently of the founder, and is willing to collaborate if the right partner and project is found, then the organization has potential.

Problem: Too Much Work and Not Enough Time

The problem with consulting is that it seems to be either feast or famine. You network, develop, and present proposals and then nothing seems to happen. Suddenly, all the seeds you planted sprout at once. Now you're overwhelmed with work and worry that you'll never get it done on time.

Solution: Try to avoid taking on too many simultaneous projects. You really can't do top-quality work when you're exhausted.

See if clients would be willing to start in four to six weeks. Perhaps there is a portion of the work that staff could be doing while you finish up with other clients. Remember that everyone always wants what they can't have. If you're in high demand, that might increase your desirability with clients. Finally, consider developing a group of subcontractors that can step in and help you.

Problem: You Don't Get the Job

Solution: Sometimes it's unexpected, sometimes it's not. In either case, it hurts. Weep, gnash your teeth, and get over it. Send a letter thanking the client for inviting you to submit a proposal and wishing the organization success. Wait two weeks and call your contact. Ask if the point person would be willing to provide you with some feedback about your proposal so that you can understand how you could have better met the organization's needs. Be non-confrontational, sincere, and genuinely interested in their feedback. If you handle it well, the client will likely remember you the next time it needs a consultant.

It can be even more surprising when a past client starts working with another consultant. The only thing you can do is be sure to follow-up with every client once you finish the project. Ask what went well, what could be improved, and whether your contact would provide a testimonial. Continue to cultivate your clients just like nonprofits cultivate donors.

Last Words

There are banana peels all around us. With careful preparation, diligence, and quality work, we can avoid most of them. Others we won't see until we've stepped on them and begun to slip. However, with a little help from our peers we'll be able to regain our balance and continue trying to make a positive difference in the world.

The Case for Margins in Business Planning

By M. Kent Stroman, CFRE

During my first year as an independent consultant, I generated over $100,000 in revenue.

While my first year's consulting revenue might be nothing to brag about compared to the salary many of us earned while serving as senior staff members, it's nothing to sneeze at either. Most people would have said it was impossible. There were some times when I would have said that myself. During these early months the outlook was promising. It caused me to feel optimistic.

But there were other times when I wondered if this consulting thing was sustainable. The most serious of these doubts screamed in my face on the seventy-second day after I launched Stroman & Associates.

I spent that sunny Tuesday morning in September driving to a nearby city to make a presentation for campaign consulting services. When I arrived at my destination, a few minutes early, I was politely asked to wait in the reception area until called. No problem. I spent these moments reviewing the details of my carefully crafted proposal, knowing it would be irresistible to the soon-to-be client. Little did I know what was about to unfold.

Shortly, a friend of mine, who served on the board of the organization, stepped into the waiting room and said, "Kent, you've got to see this." It certainly wasn't the greeting I expected, but I readily followed him to the board room.

Immediately I noticed a television with live news coverage of a breaking story taking place in New York City. The announcer said something about airplanes colliding with the World Trade Center towers. None of this made any sense to me...I had been totally oblivious to the dramatic events of that morning.

As you may have already guessed, the agenda for that day's meeting was suddenly altered. My proposal that had been so diligently prepared now became ultra-trivial. Oh, we went through the motions of the presentation, followed by a lackluster Q&A session, but it all rang hollow. Everything was overshadowed by an oppressive cloud of uncertainty that could not be ignored. I packed my briefcase and went away.

On my drive back to the office I began to hear the rest of that day's news. I wondered what the events meant for the world. What did this mean for the United States of America? What did it mean for me? For my family? My business?

A dark sense of fear enveloped me. I desperately missed the security of the university environment I had stepped out of just eleven weeks earlier. I was near panic!

I tell this story to make an important point. If you are going to be in business for yourself, you have to prepare for circumstances that you cannot predict. Or, as my mother-in-law would sometimes say, "You never know what to expect when you least expect it!" I couldn't have said it better myself.

What I can assure you of is this: The unexpected *will* happen. We can't know when. We can't know what. We can't know where. We can't know why. We can just be certain that the unexpected will happen.

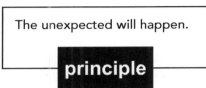

The unexpected will happen.

principle

Unfortunately the plans we make and the reality we experience usually diverge. We carefully calculate, project, estimate, and anticipate. It all comes together in a tidy spreadsheet. Using dollars as a common denominator, we forecast results.

The problem is this: things *never* go exactly according to plan. Sometimes the unexpected is good. Sometimes it is not. And if our business is going to survive, we have to be prepared for what we cannot fully prepare for.

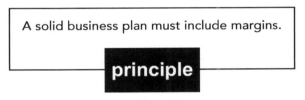

A solid business plan must include margins.

principle

This brings me to the best advice I can offer. Your business plan must include what I call margins. A margin is the white space between the text and the edge of this page. If the margin is narrow there is little room to express additional thoughts. If the margin is wide it will accommodate numerous notes, questions, and comments. Margins provide options. And in business if you don't have options, you won't last long.

What areas require margins in planning for a consulting business? What unforeseen circumstances should we expect? I would suggest these five:

1. Timing
2. Income
3. Expense
4. Cash
5. People

Margin: "An amount allowed or available beyond what is actually necessary: to allow a margin for error."

—Dictionary.com

definition

Timing

Events will not follow your timeline. Whether it is approval by a regulatory agency, orders for equipment and supplies, or board action by a prospective client to approve your proposal, things

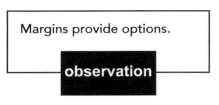

> Margins provide options.
>
> **observation**

take longer than expected. You will not be in control of the most critical factors. Your attempts to create urgency will only serve to derail the entire process. As you plan, create margins in your timeline. Make your best projections of the time needed for each step. Then double it. Remain flexible. And be prepared to wait—patiently.

Income

When I prepared my business plan, it was based on securing five clients by my launch date. I worked to that end. I hoped to that end. I prayed to that end. And I planned to that end. On my D-Day I had exactly two clients. I had proposals pending with two others. One was eventually accepted several months later. The other never came to fruition. My income projections for month one were blown. The same went for months two, three, four, and so on. Fortunately I had a contingency plan in place for income. Without it my business would never have made it to year two.

Expense

Your expense projections require margins as well. Costs you anticipate will come in higher than you plan. Expenditures you did not expect will show up uninvited. You'll encounter opportunities to invest in your business that will seem foolish *not* to pursue. Sometimes these surprises are large. Usually they're small. But they all add up and, if not accommodated, they'll overwhelm you. It is always a good idea to include a contingency in your expense budget. Consider using an allowance of 25 to 40 percent. If you don't need it, no problem! If you do need it, it will be a veritable lifesaver.

Cash

Cash expectations also require margins. Even if your revenues and expenses are completely on track, you can end up with a cash problem. With vendors breathing down your neck and client payments slower than desired, you may find cash to be in short supply. You cannot allow your cash-flow problems to create pressure on your client relationships. Be prepared to take measures to preserve cash that you might otherwise avoid. I had the money on hand to purchase my office furniture

> As a business owner, your priorities and problems do not matter to anyone else. They're yours!
>
> **observation**

and equipment outright at the time of launch. Fortunately, I also had the foresight to accept the vendors' installment terms and spread the payments out over several months. It seemed like a waste of interest dollars initially, but later it proved to be a small price to pay for the freedom of having cash on hand. I was glad to have this flexibility when I experienced the sudden deviations from my business plan described above. The cash flow eventually balanced itself out, but it took much longer than I would ever have predicted.

People

Finally, margins are helpful when it comes to *people*. Friends, colleagues, professional associates, and even family members will make commitments to you that you will rely on. They will be sincere when they make their assertions. But they will forget, delay, defer, and change their minds. It will seem like they are out to do you in. It will feel personal. It will hurt. But you must not let it get the best of you. You have to have a mechanism to take the pressure off. Nothing works better than margins.

During my business planning phase, I took deliberate steps to ask numerous friends and colleagues for their support and assistance in my new endeavor. I sought recommendations, endorsements, and commitments to use my services. While I received enthusiastic, positive responses from those who did respond, the outcome did not match up with the promises. I can only identify one such commitment that actually materialized. This is not a critical statement, just an observation. People want to assist. They want to encourage. They want to be helpful. But they have a tendency to go on with their lives.

Do ask for support. Do ask for endorsements. Do ask for the opportunity to do business with those you know. But don't expect anyone else to do the heavy lifting for you. The results of *your* business are largely up to *you*.

> As consultants, we are in the business of managing expectations.
>
> **observation**

In reality, being a consultant means you are really in the business of managing expectations. Each of the five areas described above consist of expectations. Lots of them. Your effectiveness in managing your own expectations will either make or break your business.

The Call You Dread

By Mary Hiland, PhD

This can't be happening to *me*. My first reaction was one of disbelief as I heard the voice on the other end of the phone line yell: "I am really angry at you!" Then, he went on, and on, and on.

I was overwhelmed and totally caught off guard. I was *not* prepared for this call; there were no clues that would have led me to expect this tirade from Sam (not his real name).

Frankly, I was grateful that Sam went on and on at the beginning of the call because it gave me the opportunity to think about how the heck I was going to respond! Of course, I don't remember everything he said or I said. I do remember that it felt bad. I was embarrassed, along with a host of other emotions.

As you can imagine, I have reflected on this experience and the conversation, if I can call it that, a lot. As a result, I have some insights about how to deal with an angry client.

Build Trust

This exchange occurred as part of a collaboration project in which I was working with several members of a group. One thing I emphasized at the beginning of my work with this group was critically important later: building trust. Any consultant knows that building trust among the parties involved is essential. I learned that building a high level of trust between *me* and the parties involved was also essential. Ironically, I believe Sam really trusted me. That trust created the safety that underpinned his tirade—directed *at* me, but, thankfully, not so much *about* me.

Listen

I love the wisdom of St. Francis of Assisi, something that Steven Covey borrowed in *Seven Habits of Highly Effective People*: "Seek to understand before you are understood." I can't take credit for being a sage here, but because I was so surprised by Sam's anger and didn't know what to do about it, I realize now that I genuinely wanted to understand his perspective. I just listened. *Listening was the most important thing I could have done.* A lesson I have learned over the years, and

---

Here are five behaviors I have identified that build trust:

1. Demonstrate that you value the other person's opinion.

2. Be vulnerable.

3. Behave consistently.

4. Give constructive feedback.

5. Receive feedback openly.

observation

need to apply more than I do, is the importance of knowing that sometimes people just want to be heard. They want to be understood. They don't really need us to jump to their rescue or come up with solutions.

Listening helped me. On the surface, I heard:

◆ "You should have gotten my approval to add that item to the agenda."

◆ "I am a volunteer; you are paid. I have a 'real' job. I have taken on a leadership role here because I can keep this project from being derailed!"

◆ "You are letting her have too much of a role. You have to let her know she can't do that!" (The "her" was another key member of the group.)

By listening at a deeper level I was able to gain empathy for Sam as I "heard" the following underneath his words:

◆ "I am the co-chair; I am responsible." (It wasn't power or ego really. Sam felt responsible. Most board members do.)

◆ "I am overwhelmed; I have no more time to give to this, but I'm stuck in it."

◆ "I don't feel supported in this process."

Focus on the Outcome

During Sam's call, I was able to draw his attention to results. I asked him to think not about how others in the group were presenting themselves, but about the group's actual final agreements. He didn't like the way I facilitated a particular meeting's discussion, expecting me to "manage" the discussions more proactively, but he did agree that the outcome was on target.

Initially I didn't agree with Sam's version of how that particular meeting unfolded, but as he went on, I had to acknowledge that I might have been too passive in that part of the meeting. Maybe I did defer, letting others dominate the conversation too much. As I encouraged Sam to focus on the outcome, I

There are three levels of listening. In challenging conversations, it is easy to be in the first, but we are most effective when we are in the third!

1. Evaluating/comparing: We are more interested in promoting our point of view than understanding the other person.

2. Attentive but passive: We are interested and assume we have understood.

3. Active: We confirm our understanding and are also genuinely interested in what the other person is feeling or what the message *means*.

food for thought

did too, and that helped me: it helped me avoid being defensive, which would have escalated the conversation and invalidated Sam's experience.

When we find ourselves in difficult conversations, we can get into trouble. Why?

◆ We experience emotions that don't help us respond constructively.

◆ We focus on trying to change the other person's view.

◆ A few things can help: Take a few deep breaths before responding! Acknowledge your emotions but choose not to let them control your response. Remember Covey's advice: Seek to understand.

 practical tip

Let Go of the Outcome

Okay, I know, this sounds like a contradiction. It's actually a paradox, one I find very relevant to consulting. I have learned that I am most effective when I focus on the result I am working toward, but also let go of it. In other words, I don't try to control it. Somehow, I was able to let go of the outcome of the conversation. I didn't need to make Sam wrong or me right. I didn't try to change his mind or fix things for him. I just let the conversation flow and, as if I were an outside observer, watched what happened.

Be Authentic: Trust Your Gut

At the end of our phone call, Sam asked me for my advice: "Tell me what to do." Silence.

This was about an hour into the call and, by that time, I did have a couple of thoughts in response. I debated in the few seconds I had whether or not to share them. I *felt* that I should, so I did.

I took a risk: I told him that I thought he was being overly sensitive. I advised him to focus on the results and not to let someone else's needs and style get to him so much. I also suggested that he think about his personal capacity and see if he could work something out to wind down his role in some of the minutiae and focus on the bigger issues. Given how he felt, I thought this last suggestion would go over like a lead balloon!

He got quiet. Said he would think about it, and then, "I have to go. Sorry I top so much of your time," and hung up.

About a week after Sam's call, he took part in a group phone meeting. He was quiet and participated marginally. I sensed that he had decided to withdraw from the process. I reached out to him, asking for his input, which he gave when asked. I wondered what was to come. He wasn't able to attend our next, and last, monthly in-person meeting. I trusted his excuse: he was traveling on business. I never saw him again.

I ask all my clients to do an evaluation when our work is completed. For this group, that came a few months later. A colleague interviewed Sam for me. Sam fully participated.

He raved about my work. He held to his objections about the part of the process he had been so angry about. But, in spite of them, he said he would highly recommend me to any other nonprofit. Go figure.

So What Did I Learn?

◆ Commit to building trust at every opportunity with everyone involved.

◆ Seek to understand by listening deeply and seeking the underlying messages.

◆ Don't be defensive!

◆ Gain agreement about desired results proactively and then focus on them.

◆ Trust the process; let the results unfold. Give up control.

◆ Stay true to yourself, be yourself, trust yourself!

Part Three

Sticking It Out

It's never too early to think about where you'd like to end up. As your business matures, it's reassuring to know that some of our field's best consultants have had moments of doubt, even years into their practices. They have been frustrated by the ebb and flow of their workload. They have wondered how much community service was too much. They have grown tired of their core competency—the very skill that led them to consulting success in the first place!

The contributors to this section tackle some of the perennial issues that face consultants throughout our careers, all with reassuring strategies to offer. The section opens with some inspiring transformations of consultants and their practices. You'll then read about tactics to get yourself through slow spells, and you'll see why giving back to the nonprofit sector is such a rewarding part of nearly all consultants' lives.

We'll close with three practitioners who have wound down, transferred ownership of, or closed their practices. These can be difficult steps to ponder, but as you'll see, the more planning you do, the easier the transition as you ride your white horse into the consultant's sunset.

Chapter Eleven

Reinventing Yourself

We're betting that many of you are considering, or have entered, the field of consulting because you grew tired of the same old routine day in and day out.

Guess what? Consulting sometimes gets stale too.

But it doesn't have to be that way. Three consultants tell you about the various reinventions of their consulting practice, each in a very different way.

Linda Lysakowski first asks if you really can do what you love and have the money follow, or if you have to be more strategic in choosing, and sometimes changing, what kind of practice you will have.

Sandy Rees changed her practice by monetizing some of her services and creating packages of products.

Jean Block provides a first-hand account of what it's like to retire services, add new ones, and even bring back the ones you previously eliminated.

Do What You Love and the Money Will Follow. Maybe.

By Linda Lysakowski, ACFRE

Shortly after I started my business, there was a lot of buzz about a book that claimed that if you start a business or follow a career path that you are passionate about, you will be successful. Well, maybe. There are a lot of people who are passionate about nonprofit work, but are not successful when they try their hand at consulting.

In high school when we all had to fill out those career surveys (mine always suggested I was suited to be a detective or reporter), I always knew there were two things I *didn't* want to be: a banker or a teacher. Yes, my first career was none other than banking! As you'll read later, my latest career is pretty much teaching. So much for knowing it all when you're young. But I did know I wanted to be successful.

◆ What are your goals?

◆ How would you prioritize them?

◆ How can your consulting career help you achieve them?

food for thought

As others in this book have said, you have to define what success means for you. Is it money? Travel? The opportunity to be independent? Setting your own hours? A passion for a cause? I knew which of these was most important to me and I would probably list them in this order: (1) feeling good about what I do, (2) independence, (3) travel, (4) setting my own hours, and (5) money.

Finding the Services That Help You Reach Your Goals

When I first started my business, I had a clear plan in mind. I was not going to do capital campaigns. Why? There were more experienced consultants and bigger firms doing those already. I was going to follow my passion. I was going to help smaller and newer, unsophisticated nonprofits start a development office, run an annual campaign, and build their boards.

That went fine for a while. It allowed me independence and the ability to set my own hours, not much travel at first, and not a lot of money. Although money was last on my

---

Will your services help you reach your goals? For example, if your goal is travel, focusing on research or writing probably won't help you reach that goal. If it's independence you want and the ability to set your own hours, you won't want to serve in interim executive director positions.

practical tip

list, reality quickly set in and I realized if I was going to maintain an office, pay staff, market my business, pay my accountant and state registration fees, and actually take some money home, I needed to rethink my services.

Fortunately at about the same time this realization set in, a number of my clients did find themselves in need of capital campaigns but could not afford to pay the "big guys" to come in from out of town and run these small campaigns. So I started off with a few small capital campaigns, under $1 million each. Before I knew it, I was running multi-million-dollar campaigns and making a lot more money. I was soon gaining a regional and then a national reputation, so I got to travel. Cross off two of my goals. And guess what, I was still passionate about what I was doing, was very much independent, and could schedule my own hours, although there were a lot less hours of my own to enjoy.

Reinventing My Company the First Time

After about five years in business, I felt my company needed to grow to be successful. I started bringing on subcontractors to help manage the client work, so that I could focus more on marketing.

I carefully tracked all my sales and the sources of clients. Besides word-of-mouth, the marketing effort that brought me the most clients was speaking, followed by networking at Association of Fundraising Professionals (AFP) meetings. So I expanded my speaking and writing engagements and joined several AFP chapters. Through this networking I found a colleague whose goals were similar to mine. We both wanted to expand our businesses, become more focused on capital campaigns, and do more teaching. So we formed a partnership, initially focused on doing workshops about capital campaigns. We began getting more campaign clients and hiring more subcontractors to help with the campaigns. At one point in time we had about six offices (still using subcontracted associates to run regional offices), and we were on the road a lot doing workshops and presentations, consulting, and working with the associates to market our business.

> If you hire staff or subcontracted associates, what kind of work will they do—client work, marketing, financial work, support services? Decide what you are good at, what you want to do, and what will bring your most desired results (money or satisfaction). Then hire people to do the rest of the work.
>
>

> Sometimes staff and associates can be more work that they are worth. Do you have someone who likes to do the client work but refuses to market for more business and expects you to go get the business and hand them the work? You need to be clear about the roles you want subcontractors to play.
>
>

Another Reinvention

My next rebirth came after my husband decided he was retiring early and wanted to move across the country from Pennsylvania to

Nevada. I was game but knew I needed to find some clients out west. So while I was building a new office in a new part of the country, my business partner decided she wanted to focus her energies in another direction. We dissolved our partnership.

For a while after the move, I maintained an office in Pennsylvania, left a car there to use when I was working, and kept my staff in place. Then all my staff members decided they would rather work at home, so we pulled out of the office lease, distributed the office equipment among the staff, and saved a bundle of money.

Expanding your geographic scope can be fun and exciting, and if travel is one of your goals, this is a great way to do it. The nice thing about consulting is that your home base can be anywhere.

I spent the next seven years consulting and teaching before the next change occurred.

The Next Reincarnation

Suddenly within the space of about six months, my associates started dropping like flies. Illnesses, spouses retiring, and a series of similar events left me alone and guess what? I loved it. For the first time, I was flying solo and marketing only to the clients I wanted to work with. I found I could spend more time writing, teaching, and actually taking time off to tour around my new home state, beautiful Nevada, with its mountains, lakes, and deserts.

The Final Re-birth (Maybe)

Well, this past year I turned 70 and my children, grandchildren, and great-grandchildren are all asking why I am still working! Simple, I love the work. But I am still reinventing my company and myself.

For the past three years, I have been focusing on writing and teaching. (Remember that other thing I never wanted to do when I grew up?) I have now presented at conferences in five countries, almost every state in the United States, and have written about a dozen books, including my first novel. I am editing and helping other authors get their books published. And I am mentoring colleagues. So how does this rebirth stack up against my first set of goals?

I still set my own hours. If I want to take a day off in the middle of the week to drive to Death Valley, Mesquite, Laughlin, the Grand Canyon, or Oatman, Arizona, I just do it. I still work about sixty hours a week, but you can write on Saturday evening and Sunday morning—when you can't consult.

Lesson learned from my computer guru son-in-law, the part-time musician who always said he would give up playing in the band when it was no longer fun: When your work is no longer fun, look at your consulting practice. See if you can re-invent your company to do something that is new and rewarding.

food for thought

I am still independent. I now only take on clients I really want to work with and projects that will allow me time to write, teach, and mentor.

Am I doing what I am passionate about? Absolutely. Adding to the body of knowledge for our profession and leaving a legacy for the future? A definite yes. You can't get any better than that!

Travel? I recently spoke in Bermuda. That was a no-brainer—an opportunity to meet new people, experience a different culture, sell my books, and take a mini-vacation!

Money? Well writing still isn't keeping bread on the table, but who needs bread anyway!

Packaging Your Services

By Sandy Rees, CFRE

I started out like a lot of other wanna-be consultants, thinking that I would change the world with my brilliant ideas and guidance. Consulting looked easy—show up in the client's office, provide some help, and collect a check. I was in for a rude awakening.

Being an entrepreneur was so much more, and there was a steep learning curve for me in areas like marketing and the dreaded one—accounting.

During those early days, I also thought that getting clients would be easy. I thought if I just had business cards made and went to a few networking meetings, clients would come. Turns out, that was also harder than I expected. The first three clients came easily. The next ones were much harder, until I learned how to package my services and market them well.

At first, I didn't have any standard consulting packages. I said "yes" to whatever someone needed. I figured out pretty fast that was a mistake. It became clear to me that it was easier to provide niche services and offer some consistent packages and programs, rather than have clients with a wide variety of needs. For one thing, I wouldn't have to create a new proposal for each client. For another, it would be easier for me to market and easier for people to understand what I offered. Now, most of my clients have roughly the same needs. It's much easier to take care of them and give them all a great experience.

When Do You Say "No"?

As my business has grown, I've said "no" to many opportunities because they didn't fit with my core competencies. It has been tough to do at times, especially when I've been hungry for business. But in the end, staying within a niche has served me well.

My advice to you is to start out doing what you know and love. Do what you're good at. Get clear on the ideal client for the services you plan to offer. Don't assume you know what they want, need, or will pay for. Ask them. Pay attention to the questions people are asking. That will give you an indication of what to offer.

> I started to notice that folks asked over and over again for help putting a fundraising plan together, so I decided to create a product to help with that. First it was a book/audio combination; then it changed to a book/video combo. I'm in my second revision of the book, adding more of what people want, and it continues to be one of my best-selling products!

 practical tip

When Do You Add Services?

Once you have your core offerings down pat, find a way to add additional products and services to meet other client needs in related areas. For example, if your core offerings are focused on annual fund consulting, you could offer an additional service to help organizations select the right donor tracking software or review their direct mail appeals for them.

For the first year or so, I offered consulting that focused on putting an annual fund in place. I started to notice that my clients not only needed help with fundraising, they needed help managing their boards and dealing with specific personalities on their staff or board. So, I added coaching services to my offerings.

Coaching services are different from consulting services. Consulting is the "how to" of fundraising, planning, or management. Coaching is the softer side. It includes dealing with interpersonal dynamics and other challenges that keep you from getting the "how to" stuff done.

From the very beginning, I set up my services in long-term agreements for the benefit of both my clients and me. I remembered from my staff days that it was not helpful to have a consultant come in, fire-hose information at me, and then leave. I didn't want to do that to my clients. So I set up my services in six-month and one-year programs. This gave us plenty of time to accomplish big things for the nonprofit, and it created a revenue stream for me.

Some of my prospects weren't ready to jump into a long-term coaching or consulting agreement, so I created a one-hour coaching option to address immediate needs and give folks a taste of working with me. I knew that many folks were struggling and didn't really know what they needed to get done, so I named the one-hour offering Clarity Power Hour, and it has been quite successful. My clients love that they can get so much from me in a one-hour call.

Finding New Revenue Streams

Offering services is great, but the drawback is that there is a limit to the amount of money you make when you trade hours for dollars. I learned from a couple of business coaches about passive and leveraged revenue streams and I was hooked!

I learned that instead of working with one executive director who was struggling with her board, I could create a small group program and include six executive directors. Small groups are a great way to leverage your time. They allow you to make more money while giving the participants a great group experience.

Then I learned that I could take the materials I used in that small group and flesh them out into a workbook and sell it on my website at a lower price point to other executive directors. When you

Passive income and leveraged income are two great ways to add to your bottom line without adding much additional work for yourself. Leveraged income results from your being able to work with more than one person at a time. So instead of working with clients one by one, you find several clients who are experiencing the same problems and you work with the group. By leveraging your time, you can earn more money and help more people. Passive income results from repurposing your work. Once you create content for a class, use it for a book or an audio. Then sell it on your website. Put the work into it once and benefit from it for years to come.

create products for one job, reusing them is a great way to create passive revenue streams. In fact, my first book, *Fundraising Buffet*, was created from the handouts from all my workshops up to that point!

When you start creating products, go back to your ideal clients and ask whether those products appeal to them. If they won't pay for them, you could be stuck with boxes of books and CDs!

Evaluate, Evaluate!

I've found that it's a good idea to periodically review product and service offerings to see what's selling well and what isn't. For those that aren't selling well, see if you can find out why. Do research. Ask around. Maybe they just need to be promoted again. Maybe the material is no longer relevant and needs to be removed from the lineup of offerings.

The market will change over time and if you don't adapt, you'll get left behind. For example, not too long after I launched my book *Get Fully Funded*, the Kindle became wildly popular. Folks started asking for a Kindle version of the book. You have to be able to adapt to things like that.

Your skills and interests may change over time, too. The more I learn about mindset, the more I teach it to my nonprofit clients, because I believe it's the key to success in raising big money. And when clients hear the concepts I share, they agree. Adding mindset to my material has been a good way to keep it fresh and updated.

The really interesting thing that has happened is the attention I'm getting from my colleagues. The more I implement what I've learned about adding products and streamlining my offerings, the more they've asked how I do it. So, late in 2011, I decided to offer a Coach the Coaches program to teach the concepts of passive and leveraged income to other coaches and consultants who work with nonprofits. It's been wildly successful and has not only added something new and interesting to my portfolio but has added a significant revenue stream to my business.

You Can Go Home Again

By Jean Block

For many consultants, the ability to be creative and find new ways to leverage our skills is one of our primary assets, regardless of the type of consulting services we deliver.

I prefer to leverage my professional assets to deliver short-term training programs rather than longer-term contracts that deliver a product or service. This usually keeps me fresh, in learning mode, and abreast of trends and other issues that affect the nonprofit sector.

However, after several years of providing the same general consulting and training programs, I realized that I was getting lazy. It was easy to roll out the same old training programs and PowerPoint presentations. Nearly all of my work came from referrals, and many training gigs were repeat performances for similar types of organizations and their annual conferences.

And, frankly, I felt there just wasn't anything new and exciting and challenging that inspired me to create systemic and lasting change in a nonprofit organization.

I knew I needed to find inspiration to keep me excited and fresh. As luck would have it, in 2002, a group of local funders invited me to attend a presentation on social enterprise. I'd never heard of this approach before and was inspired to add this skill set to my toolbox. Here was a new way to leverage my training skills and knowledge of the sector: I would produce a

> How will you stay creative and inspired?
>
>

product that could change the way nonprofits managed themselves. It would help them become more self-sustaining and less reliant on traditional funding sources!

After a three-year stint providing social enterprise training for another company, I ended the contract, spent a year developing an entirely new curriculum, and formed a second company to offer training specifically on this subject.

This addition to my training toolbox required a new website, new branding, new promotion, new everything. The "new" was a way to jump-start my creativity and energy while adding another dimension to my services.

It also added another dimension to my consulting practice—a partnership with another consultant with whom I had worked informally for several years. That was another learning experience, one that I share in **Chapter Ten.**

Adding social enterprise training also required a change in my consulting style, from the one- or two-day training program to a six- to nine-month engagement with several days of on-site training, homework and consulting in between.

It was perfect! It created a hybrid style to my consulting practice, kept me creative and excited, and allowed me the freedom and flexibility to work with a variety of client types and sizes across the country.

Lesson learned? When you get stale and uninspired, there's often something new you can learn that will motivate and inspire you as a consultant. While I assumed everything was the same-old, same-old, I stumbled upon the opportunity to stretch and develop a new approach to strengthening the nonprofit sector in a meaningful way.

Giving Core Services a Rest—Or Sending Them Out To Pasture

At some point a few years ago, I realized I was dreading every upcoming strategic planning contract. I charged more for these projects than I did for training programs, but I just couldn't get excited about another session leading a nonprofit board and staff through exercises in what began to look like futility. Frankly, I was burned out on this type of consulting, and I knew I wasn't delivering a quality product as a result.

I graphed what could happen to my annual income without offering strategic planning and it didn't look good financially, but the mere thought of another session made me cringe. So I had a decision to make: Should I keep doing something I really didn't want to do, knowing I wasn't doing it as well as I could, or should I take the risk of lost income?

> You can always send something out to pasture and bring it back.
>
>  practical tip

At that point, strategic planning facilitation was making me miserable, so I just took that service out of my lexicon, off my website and promotional materials, and referred every new request to one of my informal consulting partners. Sometimes it worked well. Sometimes it didn't. I lost one regular strategic planning client because the consultant I referred didn't follow through as I would have and the client was unhappy. However, the others were delighted, and so was I.

The fear of lost income never materialized. I had more time to spend on the consulting and training I enjoyed.

As it turned out, after a two-year break from strategic planning, I was ready to get back to it with renewed energy and enthusiasm. I seamlessly added it back to my website and promotional materials. Interestingly, former clients began to call again for strategic planning.

Lesson learned: now I know that I can take a break from whatever service is getting stale and uninspiring and get back to it if I chose.

Chapter Twelve

Where Have All the Clients Gone?

Most consultant face dry spells from time to time. No matter how successful your company is, economics, illness, and life in general can get in the way of success.

Ellen Bristol provides some strategies to deal with business fluctuations and to ensure that you always have prospective clients in your pipeline.

Kent Stroman writes that the key to steady business goes to the core of the type of business you operate. Surprise! It's not consulting.

Susan Schaefer recounts how she handled a hiatus in her consulting practice and how she used the time off to renew and reinvigorate herself.

Business Fluctuations:
What Doesn't Kill You Makes You Stronger

By Ellen Bristol

Consulting is filled with ups and downs, like any other business. Sometimes you're up and everything is going your way. Other times things don't go as well. The economy takes a nosedive. Competitors win over your clients. Your major client gets a new executive director who brings along favorite consultants. Maybe your area of expertise goes out of favor. It's probably cold comfort to hear this, but virtually every business owner goes through at least one significant rough patch during the business's life cycle. So what's a poor consultant to do?

How to Prevent Disaster—Or at Least Muffle the Blow

You've decided to capitalize on your expertise and knowledge of the sector by providing skills, goods, and services to nonprofit customers. You will likely start out working in a local geography where you are fairly well-known, so it seems like the first few contracts—maybe enough to keep you going for years—just fall into place.

But at a certain point, you are going to exhaust those friends and contacts. You'll have to start winning over strangers, people whom you don't know and therefore can't influence as easily. As uncomfortable as that may feel, it's a great time to realize that this is your chance to become a real, true-blue entrepreneur. One of the best ways to do so is to start with your exit strategy, which is the way you want to *end* your business, and work backwards.

Your Exit Strategy

Whether you're planning to launch six months from now, or you've been working for a few years already, take a step back and ask yourself the critical question: *What do I want this business to accomplish in the long run?*

Please take note that I focused on "this business" rather than what "*I* want to accomplish." Other articles in this book address your personal, emotional, and spiritual objectives, so right now think about the *business* of your business. A rule of thumb for entrepreneurs is to figure out your exit strategy pretty much as soon as you've figured out what it is you plan to sell. The exit strategy describes the objective or end result of your business. Do you want to sell it, retire from it, or morph it into a job where you're working for somebody else? When you focus on where you'd like to ultimately take your business, you can make decisions with an eye toward your long-term goals rather than by impulse. Exit strategies are many and varied, but they fall into two loose categories:

The Independent Consultant Strategy

You make enough money to meet or exceed your former salary, set aside enough cash so you can retire at some point, and keep enough projects coming in so that you're usually busy. This is a perfectly respectable business model. However, it requires you to become increasingly effective at marketing and selling your services to keep income and projects flowing in. This strategy implies that you will deliver all the work that you sell, rather than delegating your work to an employee. It also means that at some point you'll simply retire or go out of business. End of story.

The Sell-Your-Business Strategy

In this approach, your objective is to build a business with sufficient asset value so that you can actually sell it to someone else. Businesses can only be sold when they have a suite of products or services and a customer base that makes the business attractive to some other entrepreneur who is willing to buy it. For the most part, you can't sell a business in which you do all the work yourself, especially if you have not packaged or "productized" the solutions you offer. The sell-your-business strategy raises the bar significantly, since it requires that the enterprise for sale has enough financial (asset) value to be (a) interesting enough to sell and (b) able to command a price high enough to pay back your years of investment generously. If you sell the business, you can either retire or reinvest the profit in a new venture.

As you and your practice evolve, you may discover that your long-term goals change as well. Adopt the discipline of reviewing your business plan, ideas, objectives, and values on a regular basis, so you can make good decisions about your exit strategy. It's a good idea to get the help of some trusted advisors as you conduct this review.

Solutions at Every Price Point

Once you have a clear picture of the clients that are right for you, you should have a number of different solutions that they can buy at many different price points. The lower-priced products, even free ones like articles or white papers, give your prospects convenient ways to test-drive your work and try you out without making a huge commitment.

Here's the hierarchy of price points that is most desirable:

◆ Free or "for the cost of your email address"

◆ Low, like an e-book for ten or twenty dollars

◆ Moderate, such as a paid webinar, open-enrollment workshop, or service that doesn't require much customizing on your part

◆ High, for your top-level, long-term, most comprehensive solutions

"Sell" or promote free and low-cost solutions all the time, since these serve two objectives. They are marketing tools that expand your following, and the low-cost products bring in a modest stream of income.

Promote moderate-cost solutions for two additional objectives: they give new clients a way to sample your work without committing more money or time than is comfortable, and they also bring in a regular stream of income at reasonably low cost to you.

Promote high-cost solutions to maximize income, lock in clients for repeat business, and gain testimonials and referrals that will then strengthen your marketing position.

Manage the Opportunity Pipeline

The opportunity pipeline is that list of potential sales, contracts, and projects from both new and current clients that you are currently cultivating. If you allow your opportunity pipeline to run dry, you will be far more likely to encounter a period of business disruption. To put it bluntly, no opportunities in the pipeline means no business next month, next quarter, or next year. Once your opportunity pipeline has been interrupted, it can take years to bring it back to the desirable rate of flow.

Every sale goes through a cultivation process. If this sounds like fundraising, it is. First, recognize that every opportunity you attempt to win will go through a series of stages that start at "getting to know you" and end with "here's the check." If you clarify those stages, you can always figure out which stage the opportunity has reached. Here is a suggested set of opportunity-stage definitions:

> ◆ Stage 1: Prospect conveys needs and wants; you decide if the prospect wants what you offer and is worth further effort.
>
> ◆ Stage 2: Prospect indicates a willingness to review a proposal or recommendation from you; you prepare the proposal and present it.

Before determining solutions, identify your ideal client. Take the time to define the characteristics of the clients that are right for you. These are the ones who:

◆ Want what you have to offer

◆ Like the way you offer it

◆ Can afford to buy at your various price points

◆ Share your corporate values

◆ Are likely to buy from you again in the future

◆ Give you great testimonials and referrals

If you can clarify the characteristics of your ideal customer, you're less likely to chase any old business opportunity. This strategy will keep you on course to meet the goals you have set for your business.

◆ Stage 3: Prospect reviews proposal with you and either asks for changes or says the proposal makes sense; you decide what modifications, if any, you are willing to make.

◆ Stage 4: Prospect accepts your proposal and places the order. In other words, the prospect hires you. You cheer and then deliver the work.

> If you want to run an independent consulting practice, yet you find selling to be anxiety-provoking or distasteful, you're going to have a lot of trouble keeping your practice healthy. Learn to love sales and selling. Make it your business to take sales-training programs, read books on sales and selling, and get yourself a mentor or sales coach.

It is extremely unlikely that you will win every project or sale you cultivate, so the financial value of your pipeline, and the number of opportunities it contains, must be considerably larger than the amount of income you want to produce and the number of projects you can deliver at one time. So first, decide how much income you want to produce in the next twelve months. Then double or triple that amount. That's your pipeline multiplier, which produces your pipeline target. Over time, as you track your actual performance, you will find out if your pipeline target needs to be higher or lower than your multiplier. Keep your pipeline as large as possible at all times, so you never run out of pending opportunities.

It's also a very good idea to keep track of the number of opportunities in your pipeline at any given time. Track your pipeline for potential income as well as for the total number of opportunities you are cultivating. A healthy pipeline will always show a viable amount of potential income as well as a healthy number of deals. This strategy helps you avoid the trap of "the big hit." It's oh-so-tempting to pursue a big fat deal, because at some deep, subconscious level we say to ourselves, "if I can just pull off that humongous contract, I don't have to worry about this selling stuff for a while." Then if you lose it, you've got nothing left to fall back on.

Let's say you have $100,000 worth of opportunities in your pipeline, but all that potential comes from only two pending deals. Your risk factor is a lot higher than it would be if you had four or five deals totaling $100,000, where none of them is much larger than about $20,000. The loss of any one of those deals wouldn't mean the end of your cash flow.

Also consider the relative merits of many opportunities from one prospect versus many opportunities from many prospects. It's great to have clients that give you lots of opportunities to earn money, but there's also a corresponding risk, especially if the decision-makers are the same people for each of the projects. If you lose one of these projects, you could end up losing them all. When you have many opportunities *and* many prospects, your chances of success improve.

You will lower the risk of interrupting your pipeline when you have multiple opportunities at various stages of cultivation.

Don't allow yourself to stop cultivating new opportunities just because you're super busy delivering on the work you have already won. It can take months—even years—to restart your pipeline if you run out of opportunities.

Challenge yourself to add a certain number of opportunities to your pipeline every month. You will definitely lose some of them, but if you have enough deals in the works at all times, you will also win some of them.

Organize your pipeline records according to the opportunity-stage suggestions outlined earlier. Some constituent relationship management (CRM) software packages allow you to code expected opportunities and build an "opportunity funnel." Under ideal circumstances, your opportunity pipeline should always have the most opportunities at the beginning stage and the fewest at the closing stage, hence the funnel shape. In other words, every month you should expect to see a desired number of new deals coming into the pipeline. You should also expect to see a *declining* number of those deals moving to the next stage.

As you monitor your pipeline, you are also likely to see that deals pile up at one stage or another. For example, it's common to see a lot of opportunities stuck at the "ask for proposal" stage that never make it to the "review and negotiate" stage. If this happens to you, then you need to figure out why your pipeline is stalled. You're entitled to call your prospect, even several times if necessary, to find out why the deal is stalled and suggest alternatives. Remember, your prospect may feel just as uncomfortable as you do, especially if the prospect has to reject your proposal.

Keep your eye on the size of the pipeline (whether it should be two, three, or more times bigger than your total-income target), the speed at which deals flow through the pipeline, where the process encounters a bottleneck, and whether you consistently have a reasonable number of new opportunities entering it. These techniques will help you prevent disaster.

People often ask, "Won't I annoy my prospect if I call too often?" There are two answers. The first is, "Probably not." If you have provided a proposal, you are entitled to answers. The onus is now on the prospect's shoulders to give those answers to you. If you don't get the answers you need, you are ignoring your own corporate responsibilities. The second answer is, "Who cares?" Since you do not have the business at this point, you have nothing to lose.

Recovering from Business Challenges

Let's say you've become a master at managing your pipeline, your competitive distinction is established, and you offer solutions at many different price points. No matter how disciplined you may be, something will trip you up sooner or later. It's often something beyond your control, like the economic upheavals of The Great Recession. Sometimes it's closer to home: you or a family member gets sick, the local economy sags, or your biggest clients drop you.

It happened to me. In 2008, every single account cancelled due to the recession; my husband got sick and needed full-time care (he recovered completely), and I became completely overwhelmed. I had to put my practice in mothballs until I was able to turn things around. So in addition to dealing with the worst economic conditions since the 1930's, I had to handle personal issues that took up virtually all of my mind, heart, and time. It took me a couple of years to restore my practice to a healthy state.

So now let's talk about some recovery strategies.

Take Time to Rethink Things

When business grinds to a halt, it's always stressful. Even though you might want to be busy, a slow period is a good time to reexamine your goals and objectives, rethink your products and services, and evaluate your client base. The time you invest in rest, reflection, and analysis will pay off handsomely. You'll reenter the fray refreshed, and you might even discover some major innovations, breakthroughs, and new-solution ideas that will help you regain your desired level of success.

During this period of reflection, reexamine your long-term objectives. Think about the biggest issues:

◆ Do I still want to maintain my private consulting practice, or is it time for me to get a job?

◆ Do I still want to manage my practice the way I used to, or do I want to do something different, such as pursuing new areas of expertise, or offering new products or services?

◆ Do I still want the same exit strategy, or have my preferences changed?

◆ Do I still want to use the same business model, or should I change it?

◆ Do I still want to promote the same set of solutions, at the same price points, or is it time to redesign my products, services, and price points?

If you don't take this opportunity for reflection, there is a high likelihood that you'll succumb to the trap of "any business at any price." That means you'll find yourself picking up business opportunities that are unprofitable, that don't necessarily lead to repeat business, or that chew up so much time (for so little return) that it grows more difficult to cultivate and win the desirable, high-margin, profitable opportunities and relationships that are sustainable.

> Stress and worry are exhausting. When your business is in trouble, no matter how panicky and fearful you might be, take time to rest, reflect, and plan.
>
>

Reexamine or Reinvent Your Suite of Solutions

Take a look at which of your products or services sell well during good times, and which do not. Ask yourself if you should stop promoting the poor performers and put more emphasis on the high performers. Be courageous about this. It can be disheartening to consider dumping a product you spent valuable time creating.

Do some market research and see what's happening in the broader market. Ask yourself whether you will be successful promoting the same things in the future, after the market recovers. Or, is it possible that the market for those particular goods or services will not recover at all?

As you conduct this review of your products and services, figure out if you need to package what you sell in a new way. Can you put your services together in a course that someone else could deliver, and just sell the course? Can you put it together as self-paced instruction modules delivered over the Internet? Can you write a book about it? All of these suggestions allow you to *replicate* your own expertise, which makes it easier to sell.

Reexamine Your Sales and Marketing Strategies

Now, look at the *way* you've been selling and marketing your practice. Maybe you've been relying on a stream of referrals from a core of standard clients, and they have dried up. If that's the case, it's time to do some classic marketing outreach, like setting up an electronic newsletter or blog that promotes your services. Maybe you've been unwilling to participate in consultant referral networks, or take business as a subcontractor. (See **Chapter Ten** for a great article on working as a subcontractor.) If that's the case, consider the potential of such affiliations and alliances. Maybe others in your area of expertise have

> Back in the 1980s and '90s, it was popular to rely on business-management systems by Day-Timer and Filofax. For years, everybody used to schlep around these huge, overflowing diaries that contained calendars, business cards, address books, affirmations, jokes, and cartoons. The fatter and messier, the better! As soon as the market for these things took off, many competitors emerged, and all the players made a ton of money.
>
> Then the smartphone came along.
>
> Sometimes markets don't recover.
>
> **observation**

adopted new methods or mechanisms for doing your kind of work. Consider reconfiguring your approach to delivering your services.

Maybe you'll discover that you simply have to increase the size of your opportunity pipeline and assume a higher pipeline multiplier in order to reach your income targets. If you were able to win one out of every two opportunities last year, maybe this year it's only going to be one out of every three or four. This insight would be very useful, inspiring you to invest more time and energy into creating new prospects and being more aggressive in your cultivation efforts.

Look at what your most successful competitors are doing with their websites, email marketing, and social media strategies. Model your own marketing mechanisms on those of successful competitors.

Examine the products and services you're offering with a very critical eye. Ask yourself whether the market still wants what you offer, the way you offer it. Consider whether you can or should drop—or raise!—your price points. Maybe it would be useful to eliminate certain products, take on new ones, or give your current ones a face-lift to make them more appealing to your target market.

These opportunities for rethinking your business model are precious, even if they are triggered by stressful forces beyond your control. If you address these periods with a stout heart and confidence in yourself, you're more likely to weather the storm and come out of it with renewed vigor.

Closing Thoughts

Even successful entrepreneurs will run into obstacles at some point, maybe at several different points, in the life of their ventures. It's best to be prepared by having the disciplines in place that will allow you to soften the blow. Good preventive medicine will help you to recover from those inevitable disasters.

What Business Are You In?

By M. Kent Stroman, CFRE

O ne thing I did right when preparing to launch my consulting business was to seek the advice of others. I selected seven highly respected individuals who had achieved success in their given fields, and arranged to meet with each of them to pick their brains. Several had career paths similar to mine; they had worked in a corporate environment for a number of years and then struck out on their own to create a new business.

This endeavor produced more valuable results than I expected. I walked away from each interview with multiple nuggets of wisdom that continue to influence my business practices to this day.

The most unexpected advice came from someone I didn't know very well. Joe is a communications expert. He serves clients all around the world, enabling them to achieve their messaging, imaging, and positioning objectives. I showed up to learn from his experience.

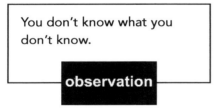

You don't know what you don't know.

observation

My primary question was this, "After being in business for yourself all these years, what would you identify as your top three factors for success?" Joe hesitated just a few moments to contemplate his response then candidly shared his top tips.

Then Joe had a question for me. He asked, "What business are you in?"

My initial thought was, "That question seems odd. I just gave Joe an overview of my business concept, target market, and expected revenue stream. Why would he be asking now, 'What business are you in?'"

I respected Joe a great deal and valued his thoughts and opinions. I had a hunch there was a deeper purpose behind his question. Something below the surface. I was about to discover exactly what that was.

I responded, "I'm in the consulting business."

Thinking I had answered his question, I eased back in the chair, waiting to hear where he was taking the conversation. I was about to learn one of the most important lessons of my career.

Joe countered, "No. You're in the marketing business." He continued, "The *product* you're marketing is consulting services. But if you do not *market* your product, on a continual basis, your consulting business will cease."

I thought he had made a good point, but I thought it was an exaggeration. I was wrong. And it didn't take very long for me to discover how wrong I was.

Thirty months later I began to wonder, "Where have all the clients gone?" I had just completed a big engagement—my first capital campaign. We had raised over $12 million toward a goal of $13.3 million. My client was well on its way to success in its capital campaign, but I had just lost my main source of revenue. My consulting business was about to cease.

> **principle**
>
> Consultants are in the marketing business.

Does that sound extreme? It felt even more extreme to me than what it may seem as you read these words. For two-and-a-half years I had been intently focused on serving the needs of this client. (I was serving other clients as well, but this had been my largest project.) There had been occasions when I was "too busy" to market my consulting business. I'd been too focused on consulting to promote my services. I had mistakenly believed that my reputation for enabling a client to reach such a monumental goal (for them) would automatically bring me other clients who wished to do the same.

"Without promotion something terrible happens: nothing."

—P.T. Barnum

Phineas Taylor Barnum

Here is the question I had failed to answer: How would anyone know about the impact of my services? I knew about it. Surely others would know it as well, right? Wrong!

Joe was right on target. My primary business is marketing. My primary service is fundraising counsel. And the fact that my skills have been honed by decades of experience is completely lost unless I have a channel for communicating the message.

One of the questions to which each consultant must provide a unique answer is, "How will anyone know about my business?" If you're unsure about how others will become aware of what you have to offer, query those who already do know about you. Ask how their awareness began. This will give you a good starting point.

The big question for us today is: How can we assure that something *does* happen? And we're not talking about just anything happening. We want to be sure the *right things* happen to move our businesses forward.

Begin by identifying your core competencies.

The largest revenue source in my business comes from campaign counsel. I have to ascertain precisely what it is that leads to campaign consulting engagements. To do so, I need to identify what I call feeders. The feeders that lead most of my campaign clients to me are:

- ❏ Friends

- ❏ Seminars

- ❏ Workshops

- ❏ Board retreats

- ❏ Books published

- ❏ Volunteer service

- ❏ Branded products

- ❏ Newsletter articles

- ❏ Coaching engagements

- ❏ Speaking engagements

- ❏ Strategic memberships

- ❏ Conference sponsorships

- ❏ Involvement in networking groups

- ❏ Testimonials from professional colleagues

- ❏ Referrals from successful clients (past and present)

This is not an exhaustive list, but these are the main sources that point prospective clients in my direction. Once a prospect's needs are matched with my capabilities, the possibility for an engagement exists.

As illustrated by the list above, there are numerous avenues through which prospective clients may connect with you. As you begin a new consulting business, it will be impossible to give equal attention to all of them. You must choose a point of initial focus—*your* place to begin. I would suggest that you limit your initial marketing efforts to the three or four targets that you believe will be most productive for you. Plan your work carefully. Then work the plan religiously.

My strategy was to concentrate my marketing and promotion activity first on the community of professional fundraisers. I attended meetings and conferences faithfully. I eagerly accepted volunteer assignments. I sought out opportunities to speak to audiences of decision-makers and influencers. I made the name of my firm synonymous with fundraising success. I marketed. And marketed. And marketed some more.

Mastering the feeders for your business will help you answer four essential marketing questions:

◆ What messages do I need to communicate?

◆ What audience needs to hear my message?

◆ What action do I want the audience to take?

◆ How will I know if the message is getting through (or not)?

Distill your message. Define your target market. Deliver the message repetitively. Provide a clear call to action. Evaluate the results. Adjust as needed.

Doing so will richly reward you—if you pay attention and act.

During downturns in my business activity, regardless of the cause, my best course of action is to evaluate which of my feeders need the most attention, and respond accordingly.

Let me share this caution, however. Becoming serious about business promotion after the clients are gone is kind of like closing the barn door after the horse has galloped away. It's the right action, but it was taken at the wrong time.

Our best marketing and promotion efforts take place when we think we don't need to do them, i.e., closing the barn door while the horse is *still in the stall*.

> Don't wait until the horse is out of the barn to close the door.
>
>  practical tip

But what do you do when the clients are gone?
My most dramatic experience with this problem occurred in November 2008. Do you remember what was happening in late 2008? The U.S. economy was experiencing its greatest challenge in over sixty years. In short, the very foundations of the American business system were being shaken. Violently.

> "We all live under the same sky, but we don't all have the same horizon."
>
> —Konrad Adenauer

Up to that point, my consulting business was operating at its peak. I was serving more campaign clients than ever. We were raising historic amounts of money. Opportunities were emerging with unprecedented frequency. But that all crumbled in a matter of six weeks.

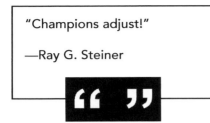

"Champions adjust!"

—Ray G. Steiner

One campaign after another went into hibernation. Nonprofit executives lost confidence. Foundations rolled back their funding levels. Some even reneged on gift commitments. Donors were paralyzed with uncertainty. A sense of desperation spread across the country.

As 2009 began, I wondered, "Will I have *any* work this year? How long will this last? Will the situation ever turn around? Is this the end of philanthropy as we know it? Can I survive?" These were serious concerns. I was fearful. The only certainty the future held was certain doom.

Fortunately, the future was not as bleak as it appeared early that year. I'm glad to report that for me, in my business, the drought didn't become as extreme as expected. It didn't last as long as predicted. The discouragement lifted sooner than anticipated. But now, five years later, there still has not been a full recovery.

"Resentment is like drinking poison and waiting for the other person to die."

—Carrie Fisher

During those dark days I had to make serious adjustments. I became more aggressive in promoting the services I had to offer. I became even more engaged in giving back to my profession. I adjusted my fees to a more affordable level.

My *key* strategy entailed evaluating my feeders and deciding to become more serious about writing. I had already been working on a book for almost a year. I was making gradual progress, but it was unimpressive, at best. The nationwide economic downturn gave me the opportunity to focus as an author in ways I never had before. I could have taken these measures at other times, but I didn't. I had convinced myself that I just didn't have the time. Suddenly that excuse was gone.

Today it's easy for me to say, "I'm glad I invested in my writing career during the uncertainty of 2009." But for me it was more out of despair than deliberation. There were other ways I could have handled my fright...I'm glad I chose this option.

"Adversity causes some men to break; others to break records."

—William Arthur Ward

The result of this focused effort was the publication of my first book, *Asking about Asking: Mastering the Art of Conversational Fundraising*™. The impact on my career has been immeasurable.

The lesson I would offer from my experience is this: be prepared to adjust when things around

Unexpected Results

My original motivation in writing a book was to satisfy an obligation described by a friend, when he said, "Kent, you owe it to your audience to leave them with more than just a memory." It has been so much more.

◆ Writing a book forced me to refine my message and methods.

◆ Writing a book made me a better fundraiser.

◆ Writing a book dramatically transformed the fundraising results I achieve.

◆ Writing a book has dramatically transformed the results achieved by countless other professional and volunteer fundraisers.

◆ Writing a book has highlighted my credibility as a fundraising expert.

◆ Writing a book has catapulted my speaking career.

◆ Writing a book grew my network of contacts within the charitable community.

◆ Writing a book ushered me into a "society" of other accomplished authors.

◆ Writing a book inspires me to be *even more impactful* on the profession I love so dearly.

stories from the real world

you change. I didn't create the financial meltdown of 2008. I didn't like it. And unfortunately, I couldn't solve it. My only real option was to choose between being passive and letting outside forces define me, or becoming intentional and defining my own response to these circumstances.

I could have become bitter. I could have been resentful. But bitterness and resentment are unproductive attitudes. The same adversity that makes some people fall apart prompts others to accomplish something new.

My Fanatical Sabbatical

By Susan Schaefer, CFRE

In over a decade of consulting, I have thankfully avoided a traditional slow spell. While the clients have been steady, I have learned that business cycles take many forms, some work-related, some not. In 2004, surgery forced me to wind down my consulting practice. I had hoped to reinstate some of my longer-term clients after a few months' rest. But during the time I was out of commission, one client's executive turnover and others' need for continuous help created the perfect storm: I'd have to start the bulk of my business all over again.

Healthy and recovered, I knew that my shallow workload had nothing to do with my abilities. Former clients had given me great recommendations. Yet it was a matter of time before my confidence began to dwindle. It's amazing how quickly that can happen. I realized that I needed to remain just as busy in my slower months as I had during my business's peak. Thus, the idea of my "sabbatical" was born.

The Name Game

You might choose to think of your slower time as a hiatus, respite, or intermission (the latter suggesting a rousing second act!). I do suggest giving a name to your transitional period. By doing so, you give it purpose. Will you choose to develop a new specialty? Will you build up the robust website you haven't had time to create? Will you reconsider your pricing and contracting practices as possible ways to attract new business? By giving name to your slower work pace, you excuse yourself, temporarily, from meeting financial goals. You redefine the scope of activities you undertake each day.

By thinking sabbatical, my involuntary time off seemed more palatable. It would be a time of professional development, renewal, and pursuit of new goals. Maybe it wasn't the traditional use of the term, but it allowed me to define my time in a way that worked for me.

This was not to be a restful sabbatical. Let's face it: consultants tend to have Type A personalities. I didn't know how to take it easy. So while the period lacked the stress of a traditional client load, it bore self-inflicted pressure to meet specific goals related to ramping up my business.

I created a business plan. It was brief but full of concrete goals. It outlined my ideal clients. It laid out when I would secure my first new one. And the second. And so on. In order to achieve those goals, the plan quantified the number of peer-to-peer meetings a month I would make, the number of articles I would write, and the gatherings I would attend. It was the basis for a daily regimen.

Reading, Writing, and Routines

I filled my calendar once again, even if some of its events took place in my home office. By scheduling things as simple as an hour of reading a day, or time spent catching up with colleagues and former clients, the full agenda worked wonders for my emotional state. Not only was it great to get up each day and have a plan, but the days quickly became more productive. It's amazing what a little note on a calendar can do.

Most of my time was spent in two broad categories: professional development and engagement in the field. There are plenty of free opportunities available while you're generating limited income. The deluge of online articles, webinars, and social media that can be overwhelming when you're busy are a lifeline for consultants looking to learn and connect.

Reading became a staple. There were many books and articles I had put aside because my schedule had been too busy. I spent each day reading up on the latest trends in philanthropy. Other days I learned about subjects new to me. I refreshed my general business knowledge, especially marketing and leadership. Not only did these readings grow my areas of expertise, but they gave me compelling things to talk about when I met colleagues or potential clients. After all, there wasn't much else of interest going on in my professional life at the time.

Lifelines to sanity when work is slow:

❑ Read

❑ Write

❑ Network

❑ Volunteer

to-do lists

I also began to write. These days, writing opportunities abound. You can start with posts on social media networks and progress to blogs, articles, and books. Some consultants' websites are virtual libraries of information, and they do get noticed by professionals in the field. I decided not to build up my website but to write articles for online forums. Not only will writing build your credibility, but the Internet's ability to connect you with your readers is tremendous. Be selective. Write for the venues that will get to the audience you desire as clients. Focus on topics that show your expertise.

Speaking engagements also let your skills shine. I spoke at a number of different venues when my client load was slow. These proved to be great opportunities to try out some new associations and membership groups that I hadn't addressed when I was busier. Not all of those venues were a great match for me, but I was happy to have had the chance to find out first hand. Some of the presentations included stipends, others eventually led to consulting jobs, and others allowed me to meet people whom I now consider close, trusted colleagues.

The obvious place to use your skills is within nonprofit organizations. In our line of work, there's little better than joining a volunteer board. The work keeps your skills sharp at a time when you may not otherwise be using them regularly. If you don't want to commit to joining a board, volunteer in some other capacity. I joined a board during my sabbatical, and my lessened workload gave me the chance to proactively interview several organizations, a luxury I didn't have time for in the past. It turned out to be such a good experience that I promised myself that I'd do the same in the future.

Where my sabbatical was most redeeming was in its overall professional development. As consultants, we're expected to keep up with fast-paced changes in the field. But let's face it, we can always use more time to learn. A reduced client load is an ideal time to learn the skills that will make you an even better consultant when you secure new jobs. Whether you're reading research reports or attending webinars, conferences, or other educational sessions, push yourself. Think of your newfound time as an opportunity to catch up on trends and learn about a new field.

There are endless opportunities to network, speak, and otherwise show your stuff. Among them:

- ❏ American Prospect Research Association (APRA)
- ❏ Association of Fundraising Professionals (AFP)
- ❏ Association of Philanthropic Counsel (APC)
- ❏ CharityChannel
- ❏ Council for the Advancement and Support of Education (CASE)
- ❏ Direct Marketing Association (DMA)
- ❏ Grants Professionals Association (GPA)
- ❏ Associations of nonprofit organizations (exact names vary by state)
- ❏ Local nonprofit umbrella organizations

Example

The Work in Networking

Clearly, you'll want to meet regularly with people in the sector. Take other consultants, past clients, and industry experts to coffee or lunch. All can provide you with insights and contacts that might lead to your next job. Follow each with a hand written note. In this digital age, that personal touch will leave a lasting impression.

Get involved with the primary professional organization in your consulting niche. Then go outside the obvious circles. Seek out small business associations or groups targeting women, minorities, or other demographic groups. Those contacts can create inroads to organizations, boards of directors, or projects not previously on your radar screen. You might even volunteer to speak at some of the groups' meetings if your past work sheds light on their areas of interest.

Other groups allow you to hone a general skill like speaking or writing, all while making valuable new contacts. Most local areas offer Toastmasters and National Speakers Association chapters. Become a master teacher or trainer. Writers' groups or centers are also great places to spread your wings.

One of my favorite activities during my transition year was attending lunch groups filled with other interesting businesspeople. The key to making valuable connections is to create a short set of parameters for participation and let a small group of your contacts invite some of *their* associates. This tactic allows you to meet new people and ensure that you all have some thread in common. Each month we agreed to talk about a pressing subject, set in advance, as well as timely business issues that arose since our last meeting. One group I belonged to included fundraisers only. Another was a group of six, whose niches ranged from fundraising to program development to communications. The criteria? We were all women who had consulted in the sector for at least three years, and we all had *toddlers*—talk about specialized! Our conversations ranged from taxes to toilet training. Valuable information all around.

Social networking didn't exist in a meaningful way when I experienced my slow spurt. Now it's a great way to solicit advice, contacts, and potential jobs. Join issue-relevant groups on the major social networking sites. There are so many ways to slice your work: you can join general philanthropy-related groups, ones that pertain to your niche, or groups that attract nonprofit consultants. Post strategic and insightful comments and you will garner interest in your expertise.

Potential clients can emerge when and where you least expect them. You never know if your dog-walker serves on the local ASPCA board or your jogging partner's church is conducting a capital campaign. No opportunity is wasted if you tell everyone you meet what you do for a living.

The Long View

Although I have maintained a full workload since my sabbatical, I'm still regularly anxious about what my client load might look like six months down the road. That anxiety is probably healthy since it forces me to plan. These days, I spend as much time ensuring that former clients keep coming back as I do developing relationships with potential ones.

When I started my consulting practice, I imagined that one of the markers of success would be that tremendous list of clients I'd seen on veteran consultants' websites. In the meantime, I have taken great pride in my relatively modest client list because it shows the commitment my clients and I have to each other—they keep coming back. This model doesn't work for every consultant, but if you work in prospect research, grant writing, or another area of specialty where it does, embrace it.

> My first post-surgery client arose when I delivered banana muffins to a new neighbor. Within a matter of minutes, she asked what I did for a living, the standard small talk around Washington, DC. She was a development director at a mid-sized nonprofit. After a long conversation about her organization's direction and needs, she hired me to help grow her grants program. All of my frenetic planning could not have prepared me for that lead!

stories from the real world

My client base includes a mix of annual contracts interspersed with large project-based ones. If your business allows it, I highly recommend this model. As a consultant who provides both fundraising counsel and proposal and other writing services, I'm lucky to work for some clients for years, while others, mostly large nonprofits, come back during campaigns or other big projects. In both cases, I put a lot of time into continuous learning about their internal and external issues. Those clients treat me like a member of their team. We celebrate successes and solve problems together.

If you want former clients to remember and re-engage you, don't fade away once your contract ends. Take a real, long-term interest in former clients' work. I call them, send notes, cards, and relevant items of interest. I even send them new funding opportunities. Why bother do this when I'm not presently contracting with them? I'm already reading about what's new in the sector. It costs me nothing to forward a relevant link with a short note. I don't spend time putting together an extensive website or even a monthly e-newsletter. Instead, I forward specific, relevant information with a personal note. That's exactly what we tell our clients to do with their donors. Whether I get hired to help secure the funding opportunity or not, the client will remember who suggested it. In my mind, that's time better spent than any mass communication vehicle.

I'm not talking about weekly communications here. This is very targeted, relevant messaging. Quarterly is a good rule of thumb, although I don't keep track. Relevance is more important than frequency.

If a former client doesn't hire me again for a while, then what? Some former clients are honest about the fact that cost is an issue. Others admit that my services were one-time pushes to take their organizations to a new level. Both types have provided referrals and references sometimes years after our work together has ended. When business is slow, and even when it's not, don't be afraid to ask clients for referrals. Sometimes even your biggest fans need a gentle reminder.

> I have worked with one client for the life of my business. In over a decade, as he has come to run larger and larger organizations, he takes me with him wherever he goes. As his responsibilities have increased, so has the scope of my projects for his organizations. Thankfully my program development and fundraising skills have proven beneficial at each of his jobs!

stories from the real world

Slow and Steady

Consider your hiatus a time of renewal. As with most things in life, time off is what you make of it. Instead of thinking of it as a sluggish period, I considered it a vehicle to meet people, read, and otherwise get to a range of things that a full workload did not allow. In retrospect, it was a great opportunity to bow out gracefully from the work that had become less interesting and delve into new areas. I emerged with projects, clients, and networks well outside of my previous realm. I was reenergized by these new challenges.

What might you have wanted to do all these years but haven't had time to tackle? Reinvent yourself. Pursue a new area of specialty. Go after a new type of client. Change your business structure.

Whether your slow spurt comes because your client load has lessened or life throws you a curve ball, above all, don't stop doing what you love.

Chapter Thirteen

Giving Back

There are many ways consultants give back to their communities—through pro bono work, through donations of time, talent, and treasure. Here three consultants share their ideas on how they give back and where they draw the line.

Gayle Gifford talks about her experience in serving on boards, committees, and task forces.

Deb Ward focuses on writing, speaking, and serving as a mentor.

Linda Lysakowski invites you to think about how you can give back to your clients, your community, and the profession.

The Work We Do For Love

By Gayle L. Gifford, ACFRE

"**S**ervice is the rent we pay for the privilege of living on this earth."

I've always loved that quote, often attributed to the remarkable Shirley Chisholm, the first African-American woman elected to the U.S. Congress.

Years before I was consulting, when I was a member of a women's anti-war group, we spoke often about what kept us moving forward when progress seemed so slow and far away.

The explanation sounded like this: "I can't *not* do it."

This was service in the sense of performing a duty, of seeing something that needed doing and doing it.

I've always felt that we have obligations that come from our roles as responsible members of any family, or any community, or any country. Voting is part of that obligation. Speaking up is part of that obligation.

And doing is part of that obligation. "Doing" to realize what we envision for the world, whether we're paid for doing it or not.

So what does doing, what does service, look like for a consultant?

I can't speak for others. But I can show you what service looks like for me.

Here are three ways I serve:

- ❑ Service to my community
- ❑ Service to my profession
- ❑ Service to the sector

Service to My Community

Some consultants I know volunteer at their houses of worship. Some bake cookies for the school bake sale.

I'm not a roll-up-your-sleeves direct service kind of gal. So I don't really enjoy volunteering for the neighborhood clean-up, or tutoring, or hammering a nail.

What I'm most enthusiastic about contributing is what I'm good at. And I'm pretty good at visioning. And strategizing. And building relationships. And promoting a cause.

Sounds like a job description for a board member, doesn't it? Yep, I'm pretty good at being a board member. Today I sit on the governing boards of two community organizations. That's the limit that I preach in my work. Even if I wanted to, I couldn't imagine having the time to take on another board and serve it well.

What's surprising to me is that both of these organizations were clients of mine.

I don't make it a practice to sit on clients' boards. Often when I'm finishing a project, I'm asked whether I'd be interested in serving on the board. I'm not surprised by the question. Through our work together, nonprofit leaders and I have built a strong partnership, and I have knowledge that might continue to benefit the organization.

But I don't accept those offers. Clients can be momentarily swayed by the enthusiasm of our work together and think that I'm the right person for the job. Clients forget that I, too, would need to go through the rigorous board recruitment and vetting process that I espouse.

For each of the two boards on which I serve, I was the one who asked. I asked because I was so impressed by the great work these agencies were doing, because I believed in the future these groups were creating, and because I felt that by serving on the board, I could make a real difference.

Now let me explain my offer, lest you think it sounds a bit like me forcing myself on these agencies.

In one case, I had been helping to develop a fundraising plan. I had so fallen in love with the incredible work this client was doing, that when my work was finished, I offered that I might consider serving on the board in a year or so, but only if I fit its profile and rolled off of another board on which I was serving. The client took me up on the offer.

I came to serve on the other board through a similar situation. I had worked with this organization to develop a strategic plan and was very vested in its success, its future, and the impact it would have on the city in which I live.

I'm sure all of your clients would love for you to work for free. I don't do that. I don't even offer the tiniest nonprofits discounts on my services because I work exclusively in the nonprofit sector.

Because I usually work on a project fee basis, I'm already putting in the hours to ensure my clients are very satisfied with our work together—even if that sometimes means spending more time than I had originally estimated.

watch out!

In this particular case, I had allowed us to evolve beyond a consulting-client relationship. I really did see myself as a volunteer. As a particularly significant volunteer project wound down, stakeholders and I talked about board service. They were shy about asking me because of our past consulting relationship, but I let them know that I would entertain a request to serve on the board. They did their due diligence. Then they asked. I accepted.

Oh yes, I fibbed a little about keeping it to two boards. I'm also on the advisory council of another former client. This is an all-volunteer organization of young people who stole my heart away. A mutual love fest. I don't have to do much as an advisory council member, just give my two cents now and then, so I don't feel that it violates my two board limit.

Now, I'm not recommending that you choose board service based on a past client relationship. But what those relationships provided was a completely unfiltered view of what the organization was about, where it was going, and how I could make a difference. I knew what I would be getting into, no rose-colored glasses. And the board leaders knew me and what I could do. This is a good way to go into a board position.

Service to My Profession

I've been a member of the Association of Fundraising Professionals (AFP) since 1988. I was certified as a CFRE and now hold the credential of ACFRE, Advanced Certified Fundraising Executive. The application for either of these professional credentials requires that you earn points for volunteer service and service to the profession.

> Only serve on the boards of organizations you love. One. Maybe two.
>
>

But long before I thought about applying for any credential, I was already very active in the work of my local AFP chapter. From my early days of membership, I found a welcoming professional home and ready camaraderie among my AFP and fund development colleagues.

So when asked by a colleague if I would serve on an event committee, I agreed.

Since then, I've served on numerous committees. I've been on the chapter board and served as its president. I helped the chapter secure a very significant grant. I've been a mentor to new professionals. And I serve in a de facto role as our chapter's government liaison, alerting the chapter to state legislation that might be of interest or concern. I'm generally just available when someone needs to ask a question or is looking for a connection to a community resource.

There are other ways to serve the profession. I'm always ready to sit down for an hour over a cup of coffee with a professional colleague looking for my advice. I've made a lot of really good friends that way.

While I also see it as an important aspect of marketing my services, I do a fair amount of writing, whether as a book author, a blogger, a contributor to this book, or an infrequent columnist. I am always humbled by the idea that sharing even very simple advice can have great value to so many in this sector.

If I spot something—a magazine article, a new report, a grant opportunity—that I know will be of value to a past client, a colleague, or even just an organization whose director I know, I pass it along.

And when I know I'm not the right person for a potential client, I pass it onto someone who is a better fit—without a fee.

Are there days when I think, I must be crazy to be spending all of this time on unpaid work? Absolutely. But ultimately, I want organizations I believe in to succeed. I want my community to be filled with vibrant nonprofits that are making a profound difference. My colleagues are an important part of that fabric. I want my colleagues to be the best they can be, and if I can help, then I'll be there. And I hope they'll help me when I need to call on them.

> The Golden Rule is still worth living by.
>
> **principle**

Serving the Sector

For the last few years, I've participated in an informal group of activist colleagues who educate our state's nonprofits about collaboration. We tout the opportunities and challenges of informal partnerships, joint ventures, and even mergers. I've spent a moderate amount of unpaid time helping to organize a workshop and a full day conference and generally lending my advice to this self-created think-and-do-tank.

Ask me to sit on a panel about the sector, to comment on a blog, or provide my thoughts in a focus group, and I'm there. When our local community foundation was exploring an initiative to build nonprofit capacity, I was delighted to serve on one of the advisory committees.

I do this because I'm a nonprofit policy wonk, because it is intellectually stimulating to me, because it helps my colleagues understand the full range of knowledge and experiences I bring to my consulting work, because I often have the opportunity to meet and work with people I might not otherwise connect with, and because I care about the impact on the sector.

Oh, yes. And then there is the work I do teaching a college class. I often teach graduate level courses on some aspect of nonprofit management. It keeps me on my toes, keeps me in touch with younger people, keeps me reading and questioning. While I do a lot of free workshops for my profession, I get paid for teaching this course, but the pay is not equivalent to the time spent.

What I really, really wish I could do, but haven't yet, is conduct some research. I'm burning for an answer to this question: What is the impact of the socioeconomic status of the founder(s) on the fundraising success of startup nonprofits?

Maybe when I'm retired.

How Do You Find Time to Give Back and Work for Pay?

It's probably a misnomer to have titled this piece "The Work We Do For Love," because I hope that even your paid work is work that brings you joy.

Perhaps a better title would have been: "The Work We Do For Love *Only*."

> There is always more to do.
>
> **food for thought**

It might sound like I don't have a lot of time for paid work. I do. I have to. I depend on paid work to put food on the table, to pay the health insurance, and to keep the lights on.

So how much free work can I do? How much can you do?

Here are a few ways to judge.

If your free work is causing you to cut corners for your clients, then you've probably taken on too much, and it's time to cut back.

Is your life feeling incredibly stressed? Have you forgotten the last time you read a book for pleasure, or went on a date with your significant other, or took a weekend off? It's probably time to cut back.

But overall, you'll decide what's right for you. That might be a little bit of volunteer work. Or a lot.

But as my late friend Herb always said, "Give till it feels good."

Ways I Make a Difference!

By Deborah Ward, MA, CFRE

I have given back in a variety of ways since I started my consulting practice in 1998, and even before then. I have always believed strongly in the concept of giving back and as a consultant, I think it is a wise investment of my time and energy, as the benefits come back many times over.

Over the years, I have served as a teacher, a mentor, a writer, and done some pro bono work. Being a teacher has fed my own desire to teach others what I know about fundraising, and more specifically, proposal writing. Sometimes I am paid to do this, and other times, I volunteer my time to present workshops or training sessions. Why is this important? There are several good reasons, both professional and personal.

Teaching

Teaching is a great marketing tool. It allows people to find out who you are, what you do, and it can plant a seed for a future work relationship. Through the years, I always have to smile when I get an email or phone call from someone who starts the conversation with, "You probably don't remember me, but I attended a workshop you did five years ago...." Unfortunately, I often don't remember people because thankfully, I have done many workshops attended by dozens of people—sometimes a hundred or more—in the audience. I just never know when someone will contact me to request consulting assistance, so I see conducting workshops for free as a worthwhile investment of my time.

I believe that there is nothing wrong with teaching people what I know and what I've learned from my years of experience. There are many organizations, especially small nonprofits, that simply cannot afford to have a fundraiser on staff. Often these same organizations do not have the funds available to pay a consultant. But if I can help them by providing a training session, then I feel good about it and believe it's a part of the "pay it forward" concept. And, if it results in an organization receiving funds for worthwhile projects, that's a good thing!

So far, I have not served as a long-term mentor to anyone starting a career as a consultant. I

When I first began my career as a consultant, I was fortunate enough to have a mentor. This individual was considered an expert, and she helped me in so many ways when I was first starting out. She gave me advice about how to structure my consulting business, she was there for me when I had questions and concerns, and she opened some doors that eventually led to my first published book. I know I wouldn't be where I am today if she had not volunteered her time and energy when I needed them the most.

stories from the real world

have, however, served as a coach to a few people who contacted me for advice about how to start their businesses. I am happy to share my own experiences. It is my way of paying it forward just like other consultants did for me when I was starting my own consulting business. Hearing first-hand information from practicing consultants was invaluable. I avoided some major mistakes related to setting boundaries and scope of practice when I started out, thanks to their words of wisdom!

Writing

Writing has been my most prolific way of giving back. I have written a monthly "Grants and Funding" column for a publication called *eSchool News* for more than ten years, and I have published two books. Over the years, I've also written columns for niche publications that deal with areas like funding for special education, technology, and the arts. For the most part, I get paid for writing these articles. But I have granted many people permission to reprint the ones for which I hold the copyright.

To me, writing is just like teaching, and it provides me with a way to reach a large group of people who otherwise probably wouldn't have an opportunity to learn about my work. My column in *eSchool News* has generated many emails over the years from readers who have questions about something I wrote about, or who want to find out if they can hire me to do consulting work for them! I love to get email from readers, especially new proposal writers in education who tell me that my last column was "so helpful" and that they appreciate my sharing my expertise.

Pro Bono Work

I have done a small amount of pro bono work, but I believe that this type of giving back is one that you must carefully monitor. Why? Because if word gets out that you will consult for free, (and believe me, in today's world of instant information, it will), you will be inundated with requests! It's hard to convince people that they need to pay you when they know that you have helped several other people for free. In some situations, I have chosen to negotiate a lesser fee for my services if potential clients convince me that they are not able to pay my customary rates. Or, I just quote lesser fees for an organization when I believe in its cause and its website shows a small organization with limited funds.

Volunteering

The final way I give back is to serve on development committees and boards in my own community. I started doing this long before I became a consultant. When board members find out that you are a fundraiser, they are quick to extend invitations for you to join them!

Balance is crucial. I cannot take on so much volunteer activity that it leaves little time for paid work. Each organization requires a different level of commitment from its volunteers and it is best,

I think, to try to get a sense of this before you actually say "yes" to an offer to join a committee or board.

For me, the question is not, "Why give back?" but, "Why not give back?" By giving of my time and talent, I learn so much and ultimately improve my consulting abilities.

Are You a Philanthropist?

By Linda Lysakowski, ACFRE

In my book *Raise More Money from Your Business Community*, I talk about the concept of corporate philanthropy. Even if you are not organized as a corporation, as a business owner, you should be socially responsible; as a nonprofit leader, you should be a philanthropist.

There are many ways you can give back: giving to your clients, giving to your community, and giving to your profession. Giving itself can come in the form of money, time, or talent.

Giving to Your Clients

There are many ways you can give to your clients. As with donors, consultants can give time, talent, and treasure. Let's talk about some of the ways you can give to your clients.

Giving Money

This is a tricky one. Do you offer to support your clients financially? What do you do when they ask for your financial support? Put yourself in the place of a donor. Donors give to organizations about which they feel passionate. Do you feel passionate about your client's mission? If so, there is nothing wrong with making a financial donation to the client. If you don't feel passionate about the cause, there is nothing wrong with saying "no" if asked for a gift.

Of course, if you're like me, you tend to work with organizations about which you do feel passionate, and you'll probably want to support them all. I admit though, while I would never work for organizations whose mission I couldn't support, there are various degrees of passion. For example, I have a son with developmental disabilities and have worked for a number of organizations that serve this population. So I am more likely to make a gift to one of those organizations than I am to some of my other clients. And sometimes my clients don't even ask me to give. Sometimes I offer, sometimes I don't. I recently broke my own rule about not giving to events in order to sponsor a client who was running a marathon. Why did I break my own rule? I believed in his cause and I believed in him.

> You're a business. Have a corporate giving policy and use it! Establish a budget for your charitable giving at the beginning of each year, just as most companies do, and weigh requests carefully. You can set up guidelines such as: we will give 5 percent of our revenues to charitable causes, and 80 percent of our gifts will go to clients. One policy I established was that I do not support event sponsorships.

 practical tip

Strictly speaking, you are a vendor to the organization. Some groups have strict rules about how they solicit their vendors. I always take it as a sign that I've taught them something about fundraising if they approach me personally and invite me to contribute to something they know I care about. I once had a client to which I made a pledge. Despite the work I did to convince this client of the importance of having a good pledge tracking system, I never received a reminder of my pledge payments. I never fulfilled my pledge. Guess you can't teach clients everything!

Giving Time and Talent

On the other side of the giving coin, what about giving pro bono work to clients? Many of us have been asked. I am sure you've heard, "But we're a nonprofit. Can't you give us a break?" I always explain to my clients that architects, accountants, and marketing firms have for-profit and nonprofit clients and can readily offer discounts to nonprofits. I work exclusively with nonprofits, so my rates are already adjusted for nonprofits. That's why I can't and won't offer discounts.

> I am always amazed by organizations that interview me along with several other consultants, hire someone else, and then add me to the solicitation list. That stings!
>
> **watch out!**

It's hard, though, to resist the temptation to offer pro bono work to groups about which you do feel passionate. But if you do too much of this, you will drive yourself crazy and not have enough time for paid clients.

> Develop a policy for pro bono work, and stick to it!
>
> **principle**

One thing I did to eliminate the numerous requests for pro bono work was to establish a policy that I would take on one pro bono client per year. I've done this most years. This policy also included an expectation of board service or other volunteer work on the part of all my employees and subcontractors, but each was free to choose the organizations for which they would volunteer.

Giving to Your Community

We all have favorite charities, and some of those might never be clients of yours. Giving to your community can be part of your overall giving strategy. How can you support community projects?

Speaking at community events or providing free workshops at your local library or nonprofit center are some of the ways many consultants give back. Serving on boards and doing other volunteer projects are other options. Volunteering to ring the bell in a Red Kettle Campaign,

For my company's tenth anniversary, we came up with a ten-month group consulting program. We invited proposals to be accepted into this training program and selected ten organizations to participate in the course at no cost. I found that being on the proposal reviewing end was much more difficult than I imagined. For our fifteenth anniversary, we held all-day workshops in four selected communities and invited all our clients, potential clients, and any nonprofits in the community to attend for free. Sometimes it takes years, but some of this did come back to us in the form of business from these attendees.

We recently celebrated twenty years in business and teamed up with three other consultants to provide a free workshop/ webinar.

stories from the real world

working at the local soup kitchen, serving as a docent for the local museum, or volunteering at your local hospital are just some of the ways you can help your community. If your "community" is national in scope, serving on a national committee can be another option. Use your imagination.

Giving to Your Profession

When I started in the development profession, the best piece of advice I got was, "Join your local Association of Fundraising Professionals (AFP) chapter and get involved." When I started my businesses, I got another great piece of advice, "Join CharityChannel and get involved." Notice the common theme—get involved in professional groups, don't just join!

My first reaction when I was told to join AFP was, "What am I going to learn meeting with a bunch of people who are raising money from the same groups I am trying to raise money from?" I quickly learned that I had a lot to learn and that my colleagues were more than willing to share ideas and mentor a newcomer. Before I knew what had hit me, I was on the board of my local chapter, then president of my local chapter, and then involved on several international committees. I have been giving back to my profession through AFP for more than twenty-five years, serving on local and national committees (I just started my second time around serving on the board of the AFP Foundation for Philanthropy), and I've loved every minute of it.

Besides helping build my reputation as a consultant, my involvement with AFP has been personally rewarding, and I've gotten to know so many fantastic professionals. I can't tell you how gratifying it is to greet colleagues at an AFP conference and have them introduce you to other colleagues

One way you can help your community and, at the same time, gain visibility for your company, is to volunteer for community projects. Your staff and/or associates might staff a booth at a health fair, clean up a river or a park, or walk in a charity walkathon. Have all your team members wear your company T-shirts, of course.

practical tip

by saying, "It's all Linda's 'fault' I am in fundraising—she encouraged me way back when." In fact, one of my mentees is now on the national AFP board.

And then, when I joined CharityChannel and saw the number of people who seemed to have endless hours to post articles on the various listservs (remember those?), I wondered if these people ever slept! Now I am the one who is being asked, "Do you ever sleep?"

My latest means of giving back is to encourage people to write for the profession and to help them brainstorm ideas for books. I am also editing other authors' books, which has made me a better writer and helped me find another way to give back. And, of course, I volunteered to co-chair the first annual CharityChannel Author's Symposium.

I find a great deal of personal satisfaction in giving back to my profession by speaking, writing, and mentoring colleagues. Do I get paid? For speaking, in most cases, yes, it is a big part of my business, but I still speak at AFP International Conferences, CharityChannel Summits, and a few other events that do not pay. For writing, yes, I get paid, but don't plan to get rich by being an author. I do it to add to the body of knowledge for our profession and leave a legacy for future nonprofit leaders. For mentoring, I never get paid, but what a rewarding experience to see someone you mentored receive the ACFRE designation, or serve on a national board, or be named the Outstanding Fundraiser of the Year for a local AFP chapter, or become a consultant.

So, giving back pays off, sometimes in dollars, but always in self-satisfaction!

> If you're a new consultant, seek a mentor. If you're a more seasoned "pro," mentor others.

> Find something you are good at—speaking, writing, mentoring, committee work, planning events—whatever you do well and enjoy. Then find a way to contribute to your profession using your skills. You will feel better about yourself, and it might even help your business! For instance, I am launching a new service to coach novice consultants. It is based on my love of mentoring those new to our field. While I will continue to do some similar work unpaid, this service is an example of how your volunteer work can give rise to new areas of consulting.

Chapter Fourteen

Winding Down

I f you're just starting your practice, you probably aren't thinking yet about winding it down. But at some point, we all face this turning point. Do you sell your company, turn it over to someone else, or just ride into the consulting sunset? Here three consultants who have taken very different paths offer their experiences.

Meri Pohutsky "heard the fat lady sing," and decided to venture back into the role of a staff person.

Bob Crandall sought out a trusted colleague and began to ease himself out of the company he built. He lays out a plan to transfer your company to a new owner.

Gene Scanlan actually closed down his business, twice! He provides step-by-step directions to follow when riding into that sunset finally looks appealing.

Is that the Fat Lady Singing?

By Meri Pohutsky

When should you consider closing or winding down your consulting business? The question can be answered by examining your income statement, personal circumstances, the business environment, and your age.

Income Statement

If you're thinking of closing shop based on your income, the primary question you need to ask yourself is: Are you making money? However, there are nuances underlying your answer.

Are You Earning What You Want to Earn?

A negative income statement is a good clue that it is time to close shop.

practical tip

Do you have a number in your head that you need to achieve in order to consider yourself successful? Maybe it's the salary you were making before starting your consulting business, or what you think you are worth. If *want* motivates you, the decision to continue or cease operations becomes easy. Either you hit your target or you don't.

Are You Making What You Need to Survive?

Is *need* your real priority? Do you make enough money to meet your basic needs? As a self-employed single mother, I required assurances that all of my family's needs were being met. I needed to provide the basics—food, shelter, health care, and some extras. Whether I could attain life's staples was my bottom-line driver in whether to continue my business.

Is "Good Enough" Good Enough?

Does your income statement show a number you consider *adequate*? If you're part of a two-income household, your consulting income might pay primarily for luxuries rather than basics. In that case, assess the bottom line. Maybe net income is $50,000 and you have $20,000 in business expenses. You are taking tax deductions on things like business meals and your home office, things that give you a sense of enjoyment outside of the strict confines of your business. In that case, you're getting some non-monetary benefits in addition to the financial ones. When those expenses are accounted for, what makes up your bottom line—gross income, net income, or intangible benefits?

I made a mental paradigm shift after a few years: quality of life took precedence over salary. I was making a gross income about twice what I made when employed, "taking home" less than when employed, but working less and spending more time with my family and in volunteer service. The old notion of the measure of workers being driven by income was no longer part of my belief system. My new philosophy related to my quality of life. This is an important consideration when thinking about whether to wind down or discontinue your consulting business. Are you satisfied with the quality of your life?

Personal Circumstances

A real danger in our field is that your self-employment can easily overtake your personal life. If your business intrudes on all aspects of your life, it may be time to go back to a staff position.

Personal circumstances may also dictate your trajectory. These can include marriage, divorce, having children, your children's life stages, relocation, an ailing parent, or your own health status.

As with all of these issues, your personality figures prominently. If you are regularly a nervous wreck living with the uncertainty of the next contract, or if you believe at least one parent needs to be home during your children's early years, your decision might be an easy one. Personally, consulting worked well for me. I found I was able to be more available to my family and friends. If a child became sick, I was home and not torn between work and family. If my mother needed help driving back from Florida, I was available. My office was, and still is, mobile. I had a smartphone, forwarded my landline to my cell, and carried my external hard drive with me when away from my home office.

If you are no longer able to maintain the work/life balance you want, it may be time to close shop.

observation

I learned to overcome the roller coaster nature of self-employment. When a contract period ended, something always seemed to come up. My fear usually drove me to start making calls and stirring the pot of potential clients. However, if you are losing a cornerstone contract (a long-term one with a decent monthly fee), and there is truly nothing on the horizon, time may be up.

Age

A midlife crisis can be a factor in changing jobs, careers, and lifestyle, not just spouses and cars. Perhaps midlife was what first drew me into consulting. I wanted to take the risk while I was still young enough to do so. But it can also be a reason to get out of consulting. You might revisit full-time employment because of all its accoutrements: health insurance, retirement plans, disability, consistent paychecks, and, perhaps, greater peace of mind.

If you are of a certain age, you will begin to consider retirement. Some in our field plan for a concrete retirement date, while others take many years to wind down. Consulting is the perfect way to ease into part-time work. Certainly, there will be a time when you either can't or don't want to maintain your current pace of work. If your consulting work requires a lot of travel, you might find that your energy level starts to decline and you need to weigh the benefits of income versus sleeping in your own bed. When you dread doing what you are doing, it is time to close shop.

Business Environment

I find there is a huge market for consulting, especially in a depressed economy. Organizations can contract for high quality expertise on an as-needed basis, avoiding the overhead of full-time employees. Nevertheless, there are times, like the financial crash of 2008, when the rules fly out the window. The trickle-down effect of the economy on your clients, or their fiscal strength and stability can make or break your business model.

Consultants are often the first costs nonprofits jettison as they face economic downturns.

Other indicators are industry-specific. If you were a typewriter repair expert in the 1970's, the advent of the personal computer was your writing on the wall to look for a new career. Twenty-first century advances in technology, business, and services are happening at an exponential rate. Step back periodically and take a macro-level look at trends in your market niche.

Since I make the bulk of my income from grant writing, the impact of the post-2008 economy was frightening. When I saw my personal investments decimated, it made sense that family and corporate foundations were going to experience the same. And despite stimulus funds from the American Recovery and Revitalization Act (ARRA) of 2009, I knew that federal grantmaking would not be sustained at that level. Grant writing was going to become more competitive, funds were going to be less available, and there would be a period of adjustment before the dust settled.

For me, the decision to wind down my business came when I was asked to work full-time for a three-year cornerstone client of mine. Although I've never specifically asked, I believe the impending release of ARRA money was a motivating force for the agency to hire me—someone they knew as a successful grant writer, especially in the realm of federal grant applications.

It was an offer I couldn't refuse. I realized I would lose this agency as a client if I didn't accept the position, and I loved working with it. My other major client was struggling, and I saw that job as tenuous. The question was, what would happen after Recovery Act funding expired? I feared a reduction in federal grantmaking post-ARRA, and private funders would take some time to rebound after the economic plummet. My youngest children had entered college and needed the consistent financial support consulting doesn't guarantee. My potential employer would allow me to continue working from my home and did not require that I move to its main office in another state.

So, my decision was based on a job offer, the economy, and the business environment for my market niche—grant making organizations.

Decision Made. Now What?

The decision about what to do with the business comes next. Do you just wind it down, let your contracts close out, and not accept any new ones? Do you close or sell it? As a sole proprietor, selling wasn't really an option for me. My business was built on my skills and connections, so it didn't feel right to try to sell the firm. I decided to wind my business down. I let my current clients know I was taking a full-time position and planned a close-out or transfer strategy. This is where my alliances with other consultants came in handy. I had a ready cadre of highly qualified colleagues to take on my various contracts.

Making the Decision

The questions to ask when considering whether to continue your consulting business, wind down, or close include those related to your income statement, personal circumstances, the business environment, and your age.

Category	Question to Ask
Income	Am I making enough money to meet my needs?
Personal	Are my family situation, health, and personal values amenable to the demands of consulting?
Personal	Do I have the stomach to live with uncertainty?
Business	Is there enough business out there?
Business	Do I have stable, reliable clients?
Age	Am I ready to retire?

food for thought

As I assumed my new position, I worked part-time for ninety days to test my new role and finish out clients' deliverables. Both my new employer and clients were fully aware of the situation. I highly recommend a period of adjustment like this. If I had started my job full-time, I would have been working sixty to eighty hours a week, and my employer and clients' work would have likely suffered.

I chose to wind down my business, which means it remains open, and I continue to accept contracts to the degree I am able. When I receive requests for consulting that would conflict with my employer's mission or are beyond my availability, I refer the jobs to my consultant colleagues. As the years have passed, there are fewer of these requests, but I remain open to them.

Working from home as a sole proprietor, I was able to wind down the business without much effort. I did not have a lease to end, equipment or furniture to move, ads to withdraw from various marketing sources, or a corporation to dissolve. I continued to work from home, so I was quickly ready to assume my new responsibilities.

The great thing about our line of business, one without inventory or much in the way of overhead, is that so many people go in and out of consulting during the course of their careers. I hope someday to reestablish my consulting firm, when I am ready to retire from full-time work, but not ready to stop contributing.

On Becoming an Entrepreneurial Empty Nester

By Bob Crandall

When nearing retirement, you begin to reflect on what is going to happen to this small company that you have built, especially if the company bears your name.

In 1995, I founded Robert J. Crandall and Associates, LLC. I employed one full-time staff person and a few part-time professionals, as needed.

When I began to think of retiring, I realized that there was little value in a company with my name on it if I were to sell it. I had no children who were in the profession and no partners in the business. However, I had hired a quality individual to work for me on a contract basis. He was younger and very bright, but he had little name recognition. When I began to think about retirement, I asked him if he might have interest in owning the company. He did. And then we began to put together a transition plan. As of this writing, we are in the final stages of transferring ownership.

There were so many steps to consider. Among the most central:

- ◆ What should the new name of the company be?

- ◆ At what point should we make the name change?

- ◆ How should we notify current and former clients?

- ◆ When should I hand over the financial end of the business?

- ◆ When should we shift responsibility for the contracts and the billing aspects of the business?

We began to consider who should make various decisions, i.e., when and how we should migrate the firm's decision-making authority. The decision that was most interesting, of course, was how best to handle income distribution between us.

We decided on a four-year process to transfer ownership to my trusted colleague, Robert N. Croft. We created a "doing business as" designation, or DBA, as an interim step. That company name identifies both our roles in the firm: Crandall, Croft & Associates. All of our business is currently done under that name, but the company still retains its original legal name—the one with my name only. This is considered a temporary step that eliminates the need for us to legally change all of our business materials. Check with your attorney for the best arrangement given your particular needs.

We considered things like who needs to know about our transition, at what point, and why. We did not do a general announcement or mailing to publicize the change, as most companies do. We simply starting using the new name and explained to our clients what was happening and why. That approach has worked well for us but might not for others.

What follows are the major goals and objectives we set for ourselves for each year of our transition plan. Again, each firm will have its own unique set of opportunities and challenges, but my experiences will give you a good idea of the major steps and reasonable timeframes:

Timeline	Major Changes	Business Side	Decision-Making Authority	Financial Division
Year One	Set up DBA designation with the state and county	Transfer billing responsibilities to new owner	Maintain original owner's decision-making authority, with the new owner to be included for informational purposes	Distribute 60 percent of net to current owner and 40 percent to new owner
	Change company name on business cards	Maintain contract and bookkeeping activities under original owner		
	Change company name on banners for conferences			
	Announce change at our local AFP chapter			
Year Two	Announce changes at additional groups that are prospective clients	Move bookkeeping responsibilities to new owner		Distribute 55 percent of net to current owner and 45 percent to new owner
	Change company name legally	Continue with all contracting done by original owner		
Year Three	Shift all business functions to new owner	Transfer contracting responsibilities to new owner	Transfer decision-making authority to new owner	Distribute 45 percent of net to current owner and 55 percent to new owner
Year Four	Shift full authority to new owner	Transfer company's legal title to new owner	Shift all decision-making authority to new owner	Enable original owner to contract with a maximum of one client at any given time
				Create provision providing an agreed-upon, one-time fee to be paid for each new client the original owner brings under contract

In year three, the new owner was to pay one-third of an agreed-upon buyout fee, with the remaining two-thirds to be paid in year four.

Special Considerations

Our plan has generally worked well but has also seen some bumps along the way. The recession of 2008 put us behind our four-year schedule, and we have since combined years three and four above to make up some of that time. Our small size has enabled that kind of flexibility, which has been quite a benefit throughout the process.

We have admittedly strayed from our financial plan a bit. As we currently find ourselves between the third and fourth year, we share all income fifty-fifty, which is a little different from that laid out in the plan, but it follows our intent. I still do all the books, but Robert is doing most of the contracts. I am mostly advising on contracts and work as needed.

The two of us discuss where we are in the schedule from time to time. We are both happy with the process we created. Soon it will be completed, and the company will be owned and operated totally by Robert. He will have the option to rename the company or retain its current name.

In general, I review the process and try to move it forward as much as possible. The remaining changes will be minor and happen quickly. Off into the sunset I will go, happy to have left a legacy to the consulting world I love.

It's Closing Time

By Eugene A. Scanlan, PhD

One of my favorite songs is "Closing Time" by Semisonic. The song is about closing a bar or pub, sending the patrons out to their other lives, and maybe going home with one of the patrons. In a way, it summarizes some key areas to consider when you make the decision to close your consulting business.

I've closed down my businesses twice(!), once when I rejoined a consulting firm I had worked for previously (it opened an office in my area, and I was the logical person to start it), and the second time when I retired, hopefully permanently. The first time I failed to understand all the steps necessary, especially in regards to state registration, taxes, and other filings. Fortunately, my attorney guided me through the steps, and probably enjoyed the fishing vacation I financed. The second time, I was more informed about what needed to be done and understood that this would be a cooperative effort of the business, the accountants, and the lawyer. I no longer thought that simply closing the doors and cancelling the phone service were all that I needed to do.

Fortunately, all of my clients were very cooperative when I gave them the news I would be shutting down my consulting business. In every case, I tried to give them the news and timelines as soon as I knew my real timeframe, which, aside from my death, was about as final as it could be. I also occasionally had to keep reminding some of my longer-term clients that, yes, I would no longer be around, although I did offer to be available by phone or email. It helped to be able to focus their thinking by telling them I was moving over 3,000 miles away. But I also asked them to keep in touch with me and let me know how things were proceeding after I left (some have and others have not).

Reasons to Close

Before I get into some of the specifics, we should look at some of the reasons you would consider closing your business:

Retirement

The most obvious one is retirement. You've decided to close down, go home, possibly move, and do all those things you've been postponing for many years. While it might seem this is something that happens at a specific date, it's often the case that, while the physical closing of the business can happen on a given day, the actual decrease in your involvement and advice giving can be spread out over a much longer time. After four plus years of "retirement," I still find myself advising colleagues and some organizations and, up until recently, participating in professional organizations.

Turning Over Your Business

A second reason, which may not really involve closing down your business, is turning it over to a partner or colleague. This might involve transferring ownership and stock, as well as other legal and organizational steps that can vary greatly depending on your corporate form and governmental requirements.

Buy-Out

A third reason might be the buy-out of your organization by another firm. This has been a sometimes dream of many smaller firms, especially when their owners start to get close to retirement. Again, there are many legal and other steps which need to be taken for this process.

Taking a Staff Position

A fourth reason might be your decision to move into a position with another firm or organization. Some of the independent consultants I knew would operate their businesses but always keep an eye out for an opportunity to move into a staff role.

Personal Reasons

Other reasons might include health issues, relocation of a partner or spouse, or other opportunities unrelated to consulting.

Some Considerations Based on Types of Organization

Whatever the reasons for closing, there will be many steps you will have to consider, based on your business designation. Are you a sole proprietorship? Are you organized as a corporation (if so, what type) or limited liability company? Are you a nonprofit? Note that these are U.S.-based classifications and other countries may have different ones.

Each type of business will have different formal requirements for shutting down or transferring ownership. States or provinces and other governmental agencies will all have a variety of procedures that need to be followed. Seek the help of a well-qualified attorney and a good accounting firm, both of which have previous experience with these issues.

Legal and Governmental Steps

Be prepared to purchase legal or other services that may be expensive, so that experts can help walk you through the necessary legal steps. My general advice concerning the legal and regulatory aspects of your business and its closing include:

◆ Notify in writing the state or provincial business registration agencies that you are planning to close by a given date and request appropriate forms. Do this several months in advance of your closing date. If there is to be a transfer of ownership, convey that message and get the appropriate forms and procedures.

◆ Also notify the federal agency, if any, where your business type and name are registered. Inform officials there of your plans to close.

◆ Notify in writing your state or provincial taxing authority of your plan to shut down the business or transfer its ownership. Get the appropriate tax and other forms from them. No matter when you shut down, you will probably have to file year-end tax returns with the state(s) where you operate and with federal tax agencies.

◆ Notify your federal taxing authority in writing and obtain the required final tax forms and other forms for shutting down.

◆ If you are registered with local governmental agencies and/or local business organizations, also notify them and obtain any necessary forms.

◆ Complete payroll records filings and ensure all social insurance and other payments required by federal or state/provincial agencies are up to date and reported as necessary.

◆ In all cases, be sure to send any correspondence by means of trackable delivery services.

◆ In many cases you may be able to obtain needed forms online or through your attorney or accounting firm.

◆ Even after your firm has closed, you may still need to file governmental forms and reports. Check with your attorney and accounting firm about these.

Employees, if any, should be notified as soon after your decision to close or transfer ownership is made so they will have sufficient time to seek other employment. You should also think through and be ready to present each employee closeout salary and benefit packages, such as lump sum payments, continuation of salary and/or benefits for a given period, and other options. Some governmental agencies may also require payments of benefits over a period of time after a business closes—check with your lawyer and accounting firm to see about any such requirements.

Notifying Your Clients and Prospective Clients

Clients should be notified of your intentions as far in advance as possible. When I decided to retire, and because a major move was involved, I had about a four-month timeline to close out client work. I immediately notified every client of my timeline. In several cases the contracts expired before or close to the end of my timeline, but in a few cases the contract extended beyond the point I would have to end my work. In these cases I discussed a few options with the clients. These included accelerating my work to finish at or near the end of my timeline (this proved a good option because my workload was lessened due to other clients' contracts ending sooner than these); agreeing to end the contract early; or altering the contract such that some of the work would not be carried out by me, but could be picked up by another consultant or carried out internally. In the latter two cases I adjusted my fees.

When you notify clients, you should also explain to each of them how you plan to complete the work specified under your contract, or when you will be canceling the contract. Ideally, all work called for should be completed. This may require adjustment of your closing schedule. If it is necessary to cancel the contract and you will not be able to complete the work called for, my best advice is to recommend two or three other consultants who could carry on with the work or who might be considered for follow-up services. For example, let's assume you are doing a feasibility study. You know you can complete it before you close up shop, but you also intend to recommend conducting a major campaign as one of the results of the study. Rather than leaving the client holding the bag, so to speak, recommend some capable consultants who could deliver such a campaign.

Be sure to provide clients with final billings and expenses so that they have sufficient time to pay you before you close up.

If you are in the process of marketing to other potential clients and you have proposals pending, let the prospects know that you plan to close and recommend other possible consultants for their consideration.

Business-Related Issues

◆ Notify office space providers. Some leases require that you notify the lessor in a specified time period before actually leaving. There may also be lease deposits that can be returned to you, and other requirements about moving out.

> Consult with a qualified attorney and accounting firm on the specific appropriate steps for your business.
>
>
> important

◆ Tell insurance and benefits providers that you are closing down. Some of these may offer transition opportunities that might allow you to convert policies to individual ownership.

◆ Prepare to return any leased equipment (computers, cars, etc.) to the lessor.

◆ Shut down or return phone and communication equipment (cable modems, cell phones, etc.) held in your business's name.

◆ Notify other service providers in advance and thank them for their services.

◆ Cancel any contracts you may have with providers of software-as-a-service, especially if you have them set up to be paid automatically by a credit card or bank account. This could include memberships in a variety of organizations. It's easy to overlook these services.

Record-Keeping

Determine requirements from governmental agencies for keeping your files and records, especially records of finances and client work. Closing your business is a good time to purge your files, but there are requirements about what types of records should be kept and for how long. Check with your lawyer, accounting firm, or government agencies about these requirements and ensure you are able to meet them. In some cases, selected records may have to be kept as long as seven years.

> Contact each of your clients as early as possible before you close shop. Ensure that the work you agreed to perform for those clients is fulfilled, either by you or another consultant.
>
>
> important

Relationships You've Established

Decide if you want to cancel or continue your memberships in professional or business organizations.

Let your friends and colleagues know your plans to close down and what you'll be doing next, even if it's moving away.

And finally, turn off the lights, close and lock the doors, and get ready for the next stage of your life!

Part Four

Consultants' Survival Kit

Some pieces of the consulting puzzle lend themselves to deep exploration and introspection. If you want to build a sustainable business, you'll need to study your personal, financial, and legal options. This section is designed to provide tools to get started or advance yourself, in some of the most crucial areas. After you read each article, continue to learn. Talk to other practitioners. Consult a lawyer or accountant. Continue to evolve your practice.

Not technical, but maybe most important, is the decision as to whether to consult in the first place. You'll learn the pros and cons of starting your own practice. If you decide to move forward, get ready to write a detailed business plan, select your business structure, and write your first—or hundred-and-first—client contract. And did you know that consultants are often required to register in the locality, state, or province in which they work? Learn the details of these rapidly changing requirements. Just to leave you with a smile on your face, you'll read about those facets of consulting that you typically learn about only through first-hand experience.

Chapter Fifteen

Building Blocks for Success

I f you are new to consulting, or if you are looking anew at your business, you want to ensure that the basic foundations are in place. The articles in this chapter are designed to get you off to a sound start—or a new beginning.

First, Sandra Migani Wall takes you on a whirlwind tour of a would-be consultant's mind: should you or shouldn't you?

Next, Helen Arnold provides a planning tool that gives you a thorough look at the issues that will shape your business for years to come.

Finally, if you have wondered which business structure suits your consulting practice best, look at Stephen Nill's creative take on how to analyze each. We guarantee you'll come away with a new appreciation for this subject when you learn to compare a sole proprietorship to a hermit crab!

Consulting, Why Not?

By Sandra Migani Wall, PhD

The opportunity to consult fell into my lap. While my decision to consult seemed inevitable at the time, the many decisions that sustain my practice have been much more deliberate.

Each of those decisions, and many others I made as a new consultant, has had a direct impact on my business, my income, and my lifestyle.

The Positives of Being a Consultant

For me, there have been many benefits to being a consultant.

Flexibility and Freedom

Since my family didn't need my income to survive, I have been able to accept projects based on my interests and availability. This helped tremendously when my daughter was younger and now, when I need to focus on my ninety-one-year-old father. Since I am the boss, I also have been able to take five- to six-week periods off whenever required due to family obligations—something I would never have been able to do with a staff job. More recently, even when I had serious health issues, I was still able to schedule my work hours around the days I felt good and maintain my annual income throughout the rough spots. I have had the freedom to choose not to be obligated for long periods to one single cause, organization, or group of people.

Variety

Through my own connections and working as an associate with other consulting firms, I have been able to work in the sectors of education, human services, justice, arts, health, wildlife, and zoological and botanical sciences. I have worked with nonprofits of all sizes, in all life cycles, and with differing geographical boundaries—local, regional, and national. Working as an associate, I have gained experience in a variety of fundraising areas in which I originally had no expertise. I have not been bored.

Pay

The hourly rate is much better than that of nonprofit staff.

Fulfillment

Being a nonprofit consultant allows me to build a business that provides a decent living, while making the world a better place. Consulting has provided me with a paid opportunity to learn about my community's needs and resources and to use this knowledge to help my clients build relationships and develop collaborations.

Camaraderie

Consultants on the whole are a very supportive group. It might not be intuitive to hang out with your competitors, but it might be one of the smartest things you can do. From them, I have received assurance that others have experienced similar issues, advice on how to handle problems, and support all along my journey. They have also referred work to me and served as references, saying that I can deliver what I promise.

> Deciding to become a consultant is not an irreversible decision. In fact, the breadth and variety of your experiences as a consultant will increase your worth as an employee. Many employees consult on the side. Many consultants eventually go back to full-time employment, either permanently or for a few years, before becoming a consultant again.
>
> **observation**

Wardrobe

I can work from my home in my pajamas if I so desire. While this is a definite advantage some days when you're trying to meet impossible deadlines and don't have to commute, it can also be a trap. Who feels like working while they're in bedclothes?

I Have Learned a Heck of a Lot

I constantly learn about time management, communicating effectively with others, networking, budgeting, technology, and marketing. I have learned a lot about myself and my own limitations. I have gained valuable insights into my community. I have also learned a lot about what nonprofits should and shouldn't do, how they go wrong, and the consequences of bad decisions.

Disadvantages of Consulting

There are, of course, some disadvantages to consulting.

Stability

Your annual income is less secure and predictable than that of staff. If you aren't out there consistently networking, developing relationships, or marketing, you will have many slow periods.

Benefits

You will have new expenses as an independent contractor. You will bear the full cost of payroll taxes, health and other insurances, and retirement plans, to name a few. If you subcontract or hire employees, you will need to pay them.

Hours

While you might be able to set your own hours, you might have to work with board members on evenings or weekends.

Perceptions

Family and friends might treat your consulting as equivalent to being unemployed and think you're free to do everything and anything. You will also soon realize that when you're not working, you're not earning money.

Workspace

You might not be able to afford an office outside of the home. Consequently, home might no longer be the sanctuary where you go to decompress. Even when you're sleeping, the wheels are turning and you wake up and find yourself going into your home office to "just finish one quick project." You consequently never get away from work.

Control

You really don't have any authority over your clients and can literally be at their mercy. Even though they might pay you good money for it, clients don't always take your advice. Or they might implement only part of your work plan, and when it fails, of course, they blame you. Some clients will not meet mutually agreed-upon deadlines or provide you with the information necessary for you to help them reach their goals.

Even if you put it in your contract, you still might not learn about the results of your work, such as the statistics about the annual fund appeal you created. Perhaps the client just doesn't see the need to track the data as you suggested or it is short-staffed. Or your contact just forgot to keep you in the loop. If you're results-oriented, this can be quite frustrating. And, if you want to cite examples of your successful consulting with prospective clients, you won't have the data to back up your success stories.

Sometimes as a consultant, you have to compromise, subjugating your wisdom about how a program should be organized to the organization's leadership and what leadership believes its constraints to be, all while maintaining the integrity of the project and your work.

> Because of some of these negative aspects of consulting, I have occasionally gone back to being a development or executive director. I want to be able to organize the work and be responsible for the accolades—or blame— for the outcome. Then again, realistically, all nonprofits and positions have constraints that affect the work. And so, my consultant/ employee door continues to revolve.

stories from the real world

Things to Consider Before Deciding To Become a Consultant

Even though there are a tremendous number of prospective clients out there, there is also a tremendous amount of competition for consulting work.

What Skills, Talents, and Expertise Do You Have?

What's your track record and can you document it? What services can you provide and how can you differentiate yourself from everyone else? Will you focus on a specific sector (e.g., human services, education), niche (e.g., grants, capital campaigns), or take any job that comes along?

According to Guidestar, there are over 1.8 million nonprofits in the United States.

Are You Realistic about Your Abilities and Limitations?

This is critical to your survival, because if you don't provide solid, agreed-upon deliverables in a timely and effective way, you're only burning bridges and destroying avenues for future repeat business or referrals. So don't overreach or accept jobs for which you really aren't qualified.

Do You Have the Expertise Needed?

If you don't, how can you gain the added credentials and experience to remediate any weaknesses you have? Can you take classes, or partner with another consultant from whom you can learn?

Who will serve as excellent references and provide testimonials about the quality of your work?

Do you have business skills? Are you willing to learn and improve them? Recognize that the skills needed to help a nonprofit client develop a game plan and achieve it are far different from the skills needed to run a business.

What Kind of Business Do You Want?

Do you want to work part-time or full-time? Do you want to hire subcontractors when you have an excess of work? Or do you want a high-powered consulting business with staff? Will you stay local or regional, or are you interested in working in a larger geographical area? What are the registration requirements and tax consequences for consulting in the states in which you will be working?

The answers likely depend on several variables. First, are you the sole or primary economic provider for you and your family? How much money do you need to make annually to meet all of your personal and professional expenses and also save for retirement? Second, do you have other family or personal responsibilities that would affect when and how you can work, and how much time you can devote to building and maintaining your business? Third, what types of resources (financial, space, technology, accounting, legal) will you need to start your business, and do you currently have any of these, or the money to obtain them? Can you handle the anxiety of not having a regular paycheck?

How Well Do You Communicate and Exert Influence?

Can you instill confidence in others by selling yourself, your services, and your value? Can you work with culturally and socioeconomically diverse constituents and foster a participatory and inclusive environment? Can you handle any situation with good cheer, while staying above the fray? Can you inspire and motivate staff, board, and volunteers? Under stress, do you have good intuitive judgment? Can you pinpoint problems, evaluate a situation, and propose a viable course of action when others see doom and gloom? Can you make things happen?

> To be safe, I recommend having enough money to cover your personal and business expenses for a minimum of nine to twelve months. This reserve fund will see you through most periods when business is slow.

practical tip

Are you willing to network consistently within the nonprofit and business community? This persistence is critical to maintaining a pipeline for future work.

Can you effectively communicate to your family and friends that, even if you're working from home, you really are working? Can you get them to honor your work commitment?

What Is Your Work Ethic and Style?

Are you persistent? Will you persevere and not take rejection personally? Many times, work is given to consultants because of their connections to boards or staff or community leaders (another reason to network!). Sometimes, the consultant has previously worked for a nonprofit and is a known quantity. Which brings up the point, will you provide good service so that you can retain clients?

Can you face the loneliness of working by yourself? If you're very social and need to be part of a team, working independently may be a problem. You might consider joining professional associations and collaborating with colleagues.

Are You Self-Disciplined, Motivated, Results-Oriented, and Willing to Work Hard?

Can you set goals and establish and follow a plan to achieve them? Will you keep accurate records of time spent on a project, expenses, and mileage? Will you consistently send out bills on time? Can you budget your time wisely?

Can you manage multiple clients and projects? Can you deliver promised work in a timely, efficient, and cost-effective manner?

Studies show that chronically working eleven to twelve hours daily for a long time can drastically increase the risk of coronary disease and hypertension. So, be deliberate in determining the type of consulting practice that you create. No sense in jumping from the frying pan into the fire.

food for thought

Parting Words

All the choices are in your hands. Exhilarating? Scary? You bet!

My advice? Don't slide into this business. Be deliberate. If you answered "yes" to most or all of the questions above, then you have some of the qualities needed in a consultant. If you decide to start a consulting business, make it what *you* want it to be.

Plan for Success!

By Helen B. Arnold, CFRE

We have all heard the adage "plan the work, work the plan." This is never truer than when you are thinking about establishing a new consulting business. You need to think—honestly—about how you want your business to look. All of the issues listed in the sample plan below are designed to get you to think through every aspect of your practice.

You might not want to take the time to work through all the details. You might not feel like writing it all down. You might intend to work it out as you go. Ignore those thoughts.

Crisis management and shooting from the hip are not good business plans.

important

Take the time and make the effort to write down an organized, detailed business plan. The level of detail will likely depend upon how many people you plan to hire or partner with, whether you'll need start-up capital, and what kind of business you plan to operate. When complete, you will be surprised by how much you might have missed if you hadn't gone through this process. When you are finished, you will understand and be able to clearly articulate to others, what you do, how you do it, and what it is going to cost. You will also be able to recognize success because you will have clear benchmarks. The final document can be used to apply for financial support from banks or business investors, if necessary.

A well-developed plan includes a projected budget, a marketing plan, an operating plan, and legal considerations. Create a table of contents, bind the final document, and own every word of it. I have found that an outline or bulleted format works best for clarity.

This might seem overwhelming. *Eat the elephant one bite at a time.* You might or might not need the level of information below to get started. However, the more facets you have considered, the better your chances of success. In consulting, your days are filled with new and unexpected adventures. When you have a detailed plan, you can be quick and flexible in tending to the needs of your business.

Refine your plan. Regularly. This is not a one-time task. Update the plan as your business matures, or as your own tastes and life circumstances change.

Sample Business Plan Format

I.   Table of Contents

II.   Executive Summary

Write this section last. If this part does not flow easily for you at the end, then the rest of the plan is probably not solid. Go over it again. Don't make it complicated. Use the grandma method: if your grandmother can easily understand it, you are probably on the right track. Try to limit this section to two pages or less. Make it enthusiastic, professional, complete, and concise.

Include everything about your business that you would cover in a five-minute interview.

Explain the fundamentals of the proposed business: What will be your core products or services? Who will be your customers? Who are the business owners? What do you think the future holds for your business and your industry?

If applying for a loan, state clearly how much you want, precisely how you are going to use it, and how the money will make your business more profitable, thereby ensuring repayment.

III. General Company Description

This does not have to be complicated, but it does have to be clear. Again, use the grandma test.

A.   Briefly discuss what business you will be in. What will you do?

B.   State your firm's mission.

C.   Outline company goals and objectives.

D.   Create your business philosophy: What values are important to you in business?

E.   Identify to whom you will market your products.

F.   Describe your industry.

G.   Describe your most important company strengths and core competencies.

H.   State your legal form of ownership: sole proprietor, partnership, corporation, or limited liability corporation (LLC). Why have you selected this form?

IV.   Products and Services

At the outset, you may not know if you want to be a generalist or if you want to specialize. As you think about this section, the pros and cons of each may become clearer to you.

A.   Provide an in-depth description of your products or services.

B.   Identify what factors will give you competitive advantages or disadvantages. Examples include level of professional education, accreditation or certification, levels of quality, and unique or proprietary features.

C.   Convey the pricing or fee structures of your products and services.

V.   Marketing

Be prepared to spend a good deal of time researching market trends and preferences—yours and others'. I went to every independent consultant I knew and talked to each about marketing. You can get a lot of very valuable insight. Don't be shy about talking to public relations folks either. They have a lot of good advice about how to deliver your information to a potential market. Visit online blogs, nonprofit websites, any reference area you can think of.

I also listed every consultant and consulting firm I could find in my regional area. I went on their websites to review services offered, client lists, and major campaigns completed. I talked to clients listed on those sites and donors with whom I was acquainted to get a feel for how the consultants worked.

A.   Include background information on trends in nonprofit fundraising and advising, standard and/or exceptional services customarily provided to industry customers and clients.

B.   Identify the niche you plan to address.

C.   Develop your pricing strategies.

D.   Describe your target market: local, regional, national, international nonprofits; charities in a particular discipline; large or small organizations.

E.   Pinpoint marketing vehicles: social media, print, Internet (website), social media, video, CDs, speaking, conference exhibiting.

F.   Identify which community groups you will join to increase your visibility.

G.   Estimate your promotional budget, based upon the above factors.

VI. Operational Plan

It's time to make decisions about the nuts and bolts of how you will work. These logistics will directly impact your budget, income, and lifestyle that your practice will afford.

A. Establish how and where your products or services will be produced. What is your geographic practice area?

B. State where your office be located. What qualities do you need in a location?

C. Decide which legal factors should be fulfilled:

1. Insurance, where applicable

a. Office and professional equipment

b. Liability

c. Auto, if your car is company-owned

d. Worker's compensation, if applicable

e. Notary bond, if applicable

f. Health insurance, long-term disability, life insurance

g. Errors and omissions

2. Agreements for services (contracts)

a. With consulting clients: use a basic form that can be adapted to most clients. This is the place to think through your basic terms.

b. With co-partners or subcontractors: make sure that you establish clear terms for timelines and deliverables.

3. Taxes

a. Self-employment

b. Income

c. Subcontractor forms 1099

d. Quarterly withholding for employees

      e.   Quarterly estimates for you

      f.   Annual reporting requirements for employees

  4. State Registrations

     Most states require some kind of registration for fundraising consultants. Be sure to check with each state where you plan to work to make sure you have properly registered as a consultant. Fundraising consultants include fundraisers (individuals or firms that make calls on donors); advisors (do not make direct calls on donors); commercial co-venturers (for-profit companies that sell a product and give some proceeds to a nonprofit); and grant writers.

D. Decide whether you plan to work alone or with staff. What are your staffing needs? What are your employment policies?

E. Determine if you will have inventory. Because you are selling services, rather than a product, your hard inventory might be limited to office equipment, sales materials, business cards, and exhibit materials.

F. Identify your suppliers. Where will you go for outside help if co-partnering on client projects? These may include advertising/marketing firms, architectural or engineering firms, or firms that provide donor recognition items or software. Make sure these professionals have good reputations and have agreed that they are willing to partner with you.

G. Establish credit policies. Are you going to extend credit to clients beyond a typical thirty-day pay policy? Under what terms will you issue long-term credit?

H. Manage your accounts receivable. What is your policy for payments due you? Will you give a discount for payment within ten days? Charge a service fee for late payments? This should be included in your contract as well.

I. Manage your accounts payable. If clients do not pay on a timely basis, how will you support your staff and business expenses? Will you establish a line of credit with your bank? How will you support your business while you transition into the consulting universe? As a general policy, it is good to have at least three months' operating capital on hand to manage the ebb and flow of consulting work opportunities.

J. Forecast your sales. Do so for three months, six months, and one year. You might want to talk to other consultants in your area to get some feedback on reasonable consultant sales expectations, if they are willing to share. Don't get too stressed about this. Make your best guess, and know that you will have to revisit this topic often to ensure you are tracking your actual progress. You won't really have a feel for cash flow or income until you have a year under your belt. It is important to have some cash reserves to get you through the fluctuations of business in the pipeline.

VII. Management and Organization

If your business will include you alone, at least at the outset, this section is self-explanatory. But if you prefer even one partner or employee, carefully think though who will be responsible for basic business functions.

A. Finalize who will manage the business on a day-to-day basis. What experience does that person bring to the business? What special or distinctive competencies? Is there a plan for continuation of the business if this person is lost or incapacitated?

B. Create an organizational chart if you'll have more than ten employees. Show the management hierarchy and who will be responsible for key functions.

C. Include position descriptions for key employees. If you are seeking loans or investors, include resumes of owners and key employees.

VIII. Management and Operations

You will need professional and advisory support. Select individuals who can provide the following types of service:

A. Attorney

B. Accountant

C. Insurance agent

D. Banker

E. Business consultant or consultants

F. Mentors and key advisors

IX. Personal Financial Statement

Include personal financial statements for each owner and major stockholder, showing assets and liabilities held outside the business and personal net worth. Owners will often have to draw on personal assets to finance the business, and these statements will show what is available. Bankers and investors usually want this information as well.

X.   Start-Up Expenses and Capitalization

    A. Estimate your start-up costs. You will have many expenses before you even begin operating your business. It's important to estimate them accurately and then to plan where you will get sufficient capital. This is a research project, and the more thorough your research efforts, the less chance that you will leave out important expenses or underestimate them. Include expenses, which are actual, based on research, and are firm and predictable.

    B. Determine contingencies, estimated unforeseen financial needs based on your own knowledge and experience; a "buffer."

XI.   Financial Plan

You'll need to create more than just a budget. There are many pieces to putting together the financial puzzle of a successful business.

    A. Create a twelve-month profit and loss estimate showing direct and indirect expenses.

    B. Estimate your one-year profit projection.

    C. Project cash flow.

    D. Draw up your opening day balance sheet.

    E. Outline your break-even analysis:

        1. Fixed costs (in dollars). These costs are consistent month-to-month and include your own and staff salaries and benefits, rent, utilities, retirement savings, and insurance payments.

        2. Variable costs (in percentage of sales or billables). These costs differ based on what services you are providing. Examples include project-related printing, subcontractor fees, and travel. Your pricing should allow a percentage of your fees for hard costs of a project. This amount will fluctuate based on each contract amount.

XII.   Appendixes

Include details and studies used in your business plan; for example:

    A. Your brochures and advertising materials

    B. Industry studies

C. Magazine or other articles you have published

D. Letters of support

E. Any other materials needed to support the assumptions in this plan

F. Market research studies

G. List of assets available as collateral for a loan

Setting Up Shop: How to Choose the Right Entity

By Stephen C. Nill, J.D.

Consulting in the nonprofit sector, as rewarding as it can be, is nevertheless a business, with all of the challenges and attendant risks of any business. Each consulting assignment carries with it the possibility that the advice given or not given, or the work performed or not performed, falls short of the mark—or at least is perceived to have done so by the client. Disputes can arise. And sometimes, law suits.

I know about law suits. I'm now in my fourth decade of law practice. In my first ten years, I was exclusively a business litigator. In other words, I brought law suits, and I defended them, for business people. I state this up front because this early professional experience instills in me, to this day, a bias of viewing the possible forms of doing business from the point of view of protecting the consultant as well as the nonprofit client, rather than from the point of view of minimizing income taxes. But I shall try to overcome my bias, at least in part, by briefly discussing the tax implications of the various entity choices; these can be important in choosing what kind of entity to form for your consulting practice.

Perhaps your eyebrows went up a bit when I mentioned, in a book addressed primarily to consultants, that, besides protecting the consultant, I was also interested in protecting the consultant's client. Almost all of the consultants I have met in our sector have been highly experienced, competent, ethical, and diligent. They would be horrified at the thought that they might somehow let down their client, and cause economic loss. For the most enlightened consultant, it is not enough to merely create a shield from personal liability (important as that is); the consultant should also be concerned about protecting the nonprofit organization from any mistakes. So, I will briefly also discuss the use of insurance to both protect the personal assets of the consultant, and provide a means of recovery by the client, should it come to that.

One more thing before we dive in. This chapter is focused on the small shop, meaning one-person shops or firms with, say, two or three principals, operating in the U.S. Okay, here we go:

Animals in the Zoo: What Are the Entity Choices?

When my daughters were little, they had various kinds of pets. One of them had hermit crabs. These are soft little crabs that would make tasty meals for a variety of predators, except for one thing: they had the habit of inserting themselves into empty shells. Once inside the hard shell, they were well protected. It would take an immensely powerful set of predator jaws to pierce through the shell. It could be done, but it is very rare that a predator would succeed. Smart crabs!

Sole Proprietorship

A single-consultant firm in its natural state is called a sole proprietorship. In this form of entity, the consultant *is* the entity. Consulting agreements are between the individual consultant and the nonprofit. The individual consultant is personally subject to all business liabilities and taxes.

Partnership

A small shop where, say, two or three principals agree to co-own the firm and divide profits and losses is, in its natural state, a partnership. In a partnership, each partner is personally liable for business liabilities and taxes.

For these reasons, savvy consultants often take a lesson from the simple hermit crab by donning a "shell" before venturing out into the deep blue sea of consulting. Fortunately, many states have seen fit to offer consultants and other business people better alternatives. Let's take a look:

Corporation

A corporation, though a fiction, is treated as a "person" separate from its shareholders, officers, and employees. The idea is that if the corporation is sued and loses, the individual shareholders, officers and employees are protected from any resulting judgment.

A corporation is typically formed by filing articles of incorporation in the state of incorporation. A corporation may have one shareholder, as with a single-person consulting firm.

Or it may have many, as with a multi-principal firm.

Why you should avoid operating as a sole proprietorship or partnership:

Sole proprietorships and partnerships are like soft little hermit crabs without their adopted shell-homes—little more than a tasty meal for a litigation attorney representing an unhappy nonprofit client. If sued, those clients would have to pay the legal fees and costs of defending the suit, easily tens of thousands of dollars. If they lost, the consultants' personal assets would be at risk in the ensuing collection. For a partnership, it's even worse than that: each partner is liable for the actions—and *mistakes*—of each of the other partners.

I once represented a consultant whose partner was driving from the nonprofit's headquarters to the home of a prospective donor, and was giving a ride to a passenger— the organization's board chair. The partner ran a red light and caused a three-car accident, with lots of serious injuries. While the partner had auto insurance, the injuries were so severe that the partnership itself was sued, thereby exposing the assets of my client to a possible judgment. Fortunately, the case settled within the policy limits of the partner's auto policy, but not before my client expended thousands of dollars in legal fees and had to endure the stress of possible financial catastrophe.

important

A corporation must follow a strict set of guidelines. For example, it is governed in accordance with its articles of incorporation and bylaws and by the state's code governing corporations. It issues stock to its owners, called shareholders. It must have, at minimum, annual shareholders' meetings and up-to-date minutes reflecting these meetings. Its finances must be separate, and separately accounted, from the finances of the individual shareholders. When dealing with the public, including consulting clients, it must hold itself out as a corporation—meaning that its contracts must be in the name of the corporation, its letterhead and website must disclose that it is a corporation, and so on.

Because it is a separate entity, the corporate form of doing business can be a sound choice from the perspective of protecting the consultant, provided the consultant or consultants are willing to carefully adhere to the corporate formalities.

Be careful to review with a lawyer or accountant the type of corporation you create. Because it is a separate legal entity, by default your corporation will pay its own taxes. Known as a C corporation, it files its own income tax return each year, and pays its own taxes. If it then issues a dividend to the shareholders, the shareholders must report the dividends as income, resulting in a kind of double taxation: once at the corporate level and again at the shareholder level. This is not particularly a problem with nonprofit-sector consultants, as it is not very common for dividends to be paid, for the simple reason that they do not often command the kinds of astronomical fees that their counterparts in the for-profit arena sometimes do.

C corporations may deduct salaries and other compensation paid to shareholders, provided they do not exceed what is "reasonable." What is reasonable is determined on the facts and circumstances of each situation. Unfortunately, there is no bright-line test for this. If in doubt,

---

A failure to adhere to the formalities of operating as a corporation can, in some cases, enable a court to disregard the corporate "shell" and enable the plaintiff to receive a judgment against the individuals operating the corporation.

When suing corporations, a plaintiff's attorney will give serious consideration to also suing the individuals operating the corporation by seeking to "pierce the corporate veil." To pierce the corporate veil, the suit will typically allege some kind of fraudulent activity, coupled with failure to adhere to the formalities of operating a corporation. Sometimes the suit will also allege that the corporation was not adequately capitalized when it was created. Even if the court ultimately determines that the veil should not be pierced and drops the individuals from the suit—attempts to pierce the corporate veil do not often succeed—the individuals who are sued will have to defend themselves and thus endure the expense, and stress, of litigation.

There are two big lessons here. First, make certain that you understand, adhere to and carefully document the various corporate formalities. Seek advice from an attorney, if necessary. Second, consider appropriate insurance that will pay your defense costs and any judgment, such as errors and omissions insurance and business liability insurance.

watch out!

check with your accountant. If it pays "unreasonable" amounts of compensation, called excessive compensation, it will pay an accumulated earnings tax. In most cases, nonprofit consultants in small shops operating as C corporations do not typically encounter the accumulated earnings tax, since any salary that they take is well within limits of what is considered reasonable. There is also something called the personal holding company tax, which is beyond the scope of this chapter, but your accountant can discuss it with you.

If, after discussing your anticipated income and expenses with your accountant, double taxation, the accumulated earnings tax, or both are a concern, consider making an S corporation election, in which the gains and losses pass through to the individual shareholders in proportion to their shareholder ownership percentages. Shareholders then report the gains or losses on their own individual income tax returns.

Limited Liability Company

The LLC is a kind of blended creature that confers on its owners the limited liability attribute of corporations, and, by default, the pass-through taxation attribute of a sole proprietorship (in the case of a one-consultant shop) or partnership (the small shop with, say, two or three consultants).

From the perspective of formation and ease of operations, LLCs beat corporations hands down. For example, unlike corporations, LLCs are not required to have a board of directors or officers. They do not have to have meetings of the principals, such as annual meetings, as do corporations. If meetings are held, minutes need not be taken (though, as I will explain, minutes of important meetings *should* be taken). Even the titles of the principals can be flexible, such as partner, chief executive officer, president, member, manager, managing member, managing director, and so forth. For example, CharityChannel is an LLC, and I am its chief executive officer. Had I wanted to, I could have dubbed myself Chief Aardvark or Hermit-Crab-in-Chief. Note that whatever you choose to call the owners, the law calls them "members," which is akin to shareholders of a corporation.

LLCs by default are taxed as sole proprietorships, in the case of one-consultant shops, and as partnerships, in the case of two or more principals. Even so, you have an array of options in how your LLC is to be taxed, giving you much flexibility and making accountants very happy (check with yours!). Depending on your particular situation, your LLC may be taxed as a sole proprietorship, partnership, S corporation, or C corporation. The options assume that your LLC otherwise meets the requirements for such taxation; for example, on the sole proprietorship option, which would be an option for a one-person consulting shop, check with your state law to determine if it permits one-person LLCs. Many do.

LLCs are well suited for one-person shops where state law permits single-member LLCs, and are also suited for small consulting shops with two or more principals. In the case of two or more principals, you can create an operating agreement that is carefully tailored to how the principals will be working together in carrying out their consulting practice. The principals, too, might decide that income will be distributed in proportion to their relative contributions to the consulting practice, rather than on, say, the amount of capital they each contributed. Corporations are not nearly so flexible.

Remember my bias? It is in the area of protecting you, the consultant, from personal liability that LLCs have a real advantage. As I mentioned above, compared to corporations, it is very important

---

Even LLCs, which have far fewer formalities than corporations, can be pierced, though it is harder for plaintiffs to do so.

For that reason, it is important to show that you're treating your LLC as a separate business entity. Here are some of the steps you should take:

♦ Maintain separate bank accounts and records for the LLC.

♦ In consulting contracts, make it clear that you are contracting on behalf of your LLC.

♦ In letterhead, cards, your website, and any other printed materials, make sure that you are indicating that your firm is an LLC. For example, on the legal page at the front of this book, you will see that it is "published by CharityChannel Press, an imprint of CharityChannel LLC."

♦ Even though your LLC is not required to have an annual meeting, go ahead and have one anyway—and create minutes of the meeting. You can recite in the minutes such things as the firm's strategic plan, performance in the prior year, goals and objectives for the upcoming year, changes in location, changing in banking, strategic alliances with other consultants, and so on. Keep the minutes in your permanent records in case they're ever needed. And by "needed" I mean in case you're sued.

♦ If there is more than one principal in your firm, make certain that you have an operating agreement, and be sure to tailor it to your particular needs. (Consult with an attorney if necessary.) Boilerplate operating agreements, while better than nothing, are rather unconvincing to courts when a plaintiff is arguing that you weren't really operating the LLC as a separate entity.

♦ If you can, be sure to adequately capitalize the LLC. What is "adequate" is open to discussion with your attorney, and is based on the type of consulting you do. Keep in mind, too, that when you capitalize your LLC, there could be tax implications that manifest later, such as at the sale of your practice—so involve your accountant in any decision-making in this regard.

to adhere to the corporate formalities in operating a corporation-—and there are many (see above). Failure to do so, as I mentioned, could open the door to legal exposure of the shareholder or shareholders (aka you), where the plaintiff seeks to have the court pierce the corporate veil. The same principle holds true for LLCs, but here is the key difference: there are far fewer formalities to follow for LLCs. In this sense, plaintiffs have a much more difficult time asserting that you didn't adhere to the formalities of operating your LLC.

Notice that I didn't say that piercing the LLC shell was impossible. Indeed, business litigation attorneys quite naturally will often try to do so, even if their grounds for doing so are weak, because they are supposed to be zealous advocates for their clients—their *angry* nonprofit clients. See the sidebar for some tips on LLC "formalities."

Insurance

Although this article is mostly focused on choice of entity, in a larger sense it is also about mitigating risk to you personally, and about protecting your client in case you make a mistake—an error—or fail to do what you are supposed to do—an omission.

Protecting You, the Consultant

In case you have an act of omission (in other words, you screw up), or the nonprofit client thinks you did, you will be very glad that you set your consulting practice up as a corporation or LLC, believe me. But pay attention carefully. If your corporation or LLC is sued, consider this:

1. You will have to cover the costs of defense, which include attorney fees often in the tens of thousands of dollars range, and costs such as filing fees, deposition transcriptions, expert witness fees, and so on. Sure, you can just walk away from the entity and let it go down, but what, then, becomes of your reputation in the field? And there might be assets of the entity that you would not want to lose, such as cash in the bank account, accounts receivable, intellectual property, and good will.

2. The plaintiff might also name you individually, even if doing so is without justification. If this happens, you have no choice but to defend the suit.

So, what to do? Consider buying insurance designed to protect you from errors and omissions. Such insurance should cover your defense costs and pay any settlement or judgment. To keep costs as low as possible, consider having a high deductible but make sure that the deductible is something that, should the unthinkable happen, you are prepared to pay.

Protecting Your Clients from Errors or Omissions

Errors and omissions insurance does one more thing: It's a statement to your clients that, in the event you make a mistake and cause economic damage, the clients are protected by having a source of recompense should it become necessary to be made whole. What I mean by "made whole" is that they should be able to receive a sum of money to make up for their financial losses.

It takes a particularly enlightened consultant to boldly tell clients about this kind of coverage that you've taken out, because it also could provide incentive to a client to actually make a claim. Still, in my view, it's the professionally responsible thing to do.

In some cases, of course, errors and omissions insurance is not optional. Nonprofit clients sometimes require this kind of insurance of their consultants, along with other forms of insurance, depending on the consulting arrangement—such as proof of automobile insurance, and general business liability insurance. If you have employees who are assigned to work for the client, the client might require that you carry workers' compensation insurance for that employee. Owners of the company, though, are generally not required to carry workers compensation insurance on themselves.

Of course, if you are in a consulting practice where there is truly very little risk that your mistake could lead to an economic loss by the client and a corresponding suit against you, then you might decide to forego errors and omissions insurance. If you're not sure, consider speaking to an attorney to help you assess the risk of foregoing insurance.

Chapter Sixteen

Details, Details

The fine print is an ongoing concern when you run your own business. From the language you write into your client contracts to the language handed down to you by legislators, the little things really do make a difference. Begin here and make those finer points a part of your ongoing education.

Gene Scanlan opens by delving into what is often the evolving process of crafting your contracts. He shares the process by which we tend to incorporate our lessons learned into those documents—here's your chance to get ahead of the game.

Then we take a peek into the world of state registration for consultants in our field—did you know there was such a thing? If you don't, then Helen Arnold's article is a must-read.

Finally, Justin Tolan treats us to the kind of details we too-often ignore...until it's too late. He leaves you with tales of growling dogs, snowstorms, and reasons to carry a spare suit.

About Contracts: Put It in Writing

Eugene A. Scanlan, PhD

I grew up in New Jersey where "taking out a contract" had certain meanings we don't need to discuss here. When I started doing independent consulting work, written contracts were something I didn't worry about too much. After all, the client and I both seemed to understand what I would be doing for the organization, and therefore not a lot of detail was needed. A simple letter of agreement was usually sufficient. But soon I discovered that sometimes the understandings were not mutual, especially when the details of the expectations started to emerge.

For example, sometimes the client was "too busy" to do something I thought it should be doing, or I would get asked to do something I thought was unrelated to my consulting services. Of course, as with all good consultants, I wanted to keep each client happy, so I would take on the extra tasks, and, often, eat the time I had spent when I did my billings. So, over time, my written contracts evolved into documents that were quite different from the early versions, and tailored to the needs and interests of each client.

I also started to learn more about all of the other players who might be involved in my contracts, including board members who were unfamiliar with consultants, funders, staff not directly involved in my work, professional associations, lawyers, and government agencies. The content of my contracts changed radically over time and with experience.

The Even Bigger Picture

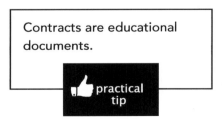

Contracts are educational documents.

practical tip

I also learned over time that contracts could be—in fact should be—educational documents. They need to explain the objectives of your services, the processes you will carry out, the methods you will use, what is expected from the organization, the basis for your fees, the timelines, and the specific outcomes of the services. Remember that many of those associated with the organization may have little or no understanding of what consultants like you actually do, so it helps if you view your contracts as educational tools as well as documents specifying your services.

Sources of Contracts

Contracts can come from several sources and there are different considerations with each.

Internal

It's nice and can appear relatively simple when the consultant or consulting firm is the source of the contract. In fact, some of the contracts I've seen from other firms consisted of large sections of boilerplate with some references to the specific client. My contracts did include some standardized sections, but those were outweighed by parts drawn up just for that client and what I was being asked to do. So, one source for a contract is you, the consultant, or, if you are part of a larger firm, the firm's usual contract language.

Client

A second source for a contract may be the client. Some clients, for a variety of reasons, wanted to provide me with the contract. This would usually mean I had to do some negotiating over the specifics, including the expected outcomes, and even the terms used. Client-sourced contracts can often be focused almost entirely on what the consultant is expected to do, with very little about what the client is responsible for doing. In some cases staff of clients pleaded they were "too busy" to supply me with information I needed to carry out my work, such as backgrounds of feasibility study interviewees, or they were unable to set up critical meetings I needed to proceed. Once, a client did not provide me with any information about a board member interviewee, who, during the interview, was appalled to find out no one told me he had founded the organization. If the client or an outside source prepares a contract, make certain that the contracts meet requirements of state registration authorities if the client is located in a state that requires approval of contracts.

Government

A third source can be a government agency. These contracts are usually very detailed and require considerable information from the consultant or firm, possibly including business registration details, financial information, and equal opportunity statements. The contract may be presented as a form which needs to be completed, and may require other attachments, such as previous year tax filings, or other details. Services, timelines, fees, and expected expenses may have to be included in a budget section or document.

Funder

A fourth source can be a funder of the organization seeking your services. Some funders may actually provide a contract or letter of agreement—this can be an unusual situation, but it does happen. It is more common for a funder, especially one that is providing a grant specifically for consulting services, to want to review the contract before it is finalized, or even meet the consultant(s) being considered.

General Purposes of Contracts

Contracts can cover a variety of services, such as feasibility studies, development audits, campaign consulting, campaign management (where the consultant or firm serves as staff for the campaign), short-term training or workshops, board development, management consulting, grant writing, events management, or other services. Some contracts may combine two or more of these into a comprehensive package of services.

If you are preparing the contract, or are negotiating with a client about a contract it or another source is providing, be sure you and the client are very clear about the real needs you will address. If the client wants to "raise more money," that expression of a seemingly simple need can have immense complications if it is the purpose of your services. The goal of your contract should be more specific and detailed, and not allow you or the client to fall into the trap of stated goals that don't take into account the many complications that can arise when you are delivering your services.

> One way to think of a contract is that it is a box that holds your responsibilities and those of the client. The box is labeled with the purposes of your services, as understood by both you and the client, and you both are clear on what the real needs are.
>
> **observation**

Once you have gotten to know the client through an initial contract, the general purposes of future contracts can be easier to define and may be broader in scope than was spelled out in your initial contract. Some of my follow-up contracts, often simpler letters of agreement, used terms as "provide general advice and assistance with…" or "provide ongoing services for the purposes of…."

Being Specific Versus Being General

People who saw my contracts often commented how detailed they were. As the contract content evolved based on my experiences, I learned there are parts of the contract that should be very specific, and other parts that needed to be more general. Some examples of being too specific are listed below.

I usually spelled out a timeline for my work ("three months from the date of signing," "…from January 1 to September 30," etc.), but learned that I also needed to include a statement that provided for things that might alter my timeframe. These could include key people who needed to be interviewed for a study but were not available for a long period of time, inability to pull meetings together due to other obligations or schedule conflicts, and even things such as staff vacations, funding issues, or other priorities of the organization. I did not list all these possibilities but did try to make it clear that my work schedule could be influenced by other factors beyond my control.

My contracts also tended to present ranges for things such as the number of interviews I would do for a feasibility study, rather than a specific number. I once had to hold off completion of a feasibility study report while we tried to do interview number thirty because our contract had said we would do thirty interviews—no more, and no less—and the client insisted we stick to that number.

And what about the issue of "dollars to be raised"—a dollar goal? I always tried to have my clients understand that my role was not to raise the money (in my type of consulting work I could not ask anyone for money), but to help the organization's staff, board, and other volunteers raise the needed dollars. I always tried to point out in my conversations with the client that there were many factors, again beyond my control, that might impact the ability to meet fundraising goals. Suppose the organization suddenly received some very negative publicity, such as the executive director embezzling funds. That would certainly impact any fundraising, but it would be out of my control.

Always think through and express in your contract those factors you can control, and those factors that might be out of your, or anybody else's, control.

A Contract's Contents

At this point you might be asking, "So what did your contracts include?" Again, remember that consulting contracts can be geared to address a variety of different services, ranging from relatively simple, such as a one-day training session or workshop, up to a multi-year engagement for a set of services. Some of my contracts, usually continuations with existing clients, were as short as three pages and as simple as a letter outlining what I would do. But let's look below at the more comprehensive version of my contracts and both what was included and why I included these areas.

Opening Lines

I usually started off the contract with a section called "Introduction, Background, and Objectives of Services." The introduction section was a brief paragraph about what led up to submission of the contract, including the fact that I reviewed materials from the organization, met with people there (I spelled out with whom), whether or not I responded to a request for proposals, and any other relevant

> Examples of objectives from sample contracts include:
>
> ◆ Determine how development and fundraising are integrated into short- and long-term planning of XYZ.
>
> ◆ Determine the effectiveness of current and recent fundraising efforts, including a list of the specific areas, such as prospect identification, research, internal systems and procedures, foundation funding, donor relations, etc.
>
> ◆ Assess the current and potential support, development, and fundraising roles of the board of directors
>
> **Example**

information. The background was a very brief summary of my understanding of the current status of the organization and recent events that led up to hiring a consultant. The objectives of the services section was where I got very specific. I started with a sentence about the outcomes of my work in summary form, including such things as stating that the work will result in specific recommendations and action steps (for a study), or other outcomes. The objectives themselves were listed, with as many as ten to twelve stated objectives.

Methodology

I next spelled out the methodology I would use to accomplish these objectives. For feasibility studies the general methodology might include, for example, internal and external reviews of recent development efforts. Ways to accomplish this included review of the organization's relevant materials (I spelled out a list of what I would need), confidential interviews with selected staff (I specified who I would interview), other interviews with board members, donors, and others, and other parts of the methodology I would use. Then I got even more detailed when I did the section called "Steps in the Process." Here I outlined each step in the order I would carry them out during the entire period of the services. If I was carrying out a study, for example, each step in the study process was defined, such as meetings to select interviewees, creation of the interview list, development of draft questionnaires and the approval process, the actual interview process, the number of interviews to be carried out, what I would do with the information collected, and other steps in detail.

It was here that I also defined what I expected from the organization, including, for example, if they would arrange for the interviews, the materials they needed to provide to me, information on those I would be interviewing, and the need for them to inform me of any major issues or problems related to the organization or my work. I also indicated here what I would provide, such as a draft case for support to prep interviewees, an interview cover sheet to be completed by the organization for each interviewee, and updated reports on my progress.

Outcomes and Deliverables

I then provided a brief outline of the contents of the final report and recommendations, if such a report was part of my services. No matter what services I provided, I usually did a report to summarize what the outcomes of the services were, as well as any issues or concerns uncovered during the process. Some of the latter might be included in a "Letter to Management," which would be only addressed to certain board members and/or staff if there were sensitive issues that could not be broadly distributed. My reports were usually presented with a section outlining the service objectives defined in the contract, the processes used, the information collected, my analysis of this information, and specific action steps, plus appropriate thank–you letters and acknowledgments.

The contract, by including details of the process, methodology, steps, and an outline of the final report, thus provides a resource for the end products.

Timeframe

The next part of my contracts briefly defined the expected timeframe for my work. The timeframe would always start with the signing of the contract and often give an approximate time for completion of the work, such as three months, six months, etc. If interviews were involved, I might say, "The primary factor affecting the timeline will be the availability of key selected interviewees."

Covering Your Bases

The timeline was usually followed by a statement that if the organization desired additional services beyond the scope of the contract, these would be billed on an hourly rate for the actual time.

All of my contracts included a cancellation clause, which allowed either party to the contract to cancel upon thirty days written notice to the other party. I also made it clear that I would be reimbursed for all fees and client-related expenses incurred up to the cancellation date. A cancellation clause is protection for both you and the client. There might be very good reasons to cancel a contract if the work is completed early, if unexpected factors intervene in the process, or even if you go over a campaign goal early because of a major gift.

Registration

An area you should be concerned about is registration of both your firm and the client organization with appropriate government agencies and other organizations. I have encountered organizations that, while having their 501(c)(3), were not registered with the state or states where they operated. In one case that I am aware of, both the client and the consulting organization they contracted with were fined because the organization had failed to register with the state.

In many states consultants are also required to register, whether or not they actually ask for and/ or handle funds; some states define the latter as "solicitors" and require such things as registration and bonding. Consultants should also be registered as businesses with appropriate government agencies. Some states have guidelines about what needs to be in the contract, such as a starting date and ending date, the fee schedule, the provision for an "out" clause, and other specifications.

Given all of these issues, I included the following statement in my contracts under the "Registration" heading: "By accepting the final contract, the XYZ organization certifies that it is registered with all appropriate federal and state agencies and has met their reporting requirements."

Intellectual Property

After several years, I also learned to include a section called "Intellectual Property" in all of my contracts. This section was worded in a way that both protected the confidentiality of the materials and items I used during the consulting process and the organization's materials shared with me. I also made it clear in this section that specific items, such as individual confidential interview notes would not be shared with the organization, although my reports summarized these without connecting them to a person interviewed.

Payment

I next spelled out both the fees involved for my services and the payment schedule. Consultants differ about how this should be done. My experience led me to give the total fee for the services and the payment schedule, with the last payment usually due after completion of the work defined in the contract. I also indicated that the payment schedule might be changed during the course of the contract (sometimes this was necessary due to cash flow problems at the client), and again indicated what payment would be expected if the contract was terminated. In the case of changes in the payment schedule, I specified that the client and my firm had to reach mutual agreement on the revised schedule or a delayed payment. This was usually done informally and payment delays weren't excessive. However, other consultants I am aware of included what was basically a "stop work" provision if the firm was not paid for a period of time, such as three months on a monthly billing cycle. I stated that fees included all services defined in the contract, but additional services, such as added interviews beyond the number indicated would require additional billing for the time involved.

Expenses

Anticipated expenses were defined in the next section. These might include travel, car mileage (usually billed at the existing state or federal per-mile allowances), materials reproduction, long-distance calls (a major expense when doing interviews out of your area), and delivery services. I specified these would be billed with appropriate receipts along with the periodic billing for services. I often would also state any extraordinary expenses over an agreed-upon amount would be cleared with the organization before being incurred. At times, at the request of a client, I would also specify a cap on total expenses for the project.

> I quickly learned to define in my contracts how many copies of reports I would provide after a client asked me for over fifty copies of a seventy-page report.
>
>  **stories from the real world**

Ethics

I followed this section with a brief statement of ethical principles, including my adherence to the Association of Fundraising Professionals' code of ethics as a member of that organization, a statement that, "All billing is time or project based," and a restatement that the confidentiality of interviewees' information will be ensured. This was followed by a statement that the organization was obligated to share with the consultant any legal or ethical issues that might affect the consulting process, and that non-public information shared with the consultant would be kept confidential.

In Closing

I next listed references, if necessary, and offered to provide additional references if needed.

I closed with the background of each consultant working on the project.

Finally, I provided signature and date lines with the names and titles of those I wanted to sign the contract. Some consultants are not too concerned about who signs the contract. In most cases I prefer that both the board chair and the CEO/executive director sign. Why? Because if the board chair and the board itself are not committed to the process it may fail. Smaller scale projects may not require this caution, but major studies, campaign efforts, and more comprehensive services require board buy-in at the start. And, in some states, the regulatory authority might require a board signature.

Other Things to Consider

Over the years I sometimes included other sections, or took additional steps related to my contracts. These might reflect the nature of the client, the work I was doing, or a specific request by the client, a funder, or even an influential board member.

I occasionally included a statement about how disputes between the consultant and the client would be resolved, particularly if I anticipated problems from a client or an individual associated with the client.

I sometimes had my attorney review a sample contract to be sure that required areas, such as cancellation clauses, were included. This was done a periodic basis or when I made some major revisions to contract elements. If a client

> At times, an organization's attorney or a board member who was an attorney would review the contract. My favorite story about this was when I included a provision that an out-of-town client would provide me with office space. The attorney on the board insisted he write more specific language to define the office space, and, lowering his glasses and looking at me skeptically, came up with, "The client will provide a desk, a light, and a phone for local calls only." I immediately pointed out there was no mention of a chair and provided the following wording: "...and will also include a comfortable chair, as determined by the consultant. If the chair is not sufficiently comfortable, the organization will find another that meets the comfort standards of the consultant." He laughed and we did insert what became known as "The Comfy Chair Provision."

stories from the real world

insisted on some additional language or a major change in one of my provisions, I also would have a phone conversation with my attorney and develop some alternative language to negotiate with the client.

Final Approvals

In some states contracts between consultants and organizations must be reviewed by a state agency before they are accepted by the organization. Check your state's requirements carefully. If the organization operates in several states, be sure it is appropriately registered in each state, and, if necessary, you are also registered in these states, especially if you are doing fundraising.

In a Contract, Never Promise Something You Can't Deliver

Finally, always be sure both you and the client have a very clear understanding—in writing—of the nature and scope of your work, the client's roles and responsibilities, limitations on your time, and the outcomes expected. It is easy to be treated as if you were a member of staff. The contract is the box that contains what you will both do to ensure a successful consulting relationship.

Yes, Consultants, You Must Register Too!

By Helen B. Arnold, CFRE

Many consultants get their start at nonprofits, which, as we know, must register in the states where they solicit funds from donors. Sometimes consultants are not aware that *we* also must register in most states. In fact, more states require consultant registration than require nonprofit registration. If your work touches nonprofit income generation, training, fundraising advising, or organizational development, in whatever form, read on.

The states requiring consultant registration are not necessarily the same as the states requiring registration of charities, and some states that require no organizational registration do require consultant registration. You didn't expect this to be simple, did you?

Consultant registration is a relatively new phenomenon, and one that is increasingly enforced. The requirements change regularly and differ greatly from one state to the next. The landscape is becoming so complex that, increasingly, consultants are rethinking whether they will consider working in certain states because of the time and cost required under the regulations. So let this article be a starting point for your own continued research.

Who Must Register?

While definitions can vary slightly by geography, in the state government's eyes, there are generally four classifications of fundraising consulting services:

- ◆ Advisors or Counsel: Individuals or firms that provide advice and guidance for the client but do not directly solicit gifts from potential donors.

- ◆ (Professional) Solicitors/Fundraisers: Individuals or firms that provide advice and guidance for the client, and make solicitation calls on potential donors. Solicitors are also defined by many states as employees of Professional Fundraisers.

- ◆ Grant Writers: Individuals or firms that provide grant writing services for the client. There is no direct contact between the grant writer and potential donors, but there may be direct contact with grantors. Grant writers do not handle any funds.

- ◆ Commercial Co-venturers: A for-profit entity that sells a product or service to the general public, and donates a portion of the profit to a nonprofit organization.

Caveat: Some states have slightly different definitions than those above. Be sure to read each state's information and requirements carefully!

Read each state's registration requirements carefully!

Some states treat all types of fundraisers equally, without differentiating between types of services. Some states have laws that apply to only one or two fundraising functions: New Mexico, for example, does not require counsel (those in an advisory role only) to register. However, if soliciting for gifts, the professional fundraiser must register and post a $25,000 surety bond. For each year's annual fundraising report to the state, a nonprofit engaging a consultant must provide both a current copy of the contract and the consultant's registration number.

The Nitty Gritty

As a consultant, you are required to register appropriately in any state where you have a client, and in any state you are working for the client if it differs from the client's corporate location.

To register, you need a copy of your executed contract. However, be aware that you are required to register *prior* to starting work in that state.

Yes, there are initial and annual fees and reporting requirements. In some states, a consultant—even if the consultant does not handle the client's money—is also required to post a bond, which is an additional cost. Sometimes the bond can be waived by providing a letter of credit, a certificate of deposit or a cash escrow account with the bond amount.

A surety bond ensures that you, as the consultant, will act in accordance with the laws governing nonprofit fundraising in that state. States that require them generally provide the form you need to use as well as the insurance itself. In some states, you may have to provide your own insurance carrier. Usually this carrier can be the company that provides your business and liability insurance policies. Fees vary depending on the state and the amount of insurance required. If you have a certificate of deposit or a secured savings account in the amount of the bond required, that can be pledged as security, you might be able to ask the state to waive the actual bond requirement.

Once registered, you must file an annual report with the state pursuant to its guidelines. Some states have fees for this report, some do not. Some states require written notice from the fundraiser once the contract is complete or terminated. Renewals may be due in less than a full year. Some are required one year from the date of the initial registration. Others, such as Florida, have a date certain for renewals, where all are due March 31, with no proration of fees. Most states require a campaign and/or corporate financial statement from the charity as well.

To make your life really easy, no two states have exactly the same requirements. You must make sure the information from each state is up to date, and that you are properly registered. Changes to the law happen all the time, and it is your responsibility to know them.

I've provided a table in **Appendix B** with each state's website and/or telephone number along with basic information about consultant registration. This information is current as of this writing. Please check each state's website for updates. In most states, you can find information from the Secretary of State, the Attorney General's office, the Department of Consumer Services or the Department of Agriculture (I know that sounds strange, but such is the case in Florida and California). Some states have even established specialized charities registration departments.

My table in **Appendix B** includes an overview of registration guidelines. Since it only includes the basics, please refer to each state's website to find full details and required forms. The fees listed in that table are only the initial registration fees. Some, such as New Jersey, also charge a fee for every contract submitted for review. Some states have minimal annual renewal fees; some are quite high.

See **Appendix B** for detailed information about each state's consultant registration requirements.

important

In some states, you may be required to register in the county or city where you are working, in addition to the state. Make sure you look into this added requirement. In California, two hundred cities and counties have registration and reporting requirements in addition to the state registration.

Some states' rules go outside the realm of registration and contract submissions. Florida, for instance, has extensive regulations about what information must be included in fundraising materials: There are state-required disclosures that must appear on any and all solicitation materials offering a website and telephone number to report violations of fundraising laws.

Necessities

In each case, assume you need a copy of your contract for services. In some states, you can submit a sample contract if you do not have a currently-executed one. Sometimes you'll need not only an executed contract, but that contract must include specific verbiage or specifications. Pennsylvania, for example, requires that the contract be signed by two persons, at least one of whom is a member of the client's board. It is important that you understand there are significant fines for late registration or late annual reporting in many states.

States that require fundraiser registration may also require any or all of the following:

◆ Advance notice of solicitation

◆ Beginning, interim, or final financial reports

◆ Corporate organizational information of the fundraiser's company (articles of incorporation; bylaws; Employer Identification Numbers (EINs) or Social Security numbers of co-owners or partners with addresses, and in one state, birth dates)

Some states levy significant fines for late registration or late annual reporting by nonprofit consultants.

watch out!

If you confirm these details in advance, you will save time by ensuring that your application is not declined due to missing documentation. New York is a great example of a complicated and time-consuming registration. Start early and give yourself some time on this one. The job classifications are professional fundraisers, solicitors who are employees of professional fundraising firms, and fundraising counsel. For professional fundraisers and counsel, there is an $800 annual fee; copies of the consultant's organizational documents as well as client contracts for the last twelve months—regardless of location—must be submitted. Registration is valid for one year from the date of application. Solicitors working for fundraising firms pay a fee of $80 a year. Professional fundraisers or firms must also post bond of $10,000, with a power of attorney from a New York attorney-in-fact. Any person owning 10 percent or more of the fundraising firm must be listed with individual addresses and individual Social Security numbers.

You can see why it's important to do your homework and give yourself plenty of time to comply.

Here is one example of what can happen when you ignore consultant registration regulations:

In late 2011, the Tennessee Division of Charitable Solicitations and Gaming assessed a Florida-based professional fundraising company $720,000 for failing to follow the state's registration rules. The firm did not clearly state that it was raising funds for a charity when it contacted Tennessee residents during client phone solicitations. The violation of Tennessee Charitable Solicitations Act carried a $5,000 civil penalty for each of 144 violations.

stories from the real world

If all of this sounds overwhelming, third party providers offer registration services for a fee. If you find that you have to register in multiple states, you might want to consider hiring a firm to help you understand and comply with the guidelines, especially if you work in those states with complex regulations.

The requirements can be quite complicated and expensive. Nonprofits are required to provide the consultant's registration number when doing the organization's original registration or when giving notice of a new fundraising campaign, so again, be sure to register in advance of providing services to your client. Timing can be critical if you are working in a state where you have not worked before.

As a consultant, educate yourself about the investment you must make in terms of time and money to register in a potential client's state. You'll need to know this information *before* you write your contract so that you can accurately estimate the scope and cost of services to that client. You might need to recognize that you cannot charge enough for your work to make the required registration cost-effective in a given state.

Keep Calm and Carry On

By Justin Tolan

In your consulting career, you will undoubtedly face something you didn't expect at some point. Your work will be affected by many variables: unexpected glitches caused by your client, upheavals in the client's community, "loose cannon" volunteer fundraisers, the economy, zoning, and even catastrophic world events.

No matter what or whom you encounter along the way, the most important thing is to keep a persistent focus on the client's success so you can help your clients realize their dreams. For example, I like to think about how more people will be fed when we help a food bank build a new distribution center; how dialysis patients will receive daily treatments closer to home thanks to a new hospital wing we consulted on; and how audiences will continue to hear first-rate classical music and musicians because of the endowment we helped a symphony grow.

It's important to maintain a healthy balance of humor and patience. Your experiences will take many turns, not always glamorous, often comical, but memorable so long as you keep top of mind the vision and dreams of your clients. And when you need a refreshing pat on the back, do what I do and drive by that hospital wing, childcare center, university building or other fundraising project you helped make a reality.

Control What You Can and Adapt to What You Can't

Our job as consultants is to help our clients best avoid the potholes on the long road to achieving their missions. Sometimes, and hopefully most times, they listen, but there are those instances when they don't and pay the price.

> "Clients often refer to me as the 'campaign mom,'" says Dee Vandeventer, CFRE, of ME&V Fundraising Advisers in Cedar Falls, Iowa. "They see my role as using my knowledge and experience to keep them on track as well as to make sure they 'keep their room clean.'" But just as in real life, we don't always listen to what "mom" has to say. Such was the case for one client who was building a hospice home. The client had the land but not the necessary zoning approval.
>
> Dee continued to urge this client to bring this critical detail to closure, but was told it wouldn't be a problem. About two weeks after training a volunteer army of sixty people, the rezoning was denied. Volunteers called to say they did not want to approach donors until the issue was resolved, which took about eighteen months. Eventually the property was rezoned, the campaign exceeded its $6 million goal and the hospice home was built, but certainly not in the timeframe initially projected.

 stories from the real world

Try as you may, there are some things you just can't control. I learned that on my second week as a consultant. I had joined a colleague on a client visit in Joliet, Illinois, outside of Chicago. The campaign had just entered the public phase. Shortly after 9 a.m., a leadership committee meeting was interrupted with the news that two planes had crashed into the two World Trade Center towers. An agency employee joined us to learn more details. Many had family members working in downtown Chicago and the uncertainty of what might happen next permeated throughout the office.

The only appropriate thing was to put the campaign on a hiatus until it felt appropriate to begin again. Fortunately, grant funders such as the Kresge Foundation adjusted the timeline and the campaign did end successfully, exceeding the goal by $1 million.

Travel is Often Filled with the Unexpected

In my travels, I have conducted more than a thousand feasibility study interviews. I have done interviews in the posh office of a Fortune 500 CEO, in a closely-guarded pharmaceutical laboratory, and inside the cab of a John Deere tractor. The most stinging interview occurred when the husband of a couple I was interviewing greeted me at the front door and guided me through their living room to the kitchen table. I politely waited to take a seat as the wife tried to restrain "Spike," the little Pomeranian puppy that appeared at my feet. And no, I am not making up this dog's name.

I tried to win him over by bending down to gently pet his forehead. "Grrrrrrrr," sputtered the angry mutt, revealing sharp teeth and fur standing straight up. I wisely withdrew my gesture. The woman tried to pick up Spike, but he proceeded to dart underneath the table and then took a quick chomp on my ankle. I'm not sure the couple noticed the bite, and I thought it impolite to check my sock for blood. The woman then corralled the conquering canine and locked him away in a nearby bedroom. I proceeded to complete the interview under duress, suppressing my own desire to yelp and even cry. The minute I was safely away in my car, however, I quickly pulled over to assess my damages. Thank God I only suffered a minor tear in my slacks, without a single puncture wound!

The moral of this story? You have to prepare yourself for meeting people and even their pets in all kinds of strange places. Whatever surprises you encounter during your visits, you should usually place the relationship first and your own minor discomforts second.

Weather and Flight Delays Can Cause Havoc

Inclement weather can crimp the style and sleep of any consultant. Linda Lysakowski, ACFRE, of Linda Lysakowski, LLC, was scheduled to lead a strategic planning session at a board member's Vermont farm. Arriving at the Philadelphia airport to catch a connecting flight, she sat at the gate for a half-hour before the flight was canceled.

Frantic, Linda went to the desk and explained that she absolutely had to get to Vermont that night. After a few minutes of begging and pleading, she said, "Look, get me anywhere in New England you can get me tonight." The new flight would arrive in Manchester, New Hampshire. "Perfect," said Linda. She had a few minutes to contact the hotel and car rental company to make new arrangements. Uh-oh. The hotel chain did not have a hotel in Manchester.

Linda arrived in Manchester and just barely made it to the rental car counter before it closed. Now all she needed was a hotel for the night. It was after midnight. The volunteer staffing the information desk at the airport told Linda that there were no available rooms in Manchester or anywhere within a 100-mile radius.

By this time, she was nearly in tears and called her husband to tell that him she might have to spend the night in her car. At that moment, a young woman appeared in distress, having just missed the last train back to her university.

Now there were two wayfarers on the verge of tears. The inventive information desk volunteer suggested to Linda, "Well you've got a car." And to the college student, "You've got a room." He smiled. "So just get together."

And they did. After a three-hour sleep on the sofa in her newfound friend's dorm room, Linda drove to her destination and facilitated a full-day retreat. As Shakespeare penned, "All's well that ends well." So ended this story thanks to a creative adjustment and Linda's flexibility.

Get It in Writing

Another unexpected obstacle can happen when an organization simply refuses to honor its agreement with you for consulting services. Alice Ferris, MBA, ACFRE, of GoalBusters in Flagstaff, Arizona, experienced an unfortunate shock when dealing with a client grumbling, "Show me the money." The board of directors wanted money fast, so Alice's firm provided a report showing grants submitted, proposals under consideration and other activity. "We did so with the assumption that we had six months remaining on our agreement," Alice recalled.

"A few weeks later, a couple days into the client's new fiscal year, I received a call saying that the board had eliminated us from the budget. No notice, just 'you're done.' When we asked about our agreement that went for another six months, I was informed that the board said they never signed it, so they didn't need to abide by its terms."

Sometimes, you have to know when to pick your battles and when to quit. In this case, Alice said her firm simply walked away from this client rather than lose the time she felt they would spend in fighting to resolve the situation.

Even Consultants Are Not Invincible

Ellen Bristol of Bristol Strategy Group in Aventura, Florida, has made her living as a consultant since 1995. During her first year, she attended a workshop where a woman gave a witty talk on how to prepare properly for speaking in public. The speaker pulled out a bunch of props such as a pair of brand new pantyhose, a bottle of diarrhea medicine, and a suit on a hanger covered in plastic, in case you spilled your lunch on the one you were wearing. "I laughed my head off and said to myself, 'how amusing, of course I'll never need to do that stuff,'" recalls Ellen.

Those were indeed famous last words. Some years later, Ellen and another consultant were coming to the end of a two-day visit to a long-term client out of state. The client brought in sandwiches so they could work through lunch.

"I happily ate my turkey sub, and we completed our work and hopped in the car to drive to the airport," Ellen noted. "But before we even left the driveway, I started to get queasy. Really queasy. Good thing the other consultant was driving; I had to have her pull the car over to the side of the Pennsylvania Turnpike so I could throw myself out the door and onto the grass where I proceeded to be spectacularly sick. And managed to get traffic backed up for miles as everybody was gawking at this well-dressed middle-aged woman on her knees. By the time we got to the airport, I couldn't get on the plane and ended up in the ER instead."

Yes, it was food poisoning.

Keep a Positive Attitude

Who knows what unexpected hitches you will encounter on the road to building your consulting practice? Most likely, you will experience your own weather setbacks, travel adventures, tight timetables and more. Although you can't always anticipate the next obstacle around the bend, the right attitude will help you realize that, "this too shall pass."

Ultimately, the joy of giving—and seeing and helping it all happen—is what makes consulting the rewarding profession that it is. While we can't plan all of our adventures with our clients, we can rest assured that even the most unforeseeable events result in something for the benefit of others. Good luck, and don't forget to share *your* stories with other consultants too!

Appendix A

Suggested Reading List

Block, Peter. 2011. *Flawless Consulting: A Guide to Getting Your Expertise Used,* 3rd edition. San Francisco: Jossey-Bass.

Chait, Richard P., William P. Ryan, and Barbara E. Taylor. 2005. *Governance as Leadership: Reframing the Work of Nonprofit Boards.* Hoboken, NJ: John Wiley & Sons.

Covey, Stephen R. 2004. *The 7 Habits of Highly Effective People,* rev. ed. New York: Free Press.

Dyer, Jeffrey H., Hal B. Gregersen, and Clayton M. Christensen. December 2009. "The Innovator's DNA." *Harvard Business Review.*

June 5, 2006. "How to Name Your Business." *Entrepreneur.* http://www.entrepreneur.com/article/159678-1.

Levoy, Gregg Michael. 1997. *Callings: Finding and Following an Authentic Life.* New York: Three Rivers Press.

Lonier, Terri. 1998. *Working Solo,* 3rd ed. New York: John Wiley & Sons.

Maiser, David H., Charles H. Green, and Robert M. Galford. 2001. *The Trusted Advisor.* New York: Simon & Schuster.

Scanlan, Eugene A. 2009. *Fundraising Consultants: A Guide for Nonprofit Organizations.* Hoboken, NJ: John Wiley & Sons.

Patterson, Kerry, Goseph Grenny, Ron McMillan, and Al Switzler. 2011. *Crucial Conversations: Tools for Talking When Stakes Are High.* 2nd ed. New York: McGraw-Hill.

Senge, Peter M. 2006. *The Fifth Discipline,* rev. ed. New York: Doubleday.

Sheth, Jagdish, and Andrew Sobel. 2000. *Clients for Life: How Great Professionals Develop Breakthrough Relationships.* New York: Simon & Schuster.

Sussman, Carl. Winter 2003. "Making Change: How to Build Adaptive Capacity." *Nonprofit Quarterly*.

Wagner, Libby. 2011. *The Influencing Option.* Cranbrook, England: Global Professional Press.

Appendix B

Fundraising Consultant Registration by State

This chart is provided by Helen B. Arnold, CFRE, of Clearly Compliant LLC (ClearlyCompliant.com), to illustrate, on a state-by-state basis, the filing requirements for consultants. While every effort has been made to ensure that the chart is accurate as of press time, states can and often do change their filing requirements. Please do not rely on this chart in determining whether or not you must register with the states in which you provide services—do your own review and, of course, you should seek the advice of a qualified attorney on important questions of law.

To find specific information about a particular state, go to the website in the table and search on keywords within the site. Keyword search suggestions include these:

◆ Solicitor

◆ Professional fundraiser

◆ Charity registration

State	Website	Comments
Alaska	www.law.state.ak.us/consumer	Paid solicitors: $200 fee; $10,000 surety bond.
Alabama	www.ago.alabama.gov	Professional fundraiser: $100 fee. Commercial co-venturer: $100 fee. Professional solicitor: $25 fee; $10,000 surety bond required.
Arkansas	www.ag.arkansas.gov	All classifications including telemarketers: $100 fee. Must appoint Arkansas Attorney General as agent for service. Surety bond required for solicitor classification.

State	Website	Comments
Arizona	www.azsos.gov	Contracted solicitor: $25 fee; $25,000 surety bond.
California	ag.ca.gov/charities/	Commercial fundraisers/fundraising counsel/co-venturers: $350 fee. $25,000 surety bond required for commercial fundraisers. Can do a cash deposit in lieu of bond.
Connecticut	www.sots.ct.gov	Fundraising counsel: $120 fee; $20,000 surety bond. Solicitor: $500 fee; $20,000 surety bond; solicitation notice must be filed with the state.
Colorado	www.sos.state.co.us	Fundraising consultants must register only if they will have control or custody funds. Solicitors, who are asking for funds, must register $175 fee.
Washington, DC	dcra.dc.gov/DC	Nonprofit organizations must register and supply a copy of the consultant's contract along with a list of all employees of the consultant who will be working under the contract. Then DC will issue a card for each solicitor, which must be carried during the term of the contract for each person working under the contract.
Delaware		No registration required.
Florida	www.800helpfla.com/socbus.html	Solicitors: $300 fee; $50,000 surety bond. Fundraising consultants: $300 fee, with no surety bond.
Georgia	sos.georgia.gov/securities/paid_solicitor	Solicitors with custody or control of funds must register: $250 fee; $10,000 surety bond; must file Notice of Solicitation in advance of solicitation. Solicitor agents: $50 fee. Fundraising counsel does not have to register if no money is handled.
Hawaii	hawaii.gov/ag/charities	All classes of fundraisers must pay a $250 fee. Surety bond of $25,000 for solicitors only.
Iowa	www.iowa.gov	All fundraisers are considered commercial fundraising counsel: $10 fee; organizational financial disclosure statement required from client agencies.
Illinois	www.illinoisattorneygeneral.gov/charities	Fundraiser: must file copies of client contracts and partnership or articles of incorporation. Solicitor: $100 fee; $10,000 surety bond if money is handled. Solicitors who are employees of fundraiser must register.

State	Website	Comments
Indiana	www.in.gov./attorneygeneral	Fundraiser or solicitor: $1,000 initial filing fee; $50 renewal fee.
Kansas	www.kansas.gov	All classes of fundraisers: $25 fee.
Kentucky	ag.ky.gov	Articles of incorporation and licensing agency request form required. Promotion (campaign) must be registered. Fundraising counsel: $50 fee. Professional solicitor: $300 fee.
Louisiana	www.ag.state.la.us	Must file notice of commencement of solicitation. Surety bond of $25,000 required of those directly soliciting. $150 fee. Co-venturers must file a report and have consent of charity.
Massachusetts	www.mass.gov/ago/charities	Solicitor: $1,000 fee $25,000 surety bond. Fundraising counsel: $400 fee. Commercial co-venturer: $200 fee; $25,000 surety bond.
Maryland	www.sos.state.md.us	Fundraising counsel: $200 fee. Solicitor: $300 fee; $25,000 surety bond fee.
Maine	www.maine.gov	Solicitor: $250 fee; $25,000 surety bond. Fundraising counsel: $250 fee. Commercial co-venturer: $250 fee; $25,000 surety bond.
Michigan	www.michigan.gov	Fundraiser is defined as the entity managing each solicitor. Fundraiser: register (as a consultant or as solicitation/event); post $10,000 surety bond; no registration fee. If not Michigan-based business, might need to obtain a Certificate of Authority to Conduct Affairs in Michigan.
Minnesota	www.ag.state.mn.us	One class of professionals, called professional fundraisers: $200 fee; $20,000 surety bond.
Missouri	ago.mo.gov	Solicitor employment statements must be filed by charity. Professional fundraiser is sole class: $50 fee.
Montana		No registration required.
Mississippi	www.sos.ms.gov	Fundraising counsel: $250 fee. Professional fundraisers: $250 fee; $10,000 surety bond. Solicitors register as working for professional fundraiser.
North Carolina	www.secretary.state.nc.us	Fundraising consultant: $200 fee. Solicitor: $200 fee; $20,000-$50,000 surety bond, based on organization's contributions in the prior year.

State	Website	Comments
North Dakota	www.nd.gov/sos	Professional fundraiser covers all classes: $100 fee; $20,000 surety bond.
Nebraska		No registration required.
New Hampshire	www.doj.nh.gov	Solicitor: $200 fee; $20,000 surety bond. Fundraising counsel: $150 fee.
New Jersey	www.state.nj.us	Co-venturer: two fees totaling $40. Custody of funds: $250 fee; $20,000 surety bond. Solicitor working for fundraiser: $15 each. Fundraiser without custody of funds: $250 fee. Additional fees totaling $50 possible for all.
New Mexico	www.nmag.gov	Fundraising counsel (no custody of funds) does not have to register. Fundraiser who solicits: surety bond of $25,000. No initial fee, but $500 penalty if fundraiser does not register.
Nevada		No registration required, but grant writing contracts must include notice to the client of its right to cancel the contract within five days and information regarding the client's right to file a complaint with the Bureau of Consumer Protection/Office of the Attorney General.
New York	www.charitiesNYS.com	Professional fundraiser and counsel: $800 annual fee; $10,000 bond; copies of fundraisers' organizational documents; client contracts for last twelve months. Solicitors: $80 fee.
Ohio	www.ohioattorneygeneral.gov	All solicitors (fundraisers) must register: $200 fee; $25,000 surety bond. Counsel must register only if it will have custody or control of funds at any time.
Oklahoma	www.sos.ok.gov/Charity	Fundraisers who directly solicit: $215 fee. Solicitors who work directly for the professional fundraiser: $25.
Oregon	www.doj.state.or.us	All professional solicitors: $250 fee; notice of campaign must be filed.
Pennsylvania	www.portal.state.pa.us	Fundraiser solicits, counsel does not. Fundraiser who solicits: $250 fee; $25,000 surety bond required. All must register and be approved and receive certificate of registration before working. Fundraisers must do specific oral disclosures when soliciting. Written notice required for ending or extending contract. $1,000 fine plus $100 per day penalty for non-compliance.

State	Website	Comments
Rhode Island	www.dbr.state.ri.us	All registrations must be submitted on CD-ROM. Fundraisers who solicit: $240 fee; $10,000 surety bond. Fundraising counsel: $240 fee.
South Carolina	www.scsos.com	Professional solicitors, solicitors, and counsel: $50 fee. Commercial co-ventures: no fee or form, just file contract and solicitation forms. All must file Notice of Solicitation forms. Professional solicitors: $15,000 surety bond; .
South Dakota		No registration required.
Tennessee	www.state.tn.us/sos/charity	All classifications: $250 fee.
Texas	www.oag.state.tx.us	Telephone solicitors: $50 fee; $50,000 bond.
Utah	www.rules.utah.gov	Three classes of fundraisers, one application. Need fundraiser's articles of incorporation, bylaws. State issues a fundraising permit. Registered agent in Utah required. Must file notice of campaign in advance, no extensions. $250 fee.
Virginia	www.vdacs.virginia.gov	Counsel (no soliciting): $100 fee. Solicitor: $500 fee ($250 fine if late); $20,000 surety bond; current and prior year's client contracts.
Vermont	www.atg.state.vt.us	All fundraisers are classified together: $20,000 surety bond; notice of solicitation required; specific disclosures required during solicitations.
Washington	www.sos.wa.gov	Commercial fundraisers/solicitors: $300 initial fee; $225 renewal fee; $15,000 surety bond.
Wisconsin	drl.wi.gov	Must obtain a Wisconsin license to do business. Fundraiser who solicits and has custody of funds: $20,000 surety bond. Fundraiser not handling funds: $5,000 surety bond. Counsel: $20,000 surety bond. $75 fee for all. Must file solicitation notice and contract with Department of Safety and Professional Services.
West Virginia	www.sos.wv.gov	Professional fundraiser and fundraising counsel treated equally: $100 fee; $10,000 surety bond.
Wyoming		No registration required.

Index

T

V

W

If you enjoyed this book, you'll want to pick up the other books in the CharityChannel Press **In the Trenches™** series.

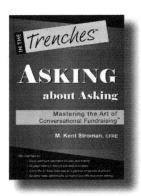

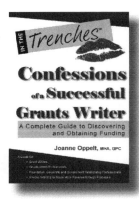

And dozens more coming soon!

www.CharityChannel.com

And now introducing **For the GENIUS® Press,** an imprint that produces books on just about any topic that people want to learn. You don't have to be a genius to read a **GENIUS** book, but you'll sure be smarter once you do!

Fundraising

for the GENIUS™

The only book you'll ever need to raise more money for your nonprofit organization.

FOR THE GENIUS IN ALL OF US™

Linda Lysakowski, ACFRE

www.ForTheGENIUS.com

67271439R00177

Made in the USA
Middletown, DE
20 March 2018